The Crisis of
Classical Music in America

The Crisis of
Classical Music in America

Lessons from a Life in the Education of
Musicians

Robert Freeman

ROWMAN & LITTLEFIELD
Lanham • Boulder • New York • London

Published by Rowman & Littlefield
A wholly owned subsidiary of The Rowman & Littlefield Publishing Group, Inc.
4501 Forbes Boulevard, Suite 200, Lanham, Maryland 20706
www.rowman.com

16 Carlisle Street, London W1D 3BT, United Kingdom

British Library Cataloguing in Publication Information Available

Library of Congress Cataloging-in-Publication Data

Freeman, Robert.
The crisis of classical music in America : lessons from a life in the education of musicians / Robert Freeman.
pages cm
Includes index.
ISBN 978-1-4422-3301-0 (hardcover : alk. paper) -- ISBN 978-1-4422-3302-7 (pbk. : alk. paper) -- ISBN 978-1-4422-3303-4 (ebook)
1. Music--Instruction and study--United States. 2. Music in universities and colleges--United States. I. Title.
MT3.U5F74 2014
780.71'073--dc23
2014009714

Printed in the United States of America

To Carol, with whom I have shared the love of 16 wonderful dogs:
Pierre Barrington, Annie Scio, Oliver Clinton, Lacy Louise, Rose, Billie
American dogs (pets of mixed heritage)
Good Time Charlie IX, Mikey, Chloe, Chaco, Tess, Chipps, Rusty, Jackson, H. Maude, Calvin,
rescue golden retrievers.
And more yet to come!

Contents

Acknowledgments

It is a special pleasure to thank my dear wife, Carol, for her strong support over the years in the preparation of this book. The most important contributors to my early education, in addition to my parents, have been my principal music teachers: pianists Marjorie Truelove MacKown, Marjorie Church Cherkassky, Gregory Tucker, Artur Balsam, and Rudolf Serkin; oboist Fernand Gillet; musicologists John Ward, Oliver Strunk, and Arthur Mendel; and Robert L. Sproull, seventh president of the University of Rochester.

I am indebted to many discussions on music's future with innumerable students whom I have had the privilege of mentoring at Princeton, MIT, Eastman, the New England Conservatory, and the University of Texas at Austin, and I have profited greatly from these conservations with young people. It is my hope that further such discussions will be facilitated in the years ahead through the appearance of this book, helping toward the broader societal impact of the art we all care so much about.

Though errors found in the text are the result of careless proofreading of mine, I am very appreciative of the help of James A. Winn and Thomas Mowrey, friends of many years' standing, for their help in reviewing the text. I am deeply grateful, finally, for the help of my editor, Bennett Graff. No one could have been more supportive, good-humored, and knowledgeable than he.

Foreword

I know of no person better suited to report on the state of musical education and to influence its development than Robert Freeman. Since 1972, as
head of three superb American institutions of higher education in music,
he has helped produce a generation of musicians who see beyond their
music stands and seek to use their talent to create a more harmonious
world. More than a quarter century ago, Dr. Freeman began to address
the educational issues that have today reached nothing less than crisis
proportions, from the disappearance of music education in the public
schools to the glut of single-minded musicians who have learned to excel
at competitions rather than at music making. I am struck by the consis-
tency of his message over that period of time. He continues to remind us
of the need for general music education in the public schools—not to
create potential professional musicians but to mold better human beings.
He still calls for a more varied curriculum in conservatories, to create
more broadly educated artists. And he still stresses the need to assess the
potential of the individual music student early on, in order to guide the
student to an appropriate, attainable, satisfying career in or out of music.
As he has always done, Dr. Freeman challenges us to develop a more
balanced and realistic approach to the way music is taught, particularly
at the highest levels of academia.

Rather than becoming a professional performer like his father and
grandfather before him, Robert Freeman earned degrees in music from
Harvard and Princeton. After serving on the music faculties of Princeton
and MIT, he was named director of the renowned Eastman School of
Music, which he led for twenty-four years. In 1996 he took the helm of the
equally celebrated New England Conservatory of Music, and in 1999
moved to the University of Texas at Austin as dean of that institution's
College of Fine Arts.

Robert Freeman's own career is the best proof of the sagacity of this
book. Briefly stated, there are many ways to make a significant contribution in music besides being a Heifetz, a Horowitz, or a Caruso. While it is
laudable to dream of a career as a renowned soloist performing to stand-
ing-room audiences in the great halls of the world, it's crucial to recognize that comparatively few musicians ever become so much as a member of an orchestra, fewer still make a living in chamber music, and an
infinitesimally small number become that celebrated soloist of legend.
Yet thousands upon thousands of other valuable opportunities in music

await the student who would set his or her sights instead on a career as composer, coach, or critic, as publisher, producer, teacher, fund-raiser, or executive.

Would you like a quick practical example of the point? Okay: a hundred musicians are on the payroll of the Boston Symphony Orchestra, while a hundred and thirty administrators draw a weekly check from the BSO.[1] A great many of the BSO administrative team bring much-valued insight to their jobs from having been serious students of music.

Further, even the student who ultimately pursues a career outside of music can take great satisfaction, and make great contributions as a knowledgeable amateur musician. I'm particularly intrigued that a person who sets the agenda for training musicians at the highest level admires the contribution of Gilbert Kaplan as an accomplished avocational conductor and scholar. While some decry the idea of a man of business conducting Mahler's Resurrection Symphony at Carnegie Hall, Dr. Freeman believes Maestro Kaplan serves to inspire. Isn't his amateur's enthusiasm what music used to be about?

Robert Freeman had the great advantage of having parents who clearly understood the music business, and who directed him early toward a rounded liberal arts and musical education. I, too, grew up in a home with professional musicians, and I continue to marvel at the wisdom and support they showed at every step of my education. It might easily have been otherwise, with very different results. The first and perhaps best decision my parents made was to send me to a series of schools that had a profound sense of the importance of musical education. Would it surprise you to know that I'm speaking of the Los Angeles public schools? I am. From 1950 to 1962, I did not attend a single private school. I didn't have to. Music was part of the curriculum in my grade school. My junior high had an orchestra and a band. Los Angeles High School had two bands, an orchestra, two choruses, and a composer-in-residence. Public schools all!

I knew early on that I would be a musician. I just didn't know what kind, because the competition in my household was daunting. Coming from an intensively musical family, I was competitive not just with my musical friends and colleagues, and not just with my very talented younger brother—now principal cellist at the New York City Ballet—but with my grandparents, parents, and uncle as well. I mean no disrespect when I say that I probably wouldn't be conducting now if my father, Felix Slatkin, had still been alive when I pursued the baton; the competition would have been too much for me. I quit violin because of competition, and I stopped playing piano seriously because I knew I'd never be as good as my uncle was.

Time and again my public school teachers stoked the fires within me. They were enthusiastic; they were good; they challenged me. They were monumental influences. After all, I saw them every day, whereas I didn't see my parents every day. These teachers applied the same kind of discipline I received in my own highly disciplined household. I well remember what that was like. Once, when I was twelve, I was practicing piano when I heard a knock on the door. It was my friends asking me to come out and play ball. I said okay. My mother, however, made it clear that I wasn't going anywhere until I finished practicing. "But I want to play ball." "If you go out to play ball, I'm going to lock the piano and you're not going to play it anymore." That seemed like a great idea at the time, so I went out and played ball. Sure enough, when I came back the piano was locked, and for a few days I worked on my career as a first baseman. After a couple of days I told my mother I wanted to practice, and she said, "No. You're not serious about it, and I'm not going to open the piano." I screamed and kicked and carried on. The message had gotten through.

As the result of my high school's representation of blacks, whites, and Hispanics, the orchestra and band were ethnically mixed, and certainly more so than in the professional organizations one sees today. Granted, my colleagues didn't all go on to pursue musical careers, but those I see every so often maintain music as an integral part of their lives. Those kids didn't come from musical backgrounds but from traditional, working-class backgrounds. The thread that held us all together was that we had music in our homes—and consistent with Dr. Freeman's vision, not just concert music. No, we listened to and conversed about the relationship of Presley to early rock; the folk music of the Kingston Trio and the Weavers; the impact of the Beatles. We'd listen to everything; music was music.[2] In my household we didn't dare categorize it. How could we? My father played at Twentieth Century Fox, while my mother and uncle played at Warner's, and hanging around the movie studios I came in contact with Alfred Newman, Erich Korngold, Max Steiner, and others. In the evenings there might be a string quartet rehearsal at our house with Stravinsky or Schoenberg showing up. And because my father was involved with the popular recording industry as well, we might have seen Sinatra one night, Danny Kaye another night, and Doris Day another. My musical perceptions were shaped by listening to New York Philharmonic broadcasts on Sunday afternoons; by watching Bernstein's Young People's Concerts with my parents; by listening to popular music on the radio; and by being taken to jazz clubs. The same was true for my classmates. Music was a point of discussion when we visited our friends. Music was just part of our lives.

As Dr. Freeman points out, the nature of the public school curriculum has altered dramatically, and music education of the sort I benefited from—call it total immersion—has virtually disappeared. We're now well into a second generation that suffers from the decline of public school arts education, and as a result, the shared commonality of the arts in any form between parents and their children has been severely damaged. Although an effort is afoot to restore the arts curriculum to its former glory, every local jurisdiction in the country ultimately has the chance to follow that course or not.

It is ironic that just as the music infrastructure in public schools of the '50s and '60s was disappearing, the quality of America's professional schools was increasing to the point that this country replaced Europe as the place to study music. Today we see a vast migration here from East Asia. The joke is, "What's the second most common language spoken at Juilliard?" The answer is English! A principal question that concerns Dr. Freeman is where all these talented kids from all over the world are going to go when they graduate. What jobs await them? I believe, as he does, that the general curriculum of our music schools fails to address this supremely practical question. I think Dr. Freeman would agree that the first questions our conservatories and music schools should ask students is, "What do you want to do? Why are you here?"

I mentioned earlier that ideal career legend. It is important for students to strive for the highest possible musical goals. I guess we all start out that way. And while very few people envision a career as an instrumentalist in an orchestra, that's precisely where most musicians who attain a measure of success will wind up. I believe that too many young people are encouraged early on to continue in impractical pursuits simply because their teachers don't communicate what the student's real potential may be. When students ask me about their future in music, I ask them where they would like to be in five years. Then I ask them where they really think they can be. I suggest that they devise a concrete method to help them achieve their goals. And I advise them to analyze their strengths and shortcomings as a person, to see which weaknesses they need to shore up to achieve their goals.

A fascinating off-Broadway show titled *Two Pianos, Four Hands* centers on two people who grew up with the aspiration to appear as duo pianists at Carnegie Hall at least four times a year. Over the course of the show they come to realize that it's not going to happen. They reflect, "We were going to be the best pianists in the country. Then, the best pianists in the city." Finally, acceptance: "All right. We're the best pianists in the neighborhood!" You see, a teacher told a friend once that he wasn't going to be good enough for a professional career as a musician, and showed him why. He's one of the few teachers I have ever encountered—real or fictional—who was willing to do that. Most don't because it seems to suggest their own failure as a teacher. As if they're admitting, "I couldn't make you a musician." Rather, the teacher should say, "I'm a good teacher, but I can only do so much." That's not failure at all. In fact, when appropriate, it's the teacher's responsibility to tell students that it's a tough world out there and that they need to excel at something else. And to do so early enough to make a difference.

Dr. Freeman is deeply concerned about a well-rounded education for musicians, and I applaud his concern. As a student, I had a wonderful time at Juilliard, which was then at Broadway and West 122nd Street. For two years I lived at Broadway and 115th. Walking to school one day, I encountered a mob of people. Mark Rudd and the Weathermen had taken over Columbia University, making history a block and a half from where I lived. I continued on my way to music class. If it seemed conscientious to do so at the time, it strikes me as benighted now, but that's how isolated I was from the rest of the world. Today's students probably know more about the world than I did, but every school should actively encourage students to discuss what's going on beyond the rehearsal room. No one can afford to be isolated anymore, and that especially includes musicians.

Who should read this eloquent and passionate summation of a lifetime of experience and vision? As the table of contents indicates, parents, students, teachers, the heads of music schools, the provosts of colleges and universities, the presidents of foundations, and the chairs of the National Endowments for the Arts and Humanities. I would also suggest this book for business executives, for a glimpse of the responsibilities and obligations they'll face as we rely more and more heavily for support from the private sector.

I believe in this book. Because, yes, it's fine to dream of playing in Carnegie Hall, but we need Dr. Freeman to remind us that it's fine, too, to play music in your living room. It's admirable to win the Tchaikovsky Piano Competition, but we need Dr. Freeman's reminder that it is no less admirable to teach a young listener how to appreciate the fine points of the winning concerto. Dr. Freeman seeks to create a new paradigm in which "our faculties and their students focus not narrowly on their careers as stars but on music's potential contribution to humanity, and on the skills one needs to affect a broader number of people through music."

Let's encourage the development of musical talent, and put it to a variety of uses for the betterment of society. We'll create happier musicians and ensure that concert music doesn't become restricted to the pleasure of an elite few. In Dr. Freeman's words, "Together we can navigate past the terrors and frustrations of the music business toward the joy of communicating one of God's greatest gifts to an enthusiastic audience."

—Leonard Slatkin, music director, the Detroit Symphony Orchestra
former music director, the St. Louis Symphony Orchestra
The National Symphony Orchestra

NOTES

1. As Charles Krusenstjerna, Eastman's very able admissions officer, used to say three graduates of Stanley Hasty's Eastman clarinet studio are employed by the Boston Symphony: Thomas Martin ('84; associate principal clarinet and principal clarinet in Pops), Marshall Burlingame ('64; orchestral librarian and international leader in the development of computer-edited orchestral parts for guest conductors), and Mark Volpe ('79; executive director). (Tom Martin's immediate predecessor in the BSO was another Hasty clarinet student at Eastman, the late Peter Hadcock, '61.)

2. This, in fact, is what Alban Berg told George Gershwin when a self-conscious young American approached the Viennese master in 1927.

Preface

This book comes from a lifetime in music that has included sixteen years of teaching in the classrooms of three major American universities and thirty-four years at the helms of three of the nation's principal collegiate music schools. My twenty-four years as Eastman director helped turn that school into a new and vibrant institution.[1] But my attempt to do something similar in Boston was thwarted in two years by internal politics and the forces of stasis. While I certainly helped strengthen the arts in Austin—assisting with the development of a splendid new eighty-five-million-dollar art museum and raising an endowment for a world-class string quartet while looking after the appointments of many superb new faculty and staff members—I was too close to the end of my administrative career to throw myself under the education reform bus in Texas in the fashion I had as New England Conservatory president. I thought instead that I would write this book, providing musicians with the road map for the future that I believe is needed by our field as a whole. The example of Orpheus, perhaps the greatest musician of all time, shows that music can have a very powerful impact. It is the purpose of my life and of the reforms proposed in this book that that impact be much more broadly shared, freeing classical music from the iron cage in which we have locked her.

The message of my book is that the current crisis in classical music comes in important measure from the obsessively narrow ways we have trained musicians for more than two centuries. Adding to the problem is our continuing production of increasing numbers of music degrees, now more than thirty thousand American collegiate degrees a year, in a field where there have never been many jobs but where there are now fewer each year. In doing so, we ignore the relationship of supply to demand. In addition, we fail to think as analytically as we should about the educational reforms that would help make "classical music," and music generally, more vibrant aspects of our national life. Howard Gardner, in his recent book *Truth, Beauty, and Goodness Reframed*, writes:

> Doing good work is never easy: conflicting demands and opposing opportunities abound. Good work is most easily achieved when all of the stakeholders in a particular line of work want the same things, roughly speaking. We call this condition *alignment*. In concrete terms, a profession is aligned when the classical values of a profession, the goals of the current practitioners, the demands of the marketplace, the lead-

ers of the institution, and the stakeholders in the broader society all want roughly the same thing.

As an example, in the last two decades in the United States, it has been relatively easy to carry out good work as a genetics researcher, because the society supports this work in a non-judgmental manner. We all want to live longer and be healthier; we look to geneticists and other biologically oriented scientists to help us achieve these goals; and we facilitate—rather than obstruct—their enterprises. (When issues like the appropriateness of stem cell research start to generate controversy, alignment may weaken or even dissolve.)[2]

It is the thesis of what follows that classical music instruction, the professional world of musical performance, and the development of an intensely interested audience are seriously misaligned enterprises, in serious need of realignment through discussion among musicians.

In what follows, I propose a new ecosystem for "classical music" in America, the development of a more holistically oriented musical community in which parents, young musicians, music professors, music deans, university provosts, and foundation directors collaborate on the development of a better world for music and musicians. In fact, without the thoughtful cooperation of these groups, I do not see how the implementation of the ideas here envisioned can be accomplished.

The culture that presently produces musicians is disjointed and badly out of date. To begin with, musical instruction as a whole is without a discernible plan, with too few people understanding why the musical training of children is so important and too few fine musicians participating in that effort.[3] Among the goals such training should achieve are the appreciation of aural beauty, the development of a work ethic, the ability to listen carefully, a pride in achievement, the ability to collaborate with others, and self-confidence in responding rapidly to unforeseen crises. Such instruction should include sight singing and ear training, keyboard playing, and learning those aspects of elementary musicianship that, like language itself, are more readily mastered at an early age. Failure to do so results in too many college music majors who are weak in basic musicianship, and in too much college work that is devoted to tasks that are both remedial and more difficult for the student than they would have been at an earlier age.

Too much time is spent in the college training of musicians who play and sing at much higher levels than ever before in history, while too little time is spent in developing skills in critical thinking, reading, writing, and speaking. Only two majors in the undergraduate curriculum, engineering and music, limit learning in basic communication skills to the degree that a music curriculum does. But there is continuing demand for engineers. In music, however, employment opportunities in existing institutions, never robust, are now in steep decline, partly because of the prolonged recession, partly for other reasons outlined in what follows. It is sad that in a great nation that has so much to be proud of, the arts that might tell our story seem irrelevant to so many Americans, especially if presentations do not entertain. This, alas, puts music in an impossible situation, since so much of the responsibility for the advocacy for music belongs to musicians—to the very people, that is, who are relatively un-skilled in verbal communication.

Though our 4,200 colleges and universities have, during the past half century, become the financial backbone for classical music in America,[4] inadequate attention is paid to the balance between undergraduate and graduate enrollment. Though I believe undergraduate enrollment should make up at least 75 percent of the whole, many faculty members under-standably prefer to work with graduate students, young people already committed to areas of relevant specialization. As a result, we produce too many young people with doctoral degrees, even as we shirk faculty and administrative commitment to help find employment for those gradu-ates. Our graduate students and assistant professors spend too much time honing their expertise in very narrow areas of specialization in order to write doctoral dissertations and achieve tenure. The faculty as a whole spends far too little time working with non-majors in ways that will make those students members of future audiences and effective board mem-bers of not-for-profit organizations. We spend too much effort protecting majors from thinking about the implications of the current world of "clas-sical music," denying them while in college the chance to develop skills that might be useful to them, after college, in coming to grips with that world. Because the introduction of classical music to America in the mid-nineteenth century implied the social and intellectual superiority of those who supported such music, we have acted as though those repertories were implicitly superior to other kinds of music, and we have imagined that audiences for the future of that great music would thus take care of themselves. Further, we have failed adequately to broaden our students' interests and skills in non-European musics, in music of the twentieth and twenty-first centuries, and in the popular music beloved by the ma-jors and the non-majors alike. We prepare too many young people whose training and backgrounds look the same, instead of asking each freshman to formulate his or her own dreams at the outset, then helping him or her toward what businesspeople call a unique selling proposition. Too few aspiring musicians have a plan B, believing with their heroes of the nine-teenth century that it is brave and noble not to think about such matters.

Juilliard,[5] the other 637 American collegiate schools of music accredit-ed by the National Association of Schools of Music (NASM), and a multi-tude of music departments are now producing more than twenty-one thousand degrees in music annually, a number that increases year by year.[6] In the past twenty years, orchestral bankruptcies have included the Birmingham, Alabama, Orchestra (1993), and the orchestras of Oakland (1994), Sacramento (1996), San Jose (2002), Tulsa (2002), the Florida Philharmonic Orchestra (2003), Honolulu (2009), Louisville (2011), and New Mexico (2011). During 2011, the Detroit Symphony spent six months in a damaging strike. In the same season, the New York City Center Opera left Lincoln Center and in the meantime has closed its doors permanently; and the Philadelphia Orchestra declared Chapter 11 bankruptcy. (It has emerged therefrom in the summer of 2012.) In the fall of 2011, the board of the Colorado Symphony Orchestra resigned, simply walking away from the organization they had pledged to protect.[7] In the fall of 2012, the Atlanta Symphony settled a strike through the reduction of musicians' salaries by 20 percent. At the same time, the Minnesota Orchestra, the St. Paul Chamber Orchestra, and the Indianapolis Symphony were all locked out.[8] (In the meantime, Indianapolis has become a chamber orchestra, while the Minnesota Orchestra settled after a sixteen-month lockout for a 15 percent salary reduction, with its inspirational music director resigning to pursue other opportunities and many of that great orchestra's members moving elsewhere. Of the three, only the St. Paul Chamber Orchestra has been able to resuscitate itself intact, under the able leadership of Bruce Coppock.) This is what happens when we convince our students that yet additional hours of practice room isolation will make it possible for them to win the gold medal in competitions. So our young musicians subject themselves to the possibility of career-ending physiological injuries and to enormous educational opportunity costs. Too many of them fail to understand that all of the young women in the Miss America Competition are pretty, that all of the pianists in the Tchaikovsky Competition play brilliantly, and that the averaged votes of the judges in both kinds of competitions are relatively meaningless. In musicology and theory, we prepare our doctoral students as though they will all dedicate their lives to teaching their subjects of specialization to future graduate students in the Ivy League, failing to remember that our highest goal ought to focus on bringing a vital interest in music of all kinds to Americans generally.

Certainly, music study is a wonderful investment for children and for adolescents. And it is a superb subject for a lifetime of avocational commitment. I am wholly in favor of undergraduate study in music, especially if there is more encouragement than at present for liberal arts study, for continuing career counseling during undergraduate years, and for the possibility of double majors. I am concerned that too many collegiate institutions encourage the enrollment of graduate students simply to fill enrollment quotas. Admissions committees in business, law, and medicine[9] are happy to welcome well-prepared young musicians who bring with them the requisite preliminary backgrounds in those areas, for it is broadly understood that successful young musicians have developed unusually strong discipline in time management and in their work and study habits.

My paternal grandfather, Harry Freeman, was a gifted professional musician who toured the world with Sousa's Band, helped found New York's Chapter 802 of the American Federation of Musicians, and was the first trumpet teacher at the Eastman School of Music when it opened in 1921. He told me as a boy that music is very seductive but a terrible way to make a living. Partly as a result, I have given thought, over a long and happy life in music, to how to raise demand for classical music without undermining its integrity as one of humanity's greatest blessings. It has been my aim to make the professional lives of musicians longer, happier, more secure, more flexible, and more fulfilling.

I have been reflecting, too, on music's origins and on why it affects us as it does. Is it true that classical music's elitist background in the United States helps persuade Americans that they cannot approach listening to it without special preparation? If so, how can we best introduce an untutored audience to the wonders of that music without implying that what they need to learn will take time they do not have? Is Schubert's beautiful little song "Heidenröslein" really a much better piece of music than Harold Arlen's "Someday Over the Rainbow," and, if so, why? Why are all the acoustic instruments treated by music schools as though they were equally difficult, with repertories of equal breadth? Why do we undervalue the roles of teachers and of amateurs? Do we all hear the same thing when listening to a work of Beethoven? Should I try to teach non-majors what I hear? How can I better understand what *they* presently hear? What do we accomplish when we imply that music studied by most musicians in college is more worthy than the music the other students care about? What will neuroscience be able to tell us about music, an area of rapidly growing interest as a result of the recent development of magnetic resonance imaging? What can be done about changing curricula in ways that encourage discussion of questions like these? With a broader musical education than was available to my grandfather in 1890, he need not have worked as a night watchman until he died at age eighty, leaving my grandmother in poverty. After he lost his front teeth in his midfifties, he had no available option but the most simple—and the most depressing.

Partly because my current office is in a building directly across from the Darrell K. Royal—Texas Memorial Stadium (seats one hundred thousand), I think often of the large numbers of young men and women in college who devote so much time to intercollegiate athletics.[10] Here, too, there is a very serious imbalance between the many who compete and the few who are chosen. But in sports, "graduate education" implies progress at least to the minor leagues, and thus to work, however brief, as a paid professional. Because athletes are keenly sensitive to the aging of their bodies and to the concomitant brevity of their careers, those unsuccessful in quantifiable competition are forced, like dancers, to leave the game at earlier stages in their lives than do musicians. They are thus provided with the need to begin professionally for a second time while still young enough to do so. In the world of professional sports, we take it for granted that it is important to develop both professional athletes and a fan base that supports them. Further, while the world of sports professionals has encouraged continuing adult participation for those who do not become professionals in baseball, volleyball, tennis, and golf, the world of music mostly encourages those who do not become professionals to put their clarinets in mothballs.[11]

That there are better models for a different musical ecosystem is evident from work ongoing in Scandinavia for the past half century. And suddenly, in China, there are 350 million classical music fans, developed since the death of Mao Tse-tung and his wife in the mid-1970s.[12] In China, the government has worked to limit the number of children born to a married couple. Parents there have apparently discovered that the dedication of love and attention required by the musical instruction of a child fosters family time spent together. And they are grateful for the work ethic that a devotion to music inspires. More and more of something positive is not always better, as persuasively argued by Garrett Hardin in his famous paper "The Tragedy of the Commons," where the gradual addition of livestock to a finite grazing area eventually undermines the best interests of the community.[13] The genesis of Venezuela's El Sistema over the past thirty-five years has produced not only a nation of two hundred youth orchestras but also a united effort all over that country to use orchestral music as a means to keep at-risk children off the streets and out of harm's way. It is an investment, on the part of several consecutive governments from both the Left and the Right, to employ music as the centerpiece of a program of national pride.

This book is addressed to the parents of potential music students, to music students, to music teachers and professors (who mold young musicians), to the deans of music schools (who have an important stake in the appointment and promotion of faculty), to the provosts and presidents of colleges and universities (who have an important role in the appointment of deans), and to the heads of foundations and the chairs of the National Endowments for the Arts and Humanities (which help underwrite music study). I have not addressed chapters to those who teach in private music studios or who teach music in our K–12 sector[14] because I have no direct professional experience in either of those important areas.

Most members of the educational establishment are stakeholders in the status quo. I believe that it is only through the thoughtful interaction of all these groups that we can produce a better balance between the supply of gifted artists and the opportunities for their professional employment.[15] I hope that all of those listed in the previous paragraph will read the whole of the book, for the messages developed in each of the chapters bear equally on music's future. Addressing chapters 4–9 as though to separate readerships is an admittedly artificial procedure, for students will eventually become parents and teachers, and some of the teachers will inevitably become deans and provosts or the heads of foundations. Were I to address these groups only as individual entities, I fear that the problems endemic to our profession will remain as they are, without an educational solution. Curricular change cannot belong to the faculty alone, nor can solutions to the problem of sexual harassment be entrusted only to the faculty and the deans.

Though I am by no means the only one concerned about the problems at hand, I am undoubtedly the person with the broadest experience in American higher education to have worked as long as I have in the trenches on reform in musical education. Greg Sandow, a Harvard and Yale graduate who is an accomplished composer, a distinguished music critic, and a member of the graduate faculty of the Juilliard School, has been at work for the past several years on a splendid blog that will shortly result in a new book, *Rebirth: The Future of Classical Music*. Sandow, whose work I greatly admire, argues that a primary responsibility of young musicians is to build new audiences. In his view, this will require three things: "making performances feel more lively, playing repertory that reflects contemporary life, and playing all music, but especially the old masterworks, more vividly," a prescription that has my enthusiastic support.

It is not my role to lay down a new track for the future of musical education. By questioning assumptions about our current musical life, however, I hope to stimulate a discussion toward a better future for music and musicians, thus bringing to more people, all over the world, a more perfect realization of the promise of Orpheus, the original title of this book. Like Sir Peter Maxwell Davies, I am eager that "musicians and music teachers of the present and future learn better than my generation has how to help preserve the wealth of wisdom and beauty that composers of the past have left us, better balancing our role as curators of musical history with our future responsibility of helping provide new music that moves and stimulates humanity of the centuries ahead."[16]

NOTES

1. Douglas Lowry, sixth dean of the Eastman School of Music, passed away in October 2013 at the tragically early age of only sixty-two. A superb and dedicated leader whose work continued the directions I had helped establish in Rochester, he addressed the problems covered in this book in his final column from the dean in *Eastman Notes*:

> Schools of music have complicated missions but one simple purpose: to educate talented young performers, composers, scholars, and teachers in the critical function of their chosen professions. We have a responsibility to furnish experiences that not only teach the art, but also bear some resemblance to the world that our students will inherit. This includes preparing them in the musical rudiments and the real-life challenge of building and inspiring an audience, knowing important aspects of the business, and be-

coming entrepreneurs. Some think that the latter components are beyond the domain of what we should be doing, suggesting that an education in the arts "should stick with the art." Yet history provides us with many examples of innovative musical entrepreneurs who not only created inspiring music but also ambitiously built careers. From Beethoven to Stravinsky, our lore is full of artists who learned how to drum up business, not afraid of posting handbills or cleverly marketing their wares. The attentive musician listens to the pulse of the times—not to curry favor with current stylistic trends, but to form an understanding of how music's presentation and enjoyment have evolved. To assume that the musical experience of 1813—how it looked, felt, dressed; where it took place—would and should remain the same in 2013 ignores some basic laws of nature.

2. Howard Gardner, *Truth, Beauty, and Goodness Reframed: Educating for the Virtues in the Age of Truthiness and Twitter* (New York: Basic Books, 2011), 90.

3. A DMA candidate in music education once came to me at Eastman with the complaint that her world class cello teacher was insisting that she was so fine a player that she "deserved" to perform in a major orchestra. She told me that she was eager to teach music in a Canadian public school, feeling that her lifelong mission. She sought—and received—my support in this.

4. Douglas Dempster, "American Medicis," commissioned by Columbia University's American Assembly, in preparation for an Arden House conference in 2004.

5. As president of the Juilliard School since 1984, Joseph Polisi is moving Juilliard in the direction of many of the goals outlined here, a task I had begun at Eastman a decade earlier. Polisi's *The Artist as Citizen* (Pompton Plains, NJ: Amadeus, 2005) is recommended reading. But his chapter "Are There Too Many Musicians?" ends with the answer, "No. We are just producing too many of the wrong kind." Nearly a quarter century later, we are producing more than thirty thousand music degrees a year instead of the twelve thousand of 1987, the date of Polisi's essay. And, in my view, too many of our graduates are still of the wrong kind.

6. Relevant data are available through HEADS, the Higher Education Administrative Data Service, information gathered annually by collegiate music's principal accreditation agency, the National Association of Schools of Music, headquartered in Reston, Virginia.

7. For a superb and very recent analysis of the economics affecting symphony orchestras worldwide, especially in the United States, see Robert J. Flanagan, *The Perilous Life of Symphony Orchestras: Artistic Triumphs and Economic Challenges* (New Haven, CT: Yale, 2012).

8. For an excellent analysis of piano competitions, see Joseph Horowitz, *The Ivory Trade* (Boston: Summit Books, 1991).

9. Lisa Wong's *Scales to Scalpels: Doctors Who Practice the Healing Arts of Music and Medicine* (New York: Pegasus Books, 2012) is full of anecdotal information on the large numbers of musically accomplished college students who end up as successful medical school students and as physicians, an area where the skills of time management, careful listening, and hard work are equally important. This is an area where demand greatly exceeds supply, especially for general practitioners.

10. For an excellent overview of the ongoing problems of sports in American colleges and universities, see James Shulman, William Bowen, Lauren Meserve, and Roger Schonfeld, *The Game of Life: College Sports and Educational Values* (Princeton, NJ: Princeton University Press, 2001).

11. Church and community choirs are an important exception to this, as are Roy Ernst's New Horizons bands, the Chamber Music Network (founded by Leonard Strauss and Helen Rice), and the Van Cliburn Competition for Amateur Pianists. These latter are amateurs not in the quality of their piano playing but in the fact that the competitors must be older than thirty-five and must not earn their livelihoods in music. For an inspiring account of a University of Chicago English professor's romance with the cello, see Wayne Booth's *For the Love of It: Amateuring and Its Rivals*

(Chicago: University of Chicago Press, 1999), of which the *Chicago Tribune*'s John von Rhein writes, "The book will be read with delight by every well-meaning amateur who has ever struggled. . . . Readers will come away with a valuable lesson for living. Never mind the outcome of a possibly vain pursuit; in the passion that is expended lies the glory." John Hitt's *Bunch of Amateurs: A Search for the American Character* (New York: Crown, 2012) is a humorous account of the history of what the author takes to be a distinctly American trait, in all sorts of domains. Lisa Wong's *From Scales to Scalpels* comprises in part a history of Boston's Longwood Symphony, where all of the performers except the conductor are professional physicians. See also William Haley, "Amateurism," *American Scholar* 45 (1976): 253–59.

12. Alex Ross, "Symphony of Millions: Classical Music in China," *Listen to This* (New York: Farrar, Straus and Giroux, 2010), 159–75.

13. Garrett Hardin, "The Tragedy of the Commons," *Science* 162, no. 3859 (December 13, 1968): 1243–48. See http://www.garretthardinsociety.org/articles/art_tragedy_of_the_commons.html.

14. For an excellent comparative summary of music in the world's public schools, see Gordon Cox and Robin Stevens, *The Origins and Foundations of Music Education: Cross-Cultural Historical Studies of Music in Compulsory Schooling* (London: Continuum, 2010).

15. Angela Myles Beeching's *Beyond Talent: Creating a Successful Career in Music* (Oxford: Oxford University Press, 2005), David Cutler's *The Savvy Musician: Building a Career, Earning a Living, and Making a Difference* (Pittsburgh: Helius Press, 2009), and Ramon Ricker's *Lessons from a Streetwise Music Professor: What You Won't Learn at Most Music Schools* (Fairport, NY: Sundown, 2011) are all excellent books, musts for the library of every musician and serious music student. My book is on a broader subject, imagining in the long term an overhaul of the whole educational system that produces musicians and their audiences.

16. Simon Johnson, "Queen's Official Composer: Youngsters are Ignorant of Classical Music Because of 'Elitist' Attitude," *Telegram*, November 17, 2013.

ONE

The Winds of Change

Having begun my teaching career in the fall of 1963 as an instructor in the Department of Music at Princeton, teaching undergraduate music history and theory, I continued as an assistant and associate professor of music in the Department of Humanities at MIT from the fall of 1968 until my appointment as director of the University of Rochester's Eastman School of Music in November 1972. Since stepping down from the deanship of the College of Fine Arts at the University of Texas at Austin in the fall of 2006, I have returned to the classroom, a quite different place from the situation I left in Cambridge during the midst of the Vietnam War. As I now tell my students at the University of Texas at Austin, a lot has changed since the time I graduated from college in 1957, in the world generally and in the field of music. And the speed of change appears to be accelerating.

To begin with, we are all part of a much smaller planet. Whenever I traveled to Europe during graduate school and as a junior faculty member, I did so by ship, and it took a week to get there. These days we all take it for granted that travel to Asia will be by plane and, while exhausting, will take but twelve to fourteen hours. Similarly, while almost all of the students in the Princeton Graduate School of the late 1950s were white males in their twenties, the students who now populate my Texas classrooms are both male and female, and they come not only from all over Texas but from all over the world, ranging in age from recent high school graduates to people in their sixties and seventies.

While the world I grew up in featured a dichotomous division between American capitalism and international communism, the collapse of the Soviet Union in the late 1980s and the development of China as the world's most populous capitalist power have in the meantime brought about a brand new world, facilitating virtually instant international com-

1

munication via the Internet. In the old days, when I held a Fulbright to Vienna for two years in the early 1960s, one called home on Christmas and perhaps on Mother's birthday. Nowadays, the cost of international phone service is trivial and, if one wishes, it is possible to *see* the person one is speaking with, or to block the calls of fund-raisers one doesn't want to speak with. During my senior year in college, the FBI returned a registered check I had sent to Berlin in a vain attempt to purchase a microfilm needed for music-historical work from an East German library, warning me never to do anything like that ever again. Hardly anyone in those days was in touch with China.

While my own student days precluded communicating with people of any race other than my own, Lyndon Johnson's civil rights legislation of the 1960s has brought about a situation in which I can learn from faculty colleagues and students from all over the world, in which I am proud that my own country is led by a black president born in Hawaii, still an American territory when I was in college. During the period 1850–1940, large numbers of young Americans completing their musical education did so in Europe, especially in Vienna, Leipzig, Berlin, Paris, and London. After World War II, the United States became the international center of education in classical music, with students coming here not only from Europe but in increasing numbers from China, Taiwan, Japan, Malaysia, Singapore, and South Korea. In our own times, it is easy to imagine that, by 2050, the international center of education in classical music may well be in Asia.[1]

While young women from Radcliffe were part of my undergraduate education at Harvard, few of them went on to graduate school or aspired to professional futures of their own, a marked difference from a world in which my daughter, married to a wonderful Chinese American actuary from MIT, is a vice president at Fidelity Investments and the mother of two terrific sons. In the old days, girls sang or played violin, cello (only in long dresses!), flute, harp, and piano. Sergiu Celibidache reportedly suffered emotional collapse in the eighties when he learned he had appointed Abbie Conant first trombone of the Munich Philharmonic after a "behind-the-screen" audition. But now women play not only every acoustic instrument but have also attained major successes as composers and conductors. Because some American values change slowly, the three areas in which American women of my childhood were allowed to have professional careers—school teaching, nursing, and clerical work—are still underpaid, producing problematic national shortages of nurses and good schoolteachers. It appears that the days when young women studied music largely as a social grace are over.

In the days of my youth, homosexuality was a forbidden subject, and in the world of music, the "don't ask, don't tell" mentality that ruled our armed forces during the period 1993–2010 characterized the whole of American society. When Serge Koussevitzky stepped down in 1949 from the music directorship of the Boston Symphony, it was rumored that Leonard Bernstein, Koussevitzky's brilliant young protégé, would have succeeded his mentor as music director had it not been for three matters: (1) Bernstein was Jewish. (2) Bernstein was said to be homosexual (the idea of bisexuality had not yet raised its head in the boardroom of the Boston Symphony). But worst of all, (3) Bernstein had written two Broadway shows (*On the Town* and *Fancy Free*). Koussevitzky had reportedly told Bernstein that it was impossible to care both about Brahms and Gershwin, the composer of *Porgy and Bess*, which I was told in college was not a real opera.

When I was a college student, life expectancy was a generation shorter than it is now. Tenured professors normally retired, whether they wanted to or not, on the June 30 following their sixty-fifth birthday. But since the early 1980s, the federal government has made it illegal to retire a tenured professor on the basis of age, eager as we now are to persuade as many septuagenarians as possible to continue working, in order not to further overburden a social security system we are often told is at long-term risk. While medical research has made great progress in dealing with all sorts of threats to health and happiness, the cost of good medical care, still not available in the United States to all Americans, continues each year to consume a larger and larger portion of our gross domestic product.

While technology makes it possible to receive international news on a 24-7 basis, it also facilitates the work of those who would harm us, as the nineteen terrorists of September 11 amply demonstrated. Because there is much more space to fill with news and commentary, there is a lot less new work on television, much more recourse to reruns of older material, the use of the radio for the stoking of angry and ill-considered opinion, the slow death of media that rely on readers, and the concomitant lessening of memory and attention spans. Those of us who were introduced to the personal computer after age sixty must learn how to deal on a daily basis with students far more at home with the new technologies than we are as senior faculty. [2]

When I was young, libraries were stocked with books, and students were guided by faculty to read what generations had come to consider the wisdom of the ages. Certainly, one understood that the synthesis of reliable information was a central part of a good education, and that to attain it a decent grasp of the principal threads of world history was important. In recent years, most libraries have moved books no longer much in demand to more remote and less expensive off-campus locations, so that we can equip our reading rooms with personal computers that now access an infinitely larger world of digitally stored and constantly reevaluated information. While Robert Layton's spoof on Dag Hendrik Essrum Hellerup in *The New Grove's Dictionary of Music and Musicians* of 1980 remained necessarily unaltered until the second printing of that encyclopedia, those responsible for the scholarly review of Wikipedia entries appear to do so on at least a monthly basis.

While the number of American institutions of higher education continues to rise, so does the cost of higher education as a percentage of the GDP. Though we continue to accept the idea that higher education produces skills needed for employment in a service-oriented economy, we appear to be losing confidence in the idea that higher education helps in the development of skills in critical thinking required to make a democratic society effective. We seem to be losing confidence, too, in the idea that higher education is not only a private good but a public one as well. This is an investment in which our principal twenty-first-century competitors, the Chinese and the Indians, believe strongly, in my view to their own long-term advantage.

If the world around us has changed markedly during the past half century, the world of music has gone through some pretty remarkable changes of its own. Fifty years ago there was a clear double line of demarcation between classical music (also known as "concert music," "good music," or "serious music") and the kind of music that appealed to a much broader spectrum of Americans, known in those days as "popular music."

Classical music, brought to the United States from Europe by the affluent after our Civil War, was said when I was young to live forever, whereas pieces of popular music, all much shorter, were promulgated on AM radio, supported by a weekly program known as *Your Hit Parade*, featuring performances of popular pieces that normally disappeared from the public consciousness with the passing of several months. Classical music was performed in auditoria for well-dressed audiences who were supposed to sit quietly, paying close attention to the music and applauding only at the ends of complete works. Popular music, on the other hand, was performed for dancing, and after the 1960s in very large venues where very loud volume, alcohol, sex, drugs, and audience participation were common. I remember being told, when I was ten, that listening to Beethoven and Brahms would make me a better human being— more intelligent, more sensitive, more caring. While the music of Gershwin was supposed to belong to the world of the Pops as I was growing up, the interest in Gershwin of such superlative artists as William Bolcom and James Levine has in the meantime helped break down the watertight division that separated Gershwin from music that was supposed to be taken more seriously. Though Alex Ross's superb *The Rest Is Noise* fully covers special twentieth-century interests in the breaking down of such musical barriers, especially during the 1920s and '30s and since the 1980s, there has been very little compensatory recognition of this in American music schools in the meantime, focused as too many of them are on European music written before the death of Debussy (1862–1918).[3]

There has been a marked change, too, in music's availability. While as a lad I had a small collection of classical 78s, it was a *very* small collection, it required a good deal of storage space, and it grew very slowly. While there was a time in my life when I had heard Brahms's symphonies numbers one, two, and four at least once each, I was eager for two or three years to hear even a single performance of the Brahms's Third. Now in my seventies, the university of which I am part owns a record collection of well over a hundred fifty thousand CDs and DVDs, any of which any student or faculty member can borrow and listen to—at home, in the office, or, as happens with the greatest numbers of Americans, in the endless commuting time between home and office that comprises several hours a week. In addition, YouTube.com and Spotify.com provide us with an almost limitless musical choice from almost anything one can think of. Music of all kinds is also more broadly available in places where one wishes it were not—in restaurants, elevators, shopping malls, super markets, and dentists' offices. One has to search hard in our time for silence.

Together with the international dissemination of all sorts of music has come, ironically, a gradual narrowing of interpretive possibility. While Kreisler, Heifetz, Szigetti, and Menuhin all had distinctive ways of playing the Beethoven Violin Concerto, today we are left only with a focus on the way Itzhak Perlman plays it. Itzhak, as we all know, is a great artist and a very special human being, worthy of emulation in many different ways. But he would be the first to acknowledge that music's house is impoverished to the degree that standard interpretations of standard masterpieces are made to substitute for the excitement produced by the Beethoven Concerto the first time Franz Clement played it in Vienna in 1806. While the recording technology available in the days of my youth produced all sorts of suboptimal recorded performances, it also spared us the antiseptic CDs of today, in which the gentle art of digital editing has eliminated any trace of performance imperfection. At the same time, we have developed a generation of splendid young artists whose standards of technical perfection, ensemble, and intonation are the highest ever. This is a conclusion inevitably reached when one compares a modern performance of a Brahms symphony by the orchestra of any of the nation's leading music schools with the recorded performance of the same work in 1920, say, by the London Symphony or the New York Philharmonic. And it is not simply that the audio engineering standards of reproduction have improved exponentially. In addition, standards of fidelity to the score, of intonation, of timbral balance, and of ensemble playing have all improved markedly as well.

Certainly, the means of music's transmission has changed. During the days of the Second War World, the nation's three radio networks broadcast weekly ninety-minute live performances of the NBC Symphony, the New York Philharmonic, and the Boston Symphony, with weekly broadcasts on Saturday afternoons of full-length operas by the Metropolitan Opera, sponsored for many years by Texaco. The expense of television production greatly limited the use of that medium for the airing of classical music events during the closing decades of the twentieth century, a situation that the development of the Internet has changed in the past twenty years. While new technology and digital piracy have undermined the traditional record business, put together to sell stars performing hits, there has developed instead a huge international market of modest niches, the aggregate of which distributes a vast variety of musical repertories all over the world. This is a phenomenon well described in Chris Anderson's persuasive book *The Long Tail.* (In preparing Debussy's "Golliwog's Cakewalk" for a recent public lecture, I found in ten seconds a dozen recorded versions of the work on YouTube, by pianists past and present, from all over the world, some with video, some with printed music displayed concurrently, by great artists and by children.)

Addicted as Texans are to Friday night football, played with six men to a team if the town is not large enough for eleven on a team, it is natural that Texas has maintained a much more extensive culture for musical instruction in the public schools than elsewhere in America. If we are to have football, we will also have a band program. And so long as we have that, we may as well have choral programs and, in the larger communities, orchestral programs. We are the only state of the fifty that is not part of MENC, the Music Educators National Conference. When I first asked the reasons, I was told, "We have our own—TMEA, the Texas Music Educators Association. It is bigger than MENC and, of course, better!"

However that may be, too many American communities have come to the conclusion that musical instruction is an educational luxury, a frill that can be cut in days of economic duress, together with a general education, clean air, and water. One notes this decline in American musical literacy in churches and restaurants all over the nation, whenever what used to be congregational singing is performed, or when the wait staff tries to sing "Happy Birthday" to the honoree of the evening. On such occasions, the first two phrases are normally performed in unison: "Happy birthday to you, happy birthday to you." But when the young waiters and waitresses get to the octave leap at the beginning of the third phrase—"Happy birthday, dear _____"—the upward leap results in half a dozen different pitches, leading to musical chaos in the final phrase. When I was a child, we all sang "Take Me Out to the Ballgame" with the seventh inning stretch. Nowadays we all get to stretch, but the music is performed by a soloist or by the organ alone. And "Take Me Out to the Ballgame" is a lot easier to sing than our National Anthem! One wonders what an audience of concertgoers who cannot perform simple tonal melodies perceives when treated to a concert of forty-minute masterpieces.

Fifty years ago music historians strove to sort out questions of attribution and dating for the works of composers who really mattered. With attention to such matters, we fostered an understandable interest in striving to make our performances fulfill the artistic intentions of their composers. We played on instruments appropriate to the period of the works' composition, improvising ornaments in the spirit of the times, using properly contemporaneous systems of tuning and temperament and instrumental ensembles appropriate to the venues of Bach's time or Mozart's. In the new millennium there is, however, a much greater willingness to acknowledge that, try as we may, having heard Wagner's *Tristan* and Berg's *Lulu*, it is impossible to be as startled as we were meant to be in 1802 by the low C-sharp of the cellos and basses in the seventh measure of Beethoven's *Eroica*. Our ears are, inevitably, of the twenty-first century.

Half a century ago opera in America was a concert in costume, sung in one (or more!) foreign languages. And chamber music was an elitist art in which few musicians participated professionally, for small and prestigious audiences. But in the meantime, with the development of supertitles, opera has become drama about greed, lust, love, anger, revenge, integrity, and pride, supported by the music of Mozart or Verdi, an unbeatable combination given the right cast of singers, a fine conductor, and a great orchestra. Though opera is understandably expensive to produce, Peter Gelb, executive director of the Metropolitan Opera, has figured out how to transmit the work of the Met to movie theaters all over America, with interviews between the acts that involve articulate musicians interviewing other musicians, and in a way that appears to increase audiences for local opera companies.

Partly because music students have become convinced that the chamber music repertory is a wonderful area for great musical pleasure, partly because universities have figured out ways of tenuring chamber ensembles in a fashion that protects both the institution and the integrity of the ensemble, partly because chamber music is not very expensive to produce, there are now more than two hundred American string quartets under artist management. Audiences like such performances because they feel they can get to know the players as individuals, and because seeing the visual interaction of the four lines of a quartet apparently helps people hear the music.

Though orchestras dominated the world of classical music in America half a century ago, it is now the symphonies that are in trouble. We were successful in convincing America that a major city cannot exist without its own orchestra. But we have to this point been unsuccessful in working out productively synergistic relationships among the seven necessary groups that underlie the life of any American orchestra: the music director, the management, the board, the players, the audience, the press, and the community. Serious budget problems, exacerbated by the current recession, even in cities like Philadelphia, Cleveland, Detroit, Minneapolis, Atlanta, and New York, demonstrate the rockiness of the road still to be traveled if American orchestras are to continue to have the role in our cultural life that Theodore Thomas (1835–1905), Serge Koussevitzky (1874–1951), George Szell (1897–1970), and Maurice Abravanel (1903–1993) once envisioned.[4]

Certainly, the role of the audience has changed. Roger Sessions's noble idea that the musically perceptive powers of composer, performers, and audience ought ideally to be close to one another in sensitivity[5] may have worked several hundred years ago. In those days, the aristocrats who hired composers and performers were themselves amateur musicians, dukes and princesses who learned music the way musicians learn it. But with the French Revolution and the disappearance of the European aristocracy, romantic entrepreneurs like Hector Berlioz began to work at filling halls of two thousand or more by introducing major works of instrumental music, itself a relatively new phenomenon, through "programs," prose to be read before listening to a piece of music, ostensibly to convey the dreams of an opium addict or the experience of traveling in Italy. While Schumann and Brahms eschewed such ideas, Liszt, Strauss, and Mahler reveled in them, though the latter tortured himself after the fact by decrying the legitimacy of programs he had already provided for his orchestral music. With the twentieth century in America came efforts initiated by Walter Damrosch and others in "music appreciation," the idea that college-educated Americans who had not studied music as children could be introduced to (primarily) orchestral repertory through information on orchestral instruments and through composers' biographies, a pursuit comparable in my view to teaching baseball through the lives of the great players and through information about how gloves and bats have evolved.

This is not to say that there is a correct way of listening to a piece of music, any more than that there is a correct way of watching a baseball game. It is to suggest that Joe Girardi, the manager of the New York Yankees, gets more out of watching a baseball game than I do, just as I get a lot more out of watching a game than did my late mother, who steadfastly refused to have anything to do with baseball. I believe that a similar spectrum probably maps the acuity of what a variety of listeners get out of listening to a piece of music. Thus, while I think that the more music one knows and loves improves the intensity with which one experiences music, I am loathe to tell anyone that I know how to listen to music, while implying that he does not.

I began to worry about the special problems of the academic world as an instructor at Princeton fifty years ago, when the questionnaire I administered after the first introductory course I taught, to three hundred young men, revealed that only one hundred of the students thought they had gotten something of value out of the course. Of the disappointed two-thirds, one hundred complained that the course had gone over their heads, while the remaining third thought the course much too simple. This suggested to me at the time, though I was not then in a position to do anything about it, both that the university would have done better at the outset to divide the class into three sections of one hundred each, and that we all had our priorities wrong. While senior faculty understandably like to teach their fields of specialization to graduate students, the field as a whole would be better off with more experienced professors teaching introductory courses, especially since students who do well in such courses will later become not only members of the audience but board members of important professional musical organizations.

Despite continuing study during the past quarter century of the long-term finances of orchestras, ticket prices have continued to escalate at rates well beyond those of the consumer price index, at a time when the world has encountered myriad forms of competition for an audience that wants to be increasingly participatory and knowledgeable, and in which the female part of the audience is as professionally active during the daytime as the male. Put another way, an art form with an elitist back-ground does not help itself by pricing itself out of an apparently declin-ing market. This has taken place during a time in our history when classi-cal music has disappeared from AM radio and television, and largely from the daily press (itself in trouble), and when we have managed to communicate to the public that special kinds of esoteric knowledge are required to get something out of a performance of classical music. How often does one hear these days, from people young, middle aged, and older, that "I don't attend orchestral concerts because I don't know any-thing about *that* kind of music"?

Though Bill Clinton plays the saxophone, classical music disappeared from the White House following the presidency of Ronald Reagan until reintroduced in 2010 by Barack Obama. Said Obama when introducing a recital in the East Room on national television, something like the follow-ing: "This sort of music is not often performed in the White House, partly because most Americans don't know when the piece is over and thus when to applaud. I am, of course, a part of that group. But Michelle knows when to clap, and she promised she would let me know when to applaud!" Put another way, the president was gently drawing our atten-tion to the fact that we all have a lot to learn about heeding, listening, remembering, synthesizing, and planning, processes that listening to mu-sic strongly supports, while at the same time reminding us that the presi-dent is not an elitist.

Part of the problem with orchestral audiences is that we are not sure who those audiences are, why they are present, whether they are satisfied or not by the experience of attending, and whether they are apt to return, recommending future attendance to their friends—all essential informa-tion for Americans interested in the sale of hotel rooms, station wagons, fast food, or shampoo. Though a good deal of market research has been published on orchestras during the last twenty years, none of it that I am familiar with tries to discover much about the music-educational backgrounds of the audience for symphony concerts, especially about the long-term efficacy of secondary and collegiate musical instruction toward the long-term development of audiences.[6] It should surprise no one that Greg Sandow will shortly publish data showing that the American audience for classical music is in fact getting older.

It is a central part of the message of this book that in a world of very rapid change, music teaching, still the predominant way musicians make a living, has been very slow to change, as have the curricula of our major music schools and the pedagogic goals toward which those curricula have been directed. The assumptions that basic study in fundamental musicianship may be put off till college, that the symphony orchestra should remain the backbone of a music school's enrollment plans, that instrumental and vocal students learn optimally from weekly private lessons from well-known specialists, and that the road to musical heaven lies straight through the practice room remain unexplored axioms inherited from the nineteenth century.

In the world of higher education, a continuing focus in our graduate schools on areas of very narrow specialization is certainly not limited to music. When Milton Babbitt published his famous article in *High Fidelity* half a century ago, "Who Cares If You Listen?" his argument was perfectly logical. If tenured professors of physics, economics, and medieval French literature normally publish for readerships limited to other academics in those disciplines, why ought professors of music not be permitted to compose for a similarly narrow audience?[7] For that matter, why ought music historians and theorists not write mostly for each other? While the perspective of narrowly focused composers reigned during my student days, the initiatives of Meet the Composer, beginning in the 1970s, together with pioneering work by leaders like Samuel Adler, William Bolcom, John Corigliano, Michael Daugherty, Donald Grantham, John Harbison, Kevin Puts, Christopher Rouse, Gunther Schuller, Joseph Schwantner, and Dan Welcher, have strengthened a conviction among young composers that their music is without much purpose if it fails to move a human audience. It is only in the past year or two that musicologists have begun to see the wisdom of treating such people as Michael Beckerman, Joseph Horowitz, Robert Greenberg, Rob Kapilow, Alex Ross, and Robert Winter, who write well beyond the confines of scholarly journals, as figures worthy of emulation by our graduate students. It is, of course, problematic that the media continue in too many cases to lead the audience to believe that anything written since the time of World War II is strong medicine with a bitter aftertaste, a long distance from the power that Orpheus's singing once exercised on Charon, persuading the figure who guarded the entrance to the underworld that Orpheus be permitted both to enter and to leave, so inspiring was the power of his singing.

Through the lens of my own experience, I have tried to put together in the chapters that follow a brief history of how we got to where we are, including suggestions on general educational directions for the future discovered during the past half century. This involves, as the reader will discover, ideas designed to encourage varying goals among the nation's 638 professional music schools, goals differentiating the schools more clearly from one another among potential future students and their parents. It includes the broadening of curricula and work toward making musicians happier and more successful human beings, while providing the visceral force in the new millennium that I believe music deserves.

NOTES

1. By this time most collegiate students of classical music are familiar with the joke in Leonard Slatkin's foreword, asking for the identity of the second most frequently spoken language at the Juilliard School. The answer is English. According to a similar modern canard, classical music can be defined as "written by Germans and taught by Russians in the United States to Asians." Any American who doubts this thesis should spend a day or two in Hamamatsu, Japan, an attractive city of more than eight hundred thousand, halfway from Tokyo to Osaka on the principal Shinkansen line. Hamamatsu is in fact the music business capital of Japan, headquarters for Yamaha, Kawai, Roland, Suzuki, and Photocon, as well as for two marvelous concert halls seating two thousand and one thousand, a luxury hotel decorated throughout with musical motifs, and a very impressive museum of musical instruments. The concert halls feature everything from fifth grade wind ensembles of Japanese schoolchildren to the Berlin Philharmonic and appear to be filled on a continuing basis with the broadest array of international performing groups and soloists and enthusiastic audiences. The thousand-seat hall has a marvelous pipe organ. Yamaha's Hamamatsu headquarters for ongoing research on acoustical instruments of all kinds is a wonder of the modern world.

2. Those of us still teaching in our seventies are referred to Marc Prensky's excellent *Teaching Digital Natives: Partnering for Real Learning* (Thousand Oaks, CA: Corwin, 2010). Craig Lambert's "Twilight of the Lecture: The Trend toward Active Learning May Overthrow the Style of Teaching That Has Ruled Universities for 600 Years" (*Harvard Magazine*, March–April 2012) also provides the professor who has been away from his classroom for many years with much to think about. The students of yesteryear busied themselves in class taking (often garbled) notes; today's students hardly ever take notes in class, preferring to participate in faculty-led discussions that promote skills of understanding rather than the memorization of material that is in any case instantly available on the web.

3. Alex Ross, *The Rest Is Noise: Listening to the Twentieth Century* (New York: Farrar, Straus and Giroux, 2007), 120–56, 473–539.

4. Thomas W. Morris, former general manager of the Boston Symphony and executive director of the Cleveland Orchestra, a year ago gave an exciting lecture to the members of a University of Texas course of mine on the history and future of the symphony orchestra. The title of Tom's lecture was "A Business in Trouble: The American Symphony Orchestra."

5. Roger Sessions, *The Musical Experience of Composer, Performer, Listener* (Princeton, NJ: Princeton University Press, 1950).

6. The sort of research I have in mind could be carried out, relatively inexpensively, by matching faculty and graduate students in universities with first-class business schools, music schools or departments, and local orchestras that pay the musicians living wages. The sorts of questions I'd advise investigating in this fashion include discovering among orchestral subscribers and attendees, sorted by age, gender, and income the following: (1) How many studied an instrument with a private teacher as a child or adolescent? (2) How many attended concerts as children with their parents? (3) How many studied music in a K–12 setting? (4) With the yellow school bus contingents that many states pay for? (5) As the result of courses taken in college? (6) With dates? (7) With other music students? (8) With other university students? (9) How many believe that an ability to read music is important? (10) How many would be interested in relevant material provided online in advance of concerts? (11) How many would really insist on music written between the days of J. S. Bach and the end of World War II? (12) How many would be interested in new work of high quality, well prepared? (13) How many would appreciate visual support at the time of the concert, or beforehand? (14) How many would like well-prepared preconcert talks? By the conductor or soloist? By members of the orchestra? (15) Do board members and other generous contributors actually attend the concerts? (16) If not, why are they motivated to give? (17) Is formal attire a significant aspect of why people attend? (18) To be seen by important community members and other peer social groups? (19) Other? Such work would offer significant opportunities for improving town–gown relationships. Shortly before this book went to press, I participated in a very successful conference, sponsored by the Houston Endowment and carried out by the Kinder Institute for Urban Research of Rice University, which demonstrated that participation in the arts by people of Caucasian, African American, Hispanic, and Asian backgrounds in Houston comprises a leading means of positive communication among those groups. *The Houston Arts Survey* is enthusiastically recommended reading for other cities seeking solutions to some of the problems posed in this footnote.

7. Babbitt protested many times in the meantime that the title assigned to his essay was not his own but the work of an editor run amuck. The original title was "The Composer as Specialist."

TWO

Where Did Musical Instruction Come From?

Whether one believes that the earth is ten thousand years old or a billion, historians and neuroscientists agree that music of some sort has been shared by humanity from the onset of our existence here, and that applying abstract rules for organizing pitches in time has been a human characteristic unshared by any nonhuman species.[1] But if the practice and perception of music is limited on earth to human beings, we have no idea of the purpose that music was originally meant to fill. To alert warriors to protect us against an oncoming attack of mastodons? To bring us all together? To help form a suitable aural context for the worship experience? To court the opposite sex, in support of the further propagation of the species? To encourage the success of tasks performed by rote? To help put squalling babies to sleep? No one knows the answer(s), though it is now clear that the human brain naturally detects organizational schemes of the kind just mentioned, and that the places in the brain responsible for such functions are broadly distributed all over the brain. It is clear that the development of such musical skills as pitch matching and the differentiating of length in a growing brain is supportive of the more general development of cognition and of attention spans, and that, like the learning of language, it is a great deal easier for human beings to acquire fundamental musical skills at age five or six than at age eighteen or twenty, the times of life when such aural skills are normally taught in college.

Though the earliest information I know of on teaching music comes from Plato and Aristotle, it concerns music's role in society and the development of a harmonious personality rather than instruction in performance, for which the ancient Greeks seem to have had relatively low regard. Says Aristotle:

13

Why need people learn to perform themselves instead of enjoying music played by others? And we may consider the conception that we
have about the gods. Zeus does not sing and harp to the poets himself.
But professional musicians we speak of as vulgar people, and indeed
we think it not manly to perform music, except when drunk or for fun. [2]

By far the most important musical repertory that survives from earlier
history, together with scant information on how that music was taught
and disseminated, comes from the music of the Roman Catholic Church.
So-called Gregorian chant, monophonic plainsong sung by the Schola
Cantorum, the trained papal choir of the Vatican, is connected by legend
with the papacy of Gregory the Great (590–604), traditionally credited
with having ordered the cataloguing of music assigned to the Mass and
to specific daily celebrations of the church's evolving liturgy. Taught
originally by rote, such music became especially important to the practice
of monastic life, at nine different occasions of daily observance celebrated
by the Benedictines. Spreading through western and central Europe during the eleventh through thirteenth centuries, plainsong seems to have
represented an effort to put both the liturgy and its music under a pedi-
gree of apparently unbroken authority—one empire, one church, one
chant—a degree of uniformity impossible without the gropingly hesitant
evolution of a notational system that made possible the learning of large
bodies of interrelated solo and choral material, greatly facilitating the
eventual development of musical polyphony.

The first institutionally organized instruction in music, apart from
preparing those charged with providing music for the liturgy of the
church, is described by Jane Baldauf-Berdes in her book on the beginnings of musical conservatories in Venice in 1510 and immediately afterward. [3] There were four such institutions—L'Ospedale della Pietà,
L'Ospedale dei Mendicanti, L'Ospedale degli Incurabili, and L'Ospedale
dei Derelitti—asylums supported on a fifty–fifty basis by the Roman
Catholic Church and the Republic of Venice, to look after (and to conserve) the welfare of young women who lacked appropriate parental
support for the dowries normally required for marriage. These institutions quickly developed music, especially choral singing, first as an informal activity, then in a more pre-professional manner, eventually as a
Venetian tourist attraction for wealthy travelers from France, Germany,
and England, who marveled at the artistic achievement of angelic choirs,
visually protected behind screens.

The development of instructional institutions for music, called conservatories, academies, colleges, institutes, and schools, spread all over Italy—to Rome and Naples in the second half of the sixteenth century,
where males equaled the young women in number, thus putting an end
to the conservation of feminine virtue through music study! The curriculum comprised sight-reading, harmony and counterpoint, figured bass

realization, and the arts of ornamentation and improvisation. After the French Revolution, Italians spread such institutions all over Europe: to Paris in 1795, to Vienna in the second decade of the nineteenth century, to London in 1822, to Madrid in 1830, Geneva in 1835, Lisbon in 1836, Copenhagen and Berlin in 1840, Antwerp in 1842, Leipzig in 1843, Rotterdam in 1845, Munich in 1846, Barcelona in 1847, Dublin in 1848, Cologne in 1850, Dresden and Stuttgart in 1856, Saint Petersburg in 1862, and to Moscow in 1866, where the founding directors were the pianist brothers Anton and Nikolai Rubinstein. In the view of Biranda Ford, an able researcher and teacher at London's Guildhall School of Music and Dance, the focus of conservatory training, beginning in Paris much more than previously, fell on specialization, on the perfection of instrumental technique, on the preservation of a growing body of classical masterworks, on performing from memory (especially in imitation of Liszt's solo piano recitals in the 1830s), on the centrality of weekly private instruction, and on a Protestant ethic of endless practicing. Such previously important matters as improvisation, ornamentation, and communication between theory and practice fell into neglect.[4] All such institutions were freestanding and anti-intellectual. In 1835 Liszt declared the Paris Conservatory "a rest home for mummies and the apotheosis of the peruke";[5] a century later, the music students of the Paris Conservatory were said to be generally illiterate. Remunerative positions were always in short supply, and the teaching of music was a principal means for a musician to make a living. Not surprisingly, societal prejudices on the proper role of women were borne out through limitations on the kinds of instruments that women were encouraged to study. Family life in nineteenth-century Germany and Austria centered around a piano in the parlor and on the expectation that any well-bred young lady would take an active interest in practicing and playing the piano, not as a way of earning a livelihood but as a social grace and as a means of attracting a good husband.[6] From the early seventeenth century onward, it was generally agreed that too much practice—especially on the recently developed violin—wasted a young man's time, rendering him unfit as a businessman or an attorney, for example. The Earl of Chesterfield wrote in 1749 to his son, then engaged in making the grand tour of Italy:

> If you love music, hear it; go to operas, concerts and pay fiddlers to play it for you; but I must insist upon your neither piping nor fiddling yourself. It puts a gentleman in a very frivolous and contemptible light. . . . Few things would mortify me more than to see you bearing a part in a concert, with a fiddle under your chin.[7]

The first institutional instruction in music in the Western Hemisphere took place with the founding of the Conservatorio de las Rosas in Morelia, Mexico, in 1763, and in the United States through Lowell Mason's interest in teaching music, immediately after Beethoven's lifetime, in the public schools of Boston, a development emulated all over America as the frontier moved west. The Music Vale Academy for Young Ladies opened in Salem, Connecticut, in 1835, about which one reads in Willis Wager's *Liberal Education and Music*: "The School taught voice, instruments, harmony, counterpoint, thorough bass, and fugue, and eventually it attracted students from all over the country and from abroad." Its earliest director, a Methodist minister named Whittlesey, after whose death in 1876 the school did not survive, conducted the school with a firm hand, says Wager, and he quotes from Frances Hall Johnson's *Music Vale Academy*, published by the State of Connecticut in 1934:

> The young ladies of Music Vale had to rise at five in the morning and practice from six to seven, and were required to dust their pianos prior to commencing practicing. No pupil was allowed to speak during practice time except to her teacher, or to leave the piano, or to play any other composition except that assigned for the practice hour.[8]

If Music Vale was the first American degree-granting institution in music, the Boston Conservatory, the New England Conservatory,[9] the Oberlin Conservatory, and the Peabody Conservatory (now a part of Johns Hopkins University) were the first music degree-granting institutions in the United States of continuous existence that still survive. They were all founded immediately after the Civil War. These institutions now aspire, with 638 American degree-granting institutions accredited by NASM, to develop graduates who can fill the nation's very small number of professional positions in the performance of classical music. The original focus, especially with an enrollment that was predominantly female, was on the development of music teachers—for the public schools, for private studios, and for one's own children. (Rose Fitzgerald Kennedy attended the New England Conservatory early in the twentieth century. During the brief period I spent as president of NEC, we awarded an honorary doctoral degree to her youngest son, the late Senator Edward Kennedy, who spoke movingly of his mother's commitment to music as a strong force for family cohesion, especially through family singing at Christmas and on birthdays.)

Following Oberlin's lead, impressive numbers of collegiate music schools were founded during the balance of the nineteenth century: at the University of Iowa in 1866, the predecessors of the College-Conservatory of the University of Cincinnati in 1875, the University of Michigan in 1880, the University of Southern California in 1884, Yale in 1894, and Northwestern University, the University of Illinois, and the University of Wisconsin in 1895, largely as a means of recognizing our burgeoning young nation's cultural development and as a way of making new land grant universities seem more civilized and less remote.

Jeanette Thurber, having founded her New York Conservatory in 1885, invited Antonin Dvorak to become its director in 1892. The Institute of Musical Art was founded in New York City in 1905, with Frank Damrosch as president. And immediately after the conclusion of World War I, three leading private music schools were founded, each with a substantial endowment: Juilliard, Eastman, and Curtis. Juilliard was developed in New York City on Claremont Avenue, as successor to the Institute of Musical Art.[10] Eastman was established as a division of the University of Rochester, with a physical plant that included a 3,500-seat theater for orchestrally accompanied silent films, making Rochester a more attractive home for the talent George Eastman was eager to recruit from Europe and the East Coast to his new film empire at Eastman-Kodak.[11] And Curtis, a small school in Philadelphia with an endowment that facilitated the recruitment of a very limited number of gifted students who paid no tuition, was founded by Mary Louise Curtis Bok Zimbalist, who twenty years earlier had founded the Philadelphia Settlement School, one of the nation's earliest community music schools, established to help develop a work ethic among the children of recent urban immigrants as a contribution to social welfare. A department of music was founded at Indiana University in 1910, transformed into a school of music in 1921, and renamed the Jacobs School of Music in 2006.[12] In 1914 the University of Texas established a department of music, dissolved by Governor Ma Ferguson in the 1920s as part of an early Texas tea party movement. Music at Texas was made part of a new College of Fine Arts in 1938, reorganized as a school of music in 1989, and renamed in 2007 as the result of a $55 million endowment gift from Sarah and Ernest Butler.[13] With the close of World War II, more than a hundred new American public universities were established, most with their own schools and departments of music. In 1971 Rice University in Houston founded its Shepherd School of Music; Vanderbilt added its Blair School of Music in 1981;[14] and in the earliest years of the twenty-first century, funds from the estate of Richard D. Colburn of Beverly Hills were used to transform what had originally been a community music school near the campus of USC into a degree-granting school directly across from Los Angeles' new Disney Auditorium, an institution planned during the 1990s as what Mr. Colburn used to call "a Curtis for the West." The Colburn School thus turned into another American music school that could afford not to charge tuition, part of a twenty-first-century triumvirate joined in 2001 by Yale as the result of an anonymous $100 million gift of endowment funds to the Yale School of Music.

The idea of founding professional American music schools during the second half of the twentieth century was partly geographic, as previously remote parts of the country became less so, partly as an expression of private donors' understandable pride in their native states and cities. In every case it resulted from a wish to make the local music school more competitive by reducing tuition payments as far as possible—in the case of Colburn, Curtis, and Yale to nothing but the investment of a student's time.

While the idea of music as a liberal art goes back to the medieval trivium and quadrivium, the cultivation of a formal interest in music's history appears to have gotten its start in England with the publications of John Hawkins (1719–1789) and Charles Burney (1726–1814), continuing with the growing European reputation of Beethoven (1770–1827) and his immediate Viennese predecessors, Haydn (1732–1809) and Mozart (1756–91), and gaining momentum with Mendelssohn's performance of Bach's *St. Matthew Passion* in Berlin in 1829.

Johann Nikolaus Forkel (1749–1818), whose biography of J. S. Bach was published in 1802, was appointed organist and music director of the University of Göttingen in 1778. François Joseph Fétis (1784–1871) stirred Paris's interest in musical history after the turn of the nineteenth century, and Edmond Henri de Coussemaker (1805–1876) cultivated an esoteric interest in the surviving writings of medieval and renaissance music theorists. August Wilhelm Ambros (1816–1876) was appointed to a professorship of music history in Prague in 1869, moving to Vienna in 1872, where he joined Eduard Hanslick (1824–1900), who had taught at the University of Vienna from 1870 and was succeeded by Guido Adler (1855–1941) in 1898. Phillip Spitta (1841–1894), whose biography of Bach was published in 1872, was appointed to a professorship at the University of Berlin in 1875. Such work established *Musikwissenschaft* (musicology) as a scholarly discipline in important German universities of the second half of the nineteenth century and inevitably had an important influence on the later development in the United States of historical and later ethno-musicology as central disciplines in American research universities, beginning with the appointment of John Knowles Paine (1839–1906) in the early 1870s at Harvard, after Paine had offered to give a series of lectures on music without compensation. This was an invitation to which the Harvard board reluctantly agreed on condition that Paine's course not count toward a Harvard degree.[15] Harmony and counterpoint were added on the same basis, though it was not until 1873 that college credit was granted for those courses and Paine was paid for teaching them, with the proviso that the repertories taught be only of the highest quality, worthy of the nation's intellectual and social leadership. This traditional Ivy League notion that music history and theory are worthy of academic credit but that musical performance is not was for many years a standard part of the philosophy of Harvard and of a small number of other American universities that followed Harvard's lead. Wrote Archibald Davison (1883–1961), for many years the highly respected chairman of music at Harvard:

> It is sometimes urged that there is an analogy between the type of ability required in the manipulation of apparatus used in the physical

lab in preparation of entrance examinations, and the merely mechanical business of playing the pianoforte, for example. This is hardly true, for the ability to handle skillfully laboratory instruments presupposes the use of logic or original thinking in the experiments that are to follow, whereas playing the pianoforte may be a purely physical matter in which the intellect plays a relatively small part.[16]

Anyone who thinks he believes this should listen to two or three different performances of the same work by artists of the first rank, separated from one another by a quarter century, say, before reflecting on the intellectual, artistic, and technical considerations that differentiate the performances. However misguided such a philosophy may be from the perspective of any thoughtful modern musician, the original design for the study of music in the United States perpetuated the European split between doing music and thinking about it, a chasm the reader will remember was introduced by Aristotle 2,500 years ago. This is a notion, repeated over the years by academics without much background as performers, whose baneful influence has been recently addressed and decisively defeated in *The Pale of Words*, a wonderful book by James A. Winn.[17]

The Harvard appointments of pianist Luise Vosgherchian in the late 1960s and of pianist-scholar Robert Levin as Vosgherchian's successor in the later 1980s have softened the Harvard dichotomy between thinking about music without doing it and doing music without thinking about it that has characterized collegiate musical education in Europe even till now. (In the spring of 2009, a distinguished and broadly based Harvard faculty committee wrote a splendid paper advocating a more synergistic relationship between theory and practice in music, though the almost simultaneous loss of more than 40 percent of the Harvard endowment has obliged the current Harvard administration to postpone further action in this vital area for what I fear will be another several decades.)[18] During the same period, Cornell moved in the same direction, with the appointment of such artist-scholars as John Kirkpatrick, Malcolm Bilson, John Hsu, and Sonya Monosoff.

While there is still a marked contrast between the educational philosophies of Harvard and Princeton, on the one hand, and Curtis and the New England Conservatory, on the other, institutions like Oberlin, Northwestern, Eastman, and several of the nation's major public universities (including Michigan, Illinois, Indiana, and Texas, for example) have for many years fostered the idea of an institution recognized worldwide as the comprehensive American music school, a school with a faculty of seventy-five or more full-time people, a student body of at least several hundred, and a curriculum that includes composition, performance, musical scholarship, pedagogy, and the liberal arts. NASM schools believe, correctly in my view, that theory and practice, isolated from one another, needlessly fracture not only music's integrity as a discipline but the possibility of its broader influence in America.

Several different kinds of undergraduate collegiate degrees with a concentration in music have arisen in the past eighty-five years, including a Bachelor of Arts degree with a concentration in music (in which studies in music history and theory comprise about a third of what is studied) and a Bachelor of Music degree (in which instrumental or vocal study comprises 50 percent, music history and theory studies an additional 25 percent, and the liberal arts a final 25 percent). There exists in addition a bachelor's degree in music education, designed to prepare K–12 music teachers, in which substantial time is taken by work in the philosophy, history, and methods of teaching. Since the music graduates whom we are producing every year as a nation far exceed the number of opportunities available to professional musicians, we have long acknowledged the importance of music *teaching* as a professional outcome for many of our graduates.[19] But while some conservatories have tried to minimize the importance of the liberal arts by labeling them with the pejorative adjective "academic," several of us worked hard during the final quarter of the twentieth century at the development of improved liberal arts studies in professional music schools, stressing the importance for musicians of learning how to think with nuance, to read with discretion, and to write and speak persuasively to others.

There will always be schools in which, no matter how comprehensive the curriculum, there is little communication among the individual faculty on subjects that really matter, a special problem in institutions where the faculty is largely part-time. Such schools certainly include a high level of artistic aspiration, but they neglect the importance of the rest of a student's education as well as the ability of our graduates to use the fruits of their training and education for further work in other fields. Howard Hanson and his contemporaries made initial progress toward such goals during his Eastman directorship (1924–1964), but there was still substantial work to be done in this direction when I became Eastman director in 1972.

I knew that Howard Hanson (1896–1981) was initially concerned that my Ivy League background would make me unsuited in this sense as Eastman director. And for a decade after my appointment, he wrote regular columns for Rochester's afternoon newspaper, the *Times Union*, often on his views about the Eastman School. I was interested, even in my letter of application for the directorship, in the possibility of bringing the practical and scholarly sides of music more synergistically together as a major challenge of my own for the school's future. This was a goal on which I hoped to make progress beyond Eastman, partly through a new consortium of leading American music schools that Philip Nelson, then dean of the music school at Yale, and I put together for the first time in 1975. This was intended as a means toward staying in touch with and influencing ongoing developments in the schools that Nelson and I regarded as the nation's leading producers of performers: Curtis, Eastman, Illinois, Indiana, Juilliard, Michigan, Oberlin, New England, Northwestern, USC, and Yale. Called the "Seven Springs Group," because our first meeting in 1975 took place at an estate called Seven Springs in Bedford Village, New York, the deans, directors, and presidents of these eleven institutions have met annually ever since as a means toward developing an informed discussion on the future of professional musical education in America. This is a discussion that I believe has helped change the professional education of musicians in the meantime, though in some institutions more than in others.

In tandem with what seemed to me in 1972 a chasm between doing music and thinking about it, I used to be bothered by the fact that the constituent parts of our national infrastructure for music focused each on itself, without much thought about the creation of synergisms with the other parts, a phenomenon reflected, not surprisingly, in the education of musicians. The public-school music people thought only about music in the public schools, just as music's liberal arts departments thought only about their work. The work of the community music schools—non-degree-granting institutions, some of them extraordinarily good—was self-contained, and the NASM-accredited collegiate schools and colleges of music focused largely on *their* own work, without much regard as to how educational outcomes from such institutions too often failed to serve the longer-term interests of the orchestras, opera houses, chamber music societies, jazz clubs, newspapers, radio and television stations, or booking agencies of West 57th Street, for example.

In the summer of 1983, as part of an Eastman conference commemorating the work of Howard Hanson, who had died two years earlier, I contributed an article titled "On the Need for Bridging Music's Islands," in which I posited an archipelago of several dozen islands, unconnected by tunnels, bridges, ferries, telephones, or smoke signals. I wrote:

> Surely, music is an important spiritual and aesthetic force, as Howard Hanson said so often and with such eloquence. But the natives of the K–12 island will remain cut off from the broader aspects of our musical culture so long as they fail to follow through on the lifelong implications of their curricula for the musical lives and interests of high school graduates that follow adolescence.
>
> Meanwhile, the professional schools bravely graduate 16,000 people each year, many too many of whom dream of careers on the stage. At Eastman we pride ourselves on the honesty with which our catalog treats the problem in "serious" music of an over-supply for a lagging demand. But the deans of too many collegiate music schools believe that any effort to introduce students to the realities of the professional world undermines the students' self-confidence, and is something akin to playing God. It is my own strong conviction that, in the years ahead,

music will need all the help we can give her. To my way of thinking, that means the development of collegiate musicians who are dedicated at least as much to the future of music as they are to the unfolding of their own careers. Certainly, it means the continuing development of young players and singers able to perform on the highest possible level. But it also implies, I think, musicians familiar with the musical literature broadly, well versed in music history and theory, and equipped to speak and write persuasively and with enthusiasm about music, and about musical coherence, to audiences of varying ages. Such professionals, we hope, will remember the importance of nurturing, throughout their careers, the love of music that brought them here in the first place.

I am sorry to say, however, that in many an institution continuing emphasis on unnecessarily long days of practice, in preparation for competitions from which there will be many more losers than winners, produces jaded musicians who view their teaching, or even performance in a major orchestra, as a kind of personal defeat. Like the inhabitants of the K–12 island, those who teach and study in the professional schools would be well advised to remember that most of the students will have to graduate, and that the other islands of the archipelago are not well served by those who believe that their destiny should be limited to the stage of La Scala or to the principal bassoon chair of the Chicago Symphony Orchestra.[20]

With our new millennium still so new, with new technologies still in their infancy, at a time with wholly new leadership in the White House, and at a time when we in the West are beginning to recognize the value and interest of musics from other parts of the world, it is easy to sense that, as in the final years of the fourteenth century in France and with the earliest years of the seventeenth century in Italy, musicians are on the threshold of whole new ways of experiencing the world. And on a smaller globe, music could be of much greater connective benefit to all of humanity in the years ahead than it is even at present.

Though I would certainly never suggest that playing and singing at very high professional levels is not important, I believe it vital to understand at the outset of a young musician's collegiate education that the prize does not go to the person who performs 1 percent more beautifully than his or her colleagues, as the result of 2 percent more practice time than his competitors will tolerate.[21]

The reader already knows that I think highly of polishing one's skills in verbal and written communication. Over the thirty years that have passed since I wrote the essay just quoted, I have been thinking about additional tools that ought to be part of the skill set of a professional twenty-first-century musician. This includes much more analysis of the characteristics of our current audience, including thinking about how productively to counteract its apparently waning interest. Collegiate musicians are urged to get to know non-music majors, abundant in great numbers on most campuses, and to get to know such people partly by convincing them of music's power. A young musician will discover in a conversation of not more than five minutes that the other students on campus are very enthusiastic about *their* music, a broad array of different kinds of music that they believe immediately accessible, unlike "classical" music, which 99 percent of them perceive as boring—too quiet, too long, too European, too demanding, and too stuck on itself to be as exciting as the music they flock to. The idea that "our" music is qualitatively better than "theirs" (some of us still call it "good music") is also offputting. "Classical music" is, to be sure, longer, more complicated, and often without a text. But young musicians are in a position enthusiastically to explain to their contemporaries what makes the beauties of "classical music" so expressive, so meaningful, so beautiful. The problem, as I see it, is that we have been busy as a nation of musicians teaching how to play the violin rather than how to understand the music and how to teach that understanding to others.

Imagine a system of baseball education in which there was mass confusion about whether learning how to swing a bat, throw a curve ball, or slide was as important to enjoying a baseball game as understanding when to bunt, when to steal home, or when to replace the pitcher. While most baseball games comprise nine innings (eight and a half if the home team is ahead), that information, while basic to understanding a ball game, is not the same as watching a home run clear the fence or admiring the greenness of the grass. Similarly, while most symphonic first movements can be described as sonata allegros, it is the *differences* in how they are all made that are interesting, not the fact that most of them can be classified normatively. Watch a good telecast of a baseball game, then compare that with an equally good version of the same game transmitted, without visual images, on the radio. Because baseball moves so slowly, there is plenty of time for the announcer (and the "color person") to provide the viewing or listening audience with all sorts of information about what just happened, about how often that sort of thing takes place, and about what may happen next, without an understanding of which a baseball game would be as boring as the cricket match I once tried to watch from a hotel window overlooking a beautiful cricket field on a summer afternoon in Cambridge, England. With the dearth of knowledge I brought to cricket, I had no idea what the players were trying to do, and the afternoon, spent alone, was perforce boring, thus discouraging me from dedicating any more of a busy life to a sport for which I have no context.

Imagine, similarly, how many friends I could attract to go with me to listen to tragedies by Euripides in the original Greek. Some friends might be willing to accompany me because they wanted me to think they knew Greek. Some might go with me because they hoped to sell me during the several intermissions on more efficient air conditioning. I might even be persuaded to give the local Classical Greek Theater ten thousand dollars a year to see my name listed in the program with those of other leading citizens of the town—at least so long as I didn't have to attend many of the productions.

The late Leonard Bernstein, before he became an international celebrity in the 1960s, was the nation's greatest music teacher—on the podium of the New York Philharmonic, playing the piano, and speaking volubly, for example, about the relationship of the sequences in the finale of the Brahms's Second to those in Elvis Presley's "I'm All Shook Up." Those Young People's Concerts by Bernstein were videotaped at the time, and in the past decade have been made available as DVDs and on YouTube, the most enthusiastic music teaching I have ever observed, highly recommended to all young musicians and to music lovers. We have, in fact, done a splendid job of allowing the elitist marketing of "classical music" to isolate us into a corner that will not be easy to escape from. A great many people associate Beethoven's Ninth Symphony and Schiller's theme of universal brother- (and sister-) hood with a human experience worth sharing, on very special occasions like the collapse of the Soviet Union and of the Berlin Wall. Young musicians reading this book are asked to consider how best we should proceed to make Brahms's Third, say, an equally communicative experience. I would maintain that that worthwhile goal can only be accomplished by better music teaching, supported, for example, by a variety of DVD and YouTube visualizations of the work, for concert preparation at home, with age-appropriate repertory choices and jargon-free language appropriate to the audience addressed. Comparing Bernstein's concerts for teenagers at Carnegie Hall in the 1960s with his lecture for adults on Mahler's Ninth as Charles Eliot Norton Lecturer at Harvard is a very illuminating experience.

There is a wealth of opportunity, too, for new ideas about thematic programming, another effective means of audience education. Among the most effective I have met in recent years are Hans Graf and the Houston Symphony in a concert titled "Mozart and Salieri," in which performances of the little Mozart G Minor Symphony, KV 183, written when Mozart was seventeen and clearly superior to the Salieri C Major Piano Concerto, performed immediately afterward, preceded a complete performance of Rimsky-Korsakov's two-scene opera *Mozart and Salieri*. There, an envious Salieri poisons Mozart because the older and politically more powerful composer envied his junior colleague's inimitable musical genius. Joseph Horowitz's use of Dvorak's exploration in the early 1890s of the meaning of American music in a nation that now spanned the whole of the Continent is equally compelling. Like Hans Graf's approach, Horowitz's makes it possible in a single evening for an audience, divorced by its (lack of) education from context, to leave the concert hall with a readily grasped musical and human experience.

Performing in surprising venues is also worth thinking about. The Ying Quartet's memorable two-year residence in Jesup, Iowa, supported in part by the NEA, not only transformed the nature of that two-thousand-person town of corn farmers but, with a strong assist from Sydney Yates, helped persuade the Congress of the United States to reauthorize the budget of the National Endowment for the Arts, then threatened by the culture wars of the early 1990s. Said an Iowan farmer to the Congress on Capitol Hill, "The Yings, through their focus on chamber music performed with enthusiasm and dedication, have changed the nature of who we are. What do you suppose there is to do night after night in an isolated community of but 2,000 souls?" Matt Haimowitz's videotaped tour of West Texas bars is an idea along similar lines, as are the Bang on a Can concerts in New York City, Fast Forward Austin, and the international work of Eighth Blackbird, the International Contemporary Ensemble (ICE), and Eastman's Signal and Alarm Will Sound. Were I still a University of Texas dean, I would move as expeditiously as possible to establish a UT musical presence on 6th Street, where our students might perform any music of their choice.

The idea is to move away from the anticipatable to at least occasional audience surprise. When Joseph Haydn decided to awaken his audience with a shocking fortissimo in the andante of his Symphony Number Ninety-Four, he was doing what Sydney Hodkinson accomplished more recently in his nine-minute theater work for clarinet and piano titled "The Dissolution of the Serial." This work begins in the style of Charles Wuorinen, turns first into something as tonal as Mahler, then to something as populist as Scott Joplin, concluding with a musical dumb show dispute between clarinetist and pianist whose climax is reached when the clarinetist, in a fit of anger, violently hurls his clarinet against the back wall of the concert stage. The examples just cited work in one way or another against normal audience expectations that a concert of classical music will include only the anticipatable.

For many musicians, this will mean a new curriculum,[22] facilitated by a willingness to work on a broader array of challenges, with a diminishment of leisure time, for none of us has more than 168 hours in a week. For many, it will mean continuing thought as to what is really important in life, for family and the meaningful interpersonal relationships that stem from family are central, but take time. In my own case, my failure as a college student to understand how time consuming my musical life would be led to an early marriage that suffered as professional opportunities and responsibilities multiplied in my thirties. That young Americans—and young musicians—are apparently marrying later during the past quarter century is, thus, a good thing from my point of view. For young musicians of the future, this book implies the development of much better skills in time management than most of us begin with, and with a better understanding of one's self than most of us have in our early twenties. The life of a musician is full of opportunity, but it is important to be prepared when opportunity knocks.

NOTES

1. Rachel Mundy, a recent NYU PhD in musicology, taught a course as a Mellon Foundation Fellow in Columbia University's Music Department on music and animals in the spring of 2012. An utterly amazing posting on YouTube under "Flea Waltz," showing two golden retrievers performing a duet under human direction on a canine keyboard, suggests that there is still a great deal to learn about animal neurology. Also on YouTube, see Menino the parrot, singing excerpts from Mozart's *Magic Flute*, and yet one more on YouTube, a twelve-bar blues in which Peter the elephant joins a human for a piano duet.

2. Oliver Strunk, *Source Readings in Music History* (New York: W. W. Norton, 1950), 17. James Winn reminds me that *mousike*, for the Greeks, comprised what we now call poetry, music, dance, and elementary education. Before the development of the alphabet, it was music that preserved the knowledge the culture needed, including the oral (i.e., musical) works of Homer. And the Greek theory of mode or ethos was not merely concerned with the development of harmonious individual personalities but with the effect of music on society.

3. Jane Baldauf-Berdes, *Women Musicians of Venice: Musical Foundations, 1515–1855* (New York: Oxford University Press, 1993).

4. Biranda Ford, "What Are Conservatoires For?" (public presentation, Guildhall School, London, March 15, 2011). Dr. Ford in the meantime has introduced me to Bernarr Rainbow's excellent *Music in Educational Thought and Practice: A Survey from 800 BC* (Woodbridge, UK: Boydell & Brewer, 2009).

5. Bernarr Rainbow, *Music in Educational Thought*, 218, quoting A. Martinet, *Histoire anécdotique du Conservatoire de musique et de déclamation* (Paris: E. Kolb, 1893), 122.

6. This is a subject well covered in Arthur Loesser's *Men, Women, and Pianos: A Social History* (Mineola, NY: Dover, 1954) and, more cogently, in James Parakilas's *Piano Roles: 300 Years of Life with the Piano* (New Haven, CT: Yale University Press, 2000).

In the late 1980s, I was invited by Bin Ebisawa to speak as a guest professor for a week at the Kunitachi College of Music in Tokyo, where six thousand music students, mostly young women, were enrolled at the time. When I asked President Ebisawa how he found employment for so many music school graduates, he told me that I did not understand Japanese culture. Said he, "Attendance at a music school is a good way of learning the social graces needed in our country to be a good wife. The husband gets home from the office at 7:30, his wife gives him a drink and plays thirty minutes of Chopin mazurkas before they have dinner together. What else do you want to know?" I told him that the situation had been much like that in America and Europe during the nineteenth century, but that in the meantime the role of women had changed markedly. Said I, "Our female graduates at Eastman expect to have the same sort of professional careers in music that our male graduates look forward to." Though he thought that such change would come to Japan slowly, I believe that subsequent experience has moved toward the West more rapidly than many Japanese of the 1980s foresaw.

In the early 1990s, a search for an additional violin professor at Eastman turned up the concertmaster of the Berlin Philharmonic in our candidate pool. When he came to Rochester, he gave an excellent recital and taught a superb master class, and he spoke and wrote excellent English. But in the Q&A session that followed his class, one of our students asked him to discuss the role of women in the Berlin Philharmonic. Though he could have solved the problem simply by indicating that Berlin was, alas, still horribly conservative about having women in the orchestra, he launched into a diatribe indicating that, in his view and that of his colleagues, the proper place for women was in the home, looking after their husbands and children. Not surprisingly, several dozen of Eastman's women students stood up and walked out. I felt obliged to tell our candidate from Berlin that the concertmaster's just-articulated social views were about a century out of date in Rochester, and I delivered him quickly to the airport, the earlier to begin his eastbound return home. The headline on the front page of the following morning's *Democrat and Chronicle* read "Eastman Students Boycott Berlin Concertmaster."

7. Rainbow, *Music in Educational Thought*, 123.

8. Willis Wager and Earl J. McGrath, *Liberal Education and Music* (New York: Columbia University Press, 1962), 36.

9. Bruce McPherson and James Klein, *Measure by Measure: A History of the New England Conservatory* (Boston: Trustees of the New England Conservatory of Music, 1995).

10. Andrea Olmstead, *Juilliard: A History* (Urbana-Champaign: University of Illinois Press, 1998).

11. Vincent Lenti is at work on what he tells me will be a three-volume history of the Eastman School, whose excellent first and second volumes appeared in 2004 and 2009, respectively.

12. George M. Logan, *The Indiana University School of Music: A History* (Bloomington: Indiana University Press, 2000).

13. E. William Doty, *A History of the College of Fine Arts, the University of Texas at Austin, 1938–1988* (Austin: Morgan Printing Company, 1989).

14. D. B. Kellogg, *The Blair School of Music: A History* (Nashville: Vanderbilt University, 2005).

15. J. Murray Somerville, "The Paine of Good Taste" (DMA dissertation, New England Conservatory, 1998).

16. Archibald T. Davison, *Music Education in America: What Is Wrong with It? What Shall We Do about It?* (New York: Harper and Brothers, 1926), 103; quoted in Wager and McGrath, *Liberal Education and Music*, 24.

17. James A. Winn, *The Pale of Words: Reflections on the Humanities and Performance* (New Haven, CT: Yale University Press, 1998).

18. Harvard University, *Report of the Task Force on the Arts*, December 2008,http://www.provost.harvard.edu/reports/ArtsTaskForce-Report_12-10-08.pdf.

19. Samuel Hope, recently retired as the able director of NASM, understands the situation described in this book and has been working at broadening current curricula to include studies in entrepreneurship, for example. But, for reasons readers of this book will understand, the speed of needed change is glacial. Relevant to this is NASM's recent policy brief of November 2008, "Creation, Performance, Multiple Relationships and Possibilities."

20. Robert Freeman, "On the Need for Bridging Music's Islands," in *In Memoriam, Howard Hanson: The Future of Musical Education in America*, ed. Donald J. Shetler (Rochester: Eastman School of Music Press, 1984).

21. For an excellent overview of musical competitions, see Joseph Horowitz, *The Ivory Trade: Piano Competitions and the Business of Music* (Boston: Northeastern University Press, 1991). My objection to the ever-increasing number of such competitions is essentially threefold: (1) With the exception of the Gilmore Competition, they unduly limit the repertories that young musicians are persuaded to study. (2) They help persuade us all that there is some Platonic standard of high performance to which young musicians ought to aspire, despite the fact that the judges of even an international competition have predictably different standards for their judgments, decisions that are often made on a partly political and often quixotic basis. (3) They no longer produce concert careers, for there are too many competitions and too few celebrity-engendered careers to make this possible. I have myself witnessed occasions when judges from one nation or another conspired behind the scenes to the hoped for political advantage of one contestant or another. Though in the 1980s I used to be

invited to help judge the "artistic" portion of the Miss America competitions, I regularly declined to do so, partly because I did not believe in the sexist nature of the competitions, partly because it seemed to me that, from a strictly artistic perspective, I could not imagine how I would deal with the judge who averred, "I like the one with the long legs" (for which one could as easily substitute "superb left hand"). Not surprisingly, I have the same feelings about the *American Idol* competition, the preliminary rounds of which rely on the audience's enjoyment of humiliating some of the competitors.

22. Shortly before this book went to press, Greg Sandow's excellent blog informed me of what Greg calls "Revolution at DePauw," an excellent account of how to accomplish curricular reform, undertaken by Mark McCoy, a new dean, in Greencastle, Indiana.

THREE

My Own Education

Because this book concerns the future of musical education, it seems appropriate that I briefly review my own education, the better for the reader to identify my own prejudices on the subject.

To begin with, the fact that I am a third-generation musician seems deeply relevant. As already noted, my paternal grandfather, born in England in the early 1870s, was a fine professional trumpet player who emigrated from England to Australia with his parents and siblings in the mid-1870s. An oil painting hung over my father's mantelpiece showing my grandfather at the age of thirteen, sitting on horseback as the newly victorious champion cornet player of Australia. Returning to England as a young man, he signed a contract to play in the Grenadier Guards Band, imagining, without bothering to read the fine print, that his duties would only be musical and ceremonial. But when the Second Boer War broke out in 1899, his bandmaster presented my grandfather with a rifle, reminding him that the band was part of the British Army. My grandfather learned to read the fine print at the cost of what amounted to a several-thousand-dollar fine that made it possible for him to leave the band and to freelance as a solo trumpeter in London, where he carefully kept a scrapbook of excellent reviews on his way to membership in Sousa's band.[1] He toured the world with that ensemble, sometimes under very difficult traveling conditions. I was cautioned never to tour without a can of Sterno in my briefcase. "If your train is marooned in subzero snow drifts, the Sterno will protect your fingers from frostbite."

His experience as a professional musician was so negative that, after he married and had three sons, he forbade any of them to study music, fearing lest they become professional musicians. The eldest of the three had an outstanding career as a successful business executive, and the youngest died as a teenager. My father, the middle brother, born in New

29

York City in 1909, was allowed to begin study of the double bass as a senior in a Rochester high school in order to play in the high school orchestra. This breach in "sensible career planning" took place because the conductor of the orchestra was a friend of my grandfather, because the orchestra had no double bass player, and because my grandfather judged it too late for a seventeen-year-old to entertain professional aspirations in music. But Dad was talented. He had an excellent teacher, and he loved playing the double bass. When he graduated from high school, he went to work in a bank, but Howard Hanson, who had just been appointed director of the Eastman School of Music, wanted to launch a career as an orchestral conductor, and he, too, had no double bass player. Before long, Dad was enrolled at Eastman as the school's first double bass major, where he met my mother, a talented and pretty young violinist. Without any professional experience and reading only the bass clef, Dad got himself a job in a pit band at a nearby silent movie house, earning sixty-one dollars a week, saving it all, and thus becoming one of the school's best-heeled students, a good bass player with a substantial bank account in the midst of the Great Depression.

After graduating from Eastman in 1930, my parents married in 1932, supporting themselves through positions they both held on the staff orchestra of radio station WHAM, while Dad performed as a member of the Rochester Philharmonic, then a per-service organization for half of its musicians. I was born in 1935, the first of two sons, both of whom graduated from Harvard and took Ivy League PhDs in musicology. Both of us spent a substantial part of our careers as college professors. My younger brother, Jim, and I grew up in a household where Mom understood the central importance of getting her sons a broader general education than she felt she had had. She practiced the standard violin concertos as Jim and I went to sleep every night, concertos that she never got to perform in public after she graduated. Listening to my parents practice their instruments went along with getting used to an inevitable double bass standing in each corner of our living room.

It has always seemed to me that the omnipresence of music in our family life provided me not only with an enviable musical education from an early age but also with the terrific advantage of parents who knew the music profession as practicing professionals. They dedicated their own time, energy, limited funds, and broad experience to ensuring that my brother and I got the best of everything, both in general education and in musical training. Not surprisingly, a great many musically talented young people do not have the advantage of ongoing advice and support from parents so familiar with the domain, and with its joys and perils.

My first musical memory comes from the age of three, sitting on my father's lap while, at the piano, he performed easy pieces by Burgmüller, making up imaginative stories for me while doing so. Before long, my mother took me to the Preparatory Department of the Eastman School and to her former violin teacher there. The quarter-size violin hurt my neck at the age of four, I cried, and that was the end of my violin studies. It had been a kind of experiment, which, while without any useful result, seemed not to disappoint anyone. Perhaps more sensibly, my parents tried me, several months later, on the piano, also at the Eastman Prep Department. While my father came to the conclusion that my parents' first choice of piano teacher had been ill advised after he attended some of the lessons, they took me before long to Marjorie Truelove MacKown, a wonderful musician with a delightful British accent.

Mom practiced the violin and saw to it that the rest of us practiced as well. In 1942, Willis Page, Dad's young double-bass-playing friend from Eastman, already a member of the Boston Symphony, was drafted by the army. When asked by Serge Koussevitzky whether he knew other fine young bass players, Page recommended Dad. I remember accompanying him to Rochester's cavernous New York Central Station to see him and his double bass off on a very crowded train to New York City. Koussevitzky, himself a distinguished bass player, was apparently impressed by Dad's playing and immediately offered him a position in the BSO, a position that Dad had to turn down because of a contract he had already signed with the Rochester Philharmonic. Koussevitzky said he was disappointed but urged Dad not to sign any further contracts in Rochester, promising that the next bass opening in the BSO would belong to my father. For the next three years, we waited on tenterhooks, anticipating another letter from Dr. Koussevitzky. Ironically, the letter arrived in February 1945, the day of the unanticipated death of Nelson Watson, Dad's and Willis's bass teacher, the principal bass of the RPO and Eastman's bass teacher since the beginning of the school's history in 1921. Though the RPO and Eastman offered my father his teacher's former position, Dad had been waiting for three years to play in the Boston Symphony. And so we were off to the "Athens of America."

While I don't remember piano practice as a special pleasure of my childhood, it was clear from my father's experience that solid practice habits really worked, a point of view enforced by my mother. She drew up formal annual contracts for her sons, specifying daily amounts of required piano practice, with longer hours for summer vacations. A bowlful of slips of paper—on which were printed D-flat major or F-sharp harmonic minor, for example—sat on a table next to the piano, where we were obliged each morning to pick at random three scales for practice in various rhythms, in contrary motion, and in thirds and sixths. Then came the arpeggios, and the études. While it was understood that there was more in life than practicing, Jim and I were often reminded that Dr. Koussevitzky had sent word to "practice the more you can," a philosophy at direct variance with the thesis of this book: "Practice as thoughtfully as you can, until you begin to lose concentration. Then switch to another activity until you are ready to practice again."

I was already something of an entrepreneur as a youngster and decided to make all that practice pay off. Rochester's CBS radio station had Sunday-morning programs for musical competitors under the age of twelve, with a weekly prize of five dollars. I played Tchaikovsky's "Skylark" reasonably well, after having told my fourth-grade teacher that I had entered the competition. She made it a class exercise for the other thirty students in the fourth grade to write letters backing my candidacy for the five-dollar prize, which I won. No wonder I have not believed in the efficacy of musical competitions since then.

THRIVING IN BOSTON

In the fall of 1945, my new life in Boston was as exciting as promised. I was accepted in the piano studio of Marjorie Church Cherkassky at the Longy School (then directed by Melville Smith, my parents' freshman theory teacher at Eastman) and permitted to travel by myself from Needham to Cambridge and back via public transit for Saturday lessons and theory classes. This was a tremendous adventure for a ten-year-old, as was receiving permission to attend Saturday-night Boston Symphony concerts on my own. Shortly afterward, my father, reminding me that "the world is full of pianists," decided that I would someday have to earn my own livelihood and that it would be a good idea for me to study an orchestral instrument. Much like what had happened to my father, the local junior high school just happened to need an oboe, and lessons began forthwith. Henry W. Kaufmann, one of my theory teachers at Longy, strongly recommended that I matriculate at Milton Academy, a private school just south of Boston, where he taught. While Milton tuition was well beyond the fiscal capacity of a BSO section player, my never-to-be-daunted mother made friends with an affluent family in Milton who, I learned sixty years later, paid for much of my Milton education, and for my brother's.

Milton was a wonderful school where I learned a lot. Founded in 1798, the school's motto was "Dare to be true," an ideal that we all followed carefully if we wanted to stay enrolled. The faculty was excellent. The classes were no more than ten or twelve in size, and we were expected to be prepared, day by day, in English, math, French, Latin, history, science, and the arts. There were regular nondenominational chapel services on Wednesday mornings, compulsory intramural sports from 3 to 5 p.m., and surprise quizzes. We were expected to wear jackets and ties, no matter how hot the weather. There were girls, but they were on the other side of a street one did not cross. I had a wonderful music class with a recent Harvard graduate and two other Milton students, where we looked at fourteenth-century isometric motets and then wrote our own, a procedure that was repeated for a month or so each for fifteenth-century frottole, Monteverdi madrigals, eighteenth-century trio sonatas, Beethoven minuets, Schumann songs, and Hindemith sonatas. My eighth-grade French instructor slowed down my overzealous class participation by announcing, in front of the class, that if I had something to say, I should raise my hand and then wait five minutes, reflecting the while on whether what I had wanted to say was still worth saying. My tenth-grade English teacher once said, again in front of the whole class, that he didn't think I was very intelligent. If I achieved good grades, said he, it was because I worked hard at studying. (While I was stunned to hear that news, it certainly cemented the idea that if I wanted to succeed, I had better work hard.)

After a year at Milton, my mother insisted that I attend the Greenwood Music Camp, a wonderful place in Cummington, Massachusetts, where seventy or so adolescents played and sang under excellent leadership, in a Berkshire environment where there was plenty of chamber and orchestral music, swimming and tennis playing, gardening and path clearing, with weekly trips for concerts at Tanglewood. The emphasis was on the joy of making music, and the students, while all talented, mostly went on to matriculate at leading liberal arts colleges rather than at professional music schools. Still, it was at Greenwood that I met Gilbert Kalish, Anton Kuerti, Peter Westergaard, and Joel Krosnick, all as fellow students. After I had played the oboe solos in Fauré's "Pelleas and Melisande" suite, a very pretty cellist told me at intermission that she thought I had played beautifully, a comment that instantly added a whole new dimension to my music making.

When the bassoonist of my woodwind quintet broke his reed in a public concert, the head of Greenwood asked me to speak to the audience about why I loved music while the bassoonist took fifteen minutes to return to the dorm for another reed. Helen Warden, a member of the audience who was impressed by my ad lib remarks, afterward suggested that in the fall she would arrange an audition for me with the famous principal oboist of the Philadelphia Orchestra, Marcel Tabuteau. When Mrs. Warden followed through, my parents, Jim, and I drove to Philadelphia so that I could play for the great man. He said he would be glad to have me as a student at Curtis but went on to question why anyone only fourteen would want to be a professional oboist. Dad sought professional counsel from someone who would surely know, Leonard Bernstein, then guest conducting the Boston Symphony. Bernstein apparently asked my father what I had wanted to do with my life a year or two earlier. When Dad conceded that I had wanted to drive fire engines, Bernstein, who had graduated from both Harvard and Curtis, suggested that I study oboe in Boston while preparing at Milton for Harvard. Said Bernstein, "No fourteen-year-old that I have ever met knows for sure what he wants to do with the whole of his life. I'm not sure that I have decided yet myself."

None of this went down very well with Marjorie Cherkassky, a dedicated artist and an excellent teacher who, as the result of previous experience of her own, was unduly nervous, my parents felt, at the thought of performing in public. This was a concern communicated to her students. From her perspective, the development of young pianists was a work requiring special focus and at least four or five hours of daily piano practice. When she questioned my father one time too many about how this commitment could be sustained by someone who needed to get top grades at Milton while playing the oboe, Dad terminated the piano lessons.

At the age of fifteen, I was urged by my Milton Academy music teacher to enter a contest for adolescent composers run by the New York Philharmonic with a piece I had written entitled "Two Movements for Oboe and Piano." I was, of course, pleased to receive a letter from an administrator at the Philharmonic praising my piece but suggesting that my title for the work had left the jury a bit cold. I responded that I had changed the title to "60 High Street," the Brookline address of my oboe teacher, Fernand Gillet, not only Koussevitzky's principal oboe for twenty-five years but also a French fighter pilot in World War I. I won second prize in the competition, and my efforts were also rewarded by a feature article in the *Boston Globe*, complimenting me on the "skill" with which I had described my oboe teacher. You can fool some of the people all of the time, they say! Thus I have always understood program music as a kind of P. T. Barnum effort to persuade the unwary that one can follow a piece of music by putting oneself in the right mood, reading the composer's program in advance.

After two summers at Greenwood, Gil Kalish and I auditioned for Tanglewood and were accepted for the summer of 1951. Naturally, the performance standards were much higher, but curiously, as Gil and I both noticed, the joy shared in music making at Greenwood was notably diminished, the result no doubt of increased pressure from the importance of doing our very pre-professional best. Though I had plenty of opportunity to play principal oboe in the Department I Orchestra at Tanglewood, my major challenge for the summer lay in playing first oboe in a performance of Stravinsky's "Symphony of Psalms," conducted by a nineteen-year-old Loren Maazel in what later became the Koussevitzky Music Shed. My father was understandably concerned that I would be nervous in playing so exposed a solo role. The score has no violins or violas, and I was seated in the place normally occupied on the apron of the stage by the principal violist. Dad gave me beforehand what I think later turned out to be white placebo pills. "Take one of these at 1 p.m., another at 5, and two just before you go on stage, the way we all do in big concerts. You will find that you have no sense of stage fright, and all will go well." I did as my father suggested and played well enough to satisfy Maazel, Monsieur Gillet, my father, and myself. When I learned later that the pills had had no medicinal power, I decided that the psychology of musical performance is a matter of real importance. So, too, is the self-confidence instilled, or withheld, by the conductor. The following summer I had the privilege of playing first oboe in a Tanglewood performance of the Beethoven Fifth, under Bernstein himself. The first time I played the thirteen-note cadenza that appears just after the beginning of the recapitulation in the first movement, I did well, and Bernstein said so. But he then proceeded to take me, in front of the orchestra, over the same thirteen notes about twenty times—a little louder here, a little faster there—until I couldn't play it at all. The following week I thought Thor Johnson was an incredibly nice man for praising every little solo I had in Bartok's Concerto for Orchestra.

While Mom saw to it that I was prepared, Dad was ever at my side for professional support. During the two years I served as organist for the local Methodist church, he often sat next to me in the organ loft, seeing to it that the music was ready when I needed it. Every season, he spent a Sunday morning sitting at the back of the second balcony of Symphony Hall, getting me to project the sound of a confident principal oboe in all the big orchestral oboe solos, one after another. (He wanted me to learn how to make reeds that were flexible and that could project over a full orchestra.) And at home, with Mom, he saw to it that I learned to sight-read in the piano trio literature (with himself playing the cello part on the bass, an octave higher), and in arrangements of a hotel trio repertory of Strauss waltzes he had acquired to teach me sight-reading. While we always took the Red Sox very seriously, there was not a lot of time for anything that interfered with studying, practicing, and playing. In a performance of Prokofieff's Quintet, Opus 39 (violin, oboe, viola, clarinet, double bass), which we prepared with two of Dad's BSO colleagues for performance at Milton Academy, I was doing what he described as "a slovenly job" on the difficult fourth movement, where the oboe wanders for thirty measures among the lowest notes of the instrument's range, legatissimo and pianissimo. I complained that the music was difficult and that I was doing the best I could. "Look," he said, "I know this is difficult, but there is no point in playing this concert at all unless you can perform at a professional level. Work at it till you get it right!"

Oboe lessons with Fernand Gillet at his home in Brookline were always a complete pleasure. He was a fine musician and a great teacher, full of wonderful diagnostic exercises that quickly solved technical problems by thinking about what the problem comprised, always impeccably dressed in a three-piece suit with tie pin. His instruction on orchestral excerpts normally included a variety of approaches, beginning with how to play the excerpt the way Koussevitzky wanted it, and continuing with advice on how to retain one's musicality by playing the music the way it was supposed to go, but in such a fashion that Koussevitzky would not notice the difference. Gillet came from a period in which thinking about reeds was not the work of a principal oboist—whatever Tabuteau thought to the contrary. As a result, I was sent on Sunday mornings to the Beacon Street apartment of the second oboist, Jean DeVergie, a nice man who sat at his kitchen table in his undershirt turning out one playable—if undistinguished—reed after another. Had Gillet been more interested than he was in reed making, perhaps I would have turned into an oboist. As things turned out, I resented reed making, an essential aspect of being a big-league oboist since the middle of the twentieth century. One or the other of my parents always attended my lessons with Gillet, taking assiduous notes on what he had to say, with the understanding that my first task once home was to transcribe the notes in typewritten form, making certain that I remembered exactly what he had said and mastering those points by the time of the next lesson.

HARVARD

When it came time to go to college, I applied to Harvard, Yale, and Pennsylvania, was admitted to all three, and decided on Harvard, partly because it was near home and in a city where I already had burgeoning musical contacts. Because Milton Academy had in fact been an excellent preparation for college, Harvard seemed comparatively easy, leaving me time for several hours a day of piano practice and a certain amount of time for oboe freelancing. When I was called by the contractor for the Boston Opera House to play second oboe and English horn for a week-long visit from the Sadler's Wells Ballet, I responded that I would love to but that I didn't own an English horn. The contractor said he would arrange for the principal oboe, who traveled with the show, to double on English horn. I agreed to a week's work on that basis, appearing half an hour early in my tuxedo. I had had no idea how exciting the evening was to be, for the principal oboe refused to double on English horn, insisting that I perform as principal. Half an hour later, the curtain went up, with Robert Irving conducting and myself playing principal oboe in Tchaikovsky's *Swan Lake*. I must have had a good reed, because once the performance was over, I was offered the principal oboe chair of the opera house. The second night, also without rehearsal like the music for the rest of the week, comprised two ballets by Stravinsky, *Petroushka* and *Sacre du Printemps*. It was an exciting week, bearing out my father's continuing advice: if you practice hard, know the repertory, read with facility, and avoid stage fright, you should never be afraid to take calculated risks. After the week with Sadler's Wells, I bought myself an English horn. Later in my freshman year, I had the privilege of playing principal oboe in Bach's *St. Matthew Passion* for a performance of the Handel-Haydn

Society in Symphony Hall—in which all the other oboe and English horn players were members of the Boston Symphony. That, too, went well, and I was rewarded by a very positive, though brief, review by Rudolf Elie in the *Boston Herald*. As in many instances in the second and third decades of my life, Dad had a good professional contact with someone who was willing to take a chance on me, an opportunity on which it was my responsibility to make good.

By the time of my sophomore year, I reasoned that Bernstein had been right. I knew essentially all of the then very limited oboe repertory and was accepted as a professional in a competitive environment, but I had gotten interested in my later teens in the piano, which has an endless repertory. As the reader already knows, Harvard, especially in those days, took a dim view of musical performance, resulting in my continuing piano study at the Longy School, half a mile away in Cambridge, with Gregory Tucker, a fine professional pianist and teacher who took a more practical view of the instrument than had Marjorie Cherkassky. Before long, he had decided that I should learn Walter Piston's Concertino for Piano and Orchestra, for performance at Harvard's Sanders Theater as part of Longy's annual spring festival there. That, too, went well, and with a word from Dad, I had a chance to play it for Arthur Fiedler, who then scheduled it at the Pops and for the opening night of Esplanade. Further, Fiedler gave me a list of piano concertos he wanted me to learn for the balance of my undergraduate studies, beginning with the Mendelssohn G Minor, Rachmaninoff Rhapsody on a Theme by Paganini, and the Ravel Concerto.

Though I felt like a budding Horowitz, at seventy-five dollars a night, my father quite rightly reasoned that a dozen very promising young pianists played annually at Pops, none of whom was ever heard of once they passed their midtwenties. He counseled me to spend the summer after my sophomore year assisting Artur Balsam at Blue Hill, playing for the violin class of Joseph Fuchs, and the summer following my junior year, at Marlboro, studying with Rudolf Serkin. From Balsam, a fine musician, I learned that the task of a collaborative artist was to be able to make on-the-spot transcriptions of all sorts of repertory. This skill enabled one, if called on Thursday, to play the required music by the following Tuesday in Carnegie Hall. Well, something that sounded to *New York Times* critics like the music in question! That sort of philosophy did not go down at all with Rudolf Serkin, an artist dedicated to practicing individual works as long as necessary in order to perform them with as great a fidelity as a human being could bring to the intentions of the composer. There was no sense of compromise in Mr. Serkin! During the first week I was at Marlboro, he scheduled me as pianist in the Mozart Quintet for Piano and Winds, KV 452, but was clearly disappointed when I appeared for the initial rehearsal. Said he, "But Bob, I thought you told me you had performed this work at Tanglewood." I responded that I had probably forgotten to tell him that I had performed it at Tanglewood as oboist. And he scheduled another pianist for the role at Marlboro.

Back at Harvard in the fall, I had a wonderfully exciting senior year. I became producer and host of a weekly half-hour radio program on WHRB, *Classical Roundtable*, in which we played prerecorded sixty-second excerpts from fairly esoteric selections and asked a panel of music students, faculty, and visiting celebrities to discuss and identify them. An offstage voice informed the listening audience of the identity of each piece, except for one weekly excerpt of the most standard sort. The audience, most of whom lived no more than half a mile from Harvard Square, were supposed to rush over to Briggs and Briggs for a free LP if they could correctly identify the piece in question, issued to as many as appeared with student IDs within fifteen minutes of the excerpt's performance on the radio. This procedure was designed to build audiences, though it occasionally resulted in fender benders.

I was also invited to perform a violin and piano recital at the Detroit Art Institute with the violinist Joseph Silverstein, shortly afterward concertmaster of the Boston Symphony. We both played well, I learned a lot of music from a splendid young violinist, we both got two excellent reviews from the Detroit press, and it was exciting to perform on the road for the first time. Promised a "generous fee," I was surprised that I ended up with fifty dollars and expenses, an important learning experience. It taught me that this was not a way of making much money and that fees have to be negotiated up front! The same season I played the ten Beethoven sonatas for violin and piano at Boston's Isabella Stewart Gardner Museum with my mother.

The capstone experience of my Harvard years was an undergraduate honors thesis on cadenzas for the two dozen Mozart piano concertos. Having performed several of these as an undergraduate, I knew that while three-quarters of the Mozart piano concertos survive with their own cadenzas, six of his most mature concertos (KV 466, 467, 482, 491, 503, and 537) do not. Further, I learned that several eighteenth-century treatises on keyboard playing discussed the cadenza problem and that dozens of eighteenth-, nineteenth-, and twentieth-century composers and pianists had provided their own cadenzas for the six concertos just listed. This included Beethoven, whose KV 466 cadenzas were composed fifteen years after Mozart's death, and Artur Schnabel, whose early twentieth-century cadenzas for KV 491 sound as though they had been written by Arnold Schönberg in 1912. I composed sets of my own cadenzas for KV 482 and 491, and performed both concertos with Harvard's Bach Society Orchestra in Paine Hall.

Because my undergraduate record comprised As and a few Bs, I was totally unprepared for the news that I was going to graduate with highest honors, partly as the result of my thesis. Since each of Harvard's departments nominated one student for what were called Sheldon Traveling

Fellowships, I was interviewed by an ad hoc committee of Harvard faculty members. Asked what I would do if provided with five thousand dollars in the year ahead to do whatever I wished, I proposed traveling all over western Europe; attending recitals, concerts, and operas; visiting all kinds of museums and libraries—and won one of the four fellowships. It had but two rules: that I write a letter to the dean of Harvard College at the end of each of the two semesters, letting him know what I had been doing, and that I let Harvard know in advance the addresses of the American Express offices to which I wanted my monthly checks mailed. The grand tour at Harvard's expense! All this had both positive and negative results. I married the girl I had been dating throughout college, Katharine Merk (daughter of a distinguished Harvard professor of American history), a dedicated sightseer with whom I saw Europe for the first time. The downside was that, by becoming a tourist for a year, I found it harder and harder to find practice pianos in each of the cities we visited. Honored to be allowed to visit in November as a member of Nadia Boulanger's Wednesday-afternoon class, I was surprised when she told the class, "This man is not a musician. He is a tourist!" I had wanted to discuss Mozart cadenzas with Mlle. Boulanger, a subject she told me could be covered only in the seventh week of the third year of study.

PRINCETON

I was encouraged by Harvard—and implicitly, I suppose, by many memorable dinnertime conversations with Professor Merk and his family—to think that I was an academic. I applied for graduate school at Princeton and was accepted there as an MFA (and later PhD) candidate in musicology, studying in classes of half a dozen with Oliver Strunk and Arthur Mendel, both dedicated teachers of young scholars. Strunk treated us not as students but as junior colleagues, at work together in a cooperative quest for truth. If he had a fault, it was that he gave me so much credit for what I clearly didn't know that I feared a day of reckoning, when the sky would publicly collapse on my ignorance. With Strunk, we worked on Richard Wagner and on plainsong, with Arthur Mendel on Schütz and on editing the *St. John Passion*. I was honored by Professor Mendel to be given the responsibility of editing my own Bach Cantata for the *Neue Bach Ausgabe*, BWV 176, my first publication. While Mendel could be very gruff in public, he was one of the gentlest and most supportive teachers I ever had in private. Four semesters of seminar participation—in which the professor introduced and concluded the semester, with the students giving afternoon-long reports in between—were supposed to prepare us for three days of written examinations, by way of qualification for PhD candidacy. We were advised to have a look at previous examinations, on file in the Music Department office. Professor Strunk urged that there was nothing to be worried about "because there are only about a dozen questions worth thinking about in the whole history of Western music." That notwithstanding, the students who took the tests in 1959 were very upset, complaining of nausea, lack of sleep, and what sounded to me like stage fright. I determined that the best way to avoid that syndrome was, of course, to be prepared, convincing myself in advance that, in the worst possible instance, if I drew nothing but blanks on all twelve topics of the first day of tests, I would confess my ignorance and write on subjects about which I was more knowledgeable. In the event, I drew no blanks, ending up with high grades.

The Princeton system involved two years of seminar enrollment, passing the general examinations with honor, and completing a doctoral dissertation that covered new ground. Because my year in Europe on the Sheldon Fellowship had introduced me to Vienna, I decided to apply for a Fulbright Fellowship for 1960–1961 to study in Austria. After winning it, I worked on an endless series of *opere serie* by Antonio Caldara, Vice Kapellmeister to the Hapsburg Court from 1716 to 1736. There he had made almost all the initial settings of the Zeno and Metastasio libretti written for the Hapsburg court. Though we had a wonderful time in Vienna for two years (my Fulbright was renewed for 1961–1962), and though I completed my doctoral degree in 1967, had I to do it over again, I would have taken a doctoral subject involving music I really cared about and whose historical significance I was clearer on than I was about Caldara in the fall of 1960. It would, for example, have made a lot more sense for me to have studied Brahms or Mahler. Put another way, graduate students should be a lot more careful than I was about an initial choice of subject for doctoral investigation.

After a third year of European study in 1962–1963 on Martha Baird Rockefeller funds, I returned to Princeton in the fall of 1963 as an instructor, teaching twelve weekly hours of undergraduate music history and theory, my first collegiate experience, with a course of my own. Because of the weekly pressure of teaching very bright Princeton undergraduates, on a comparatively weak knowledge base of my own, I made little progress on my dissertation until midway through 1964–1965. It was then that Arthur Mendel, by then my dissertation adviser, said, "There is no need to compare yourself with Joseph Kerman or Lewis Lockwood. You are neither of them, but somebody else of value to music. If you will write ten pages a week from now on, I'll review what you have done every month, and you will be finished in no more than a year." Though I had almost accepted an assistant professorship elsewhere for the fall of 1965, Princeton offered me a three-year appointment beginning with the fall of 1965, including an important new responsibility as conductor of the Princeton University Orchestra. Once more, I had had no real experience as a conductor, especially with an orchestra in which many of the players did not attend the rehearsals except as a favor to the conductor. But I had learned about the importance of taking reasonable risks, threw myself into the task with enthusiasm, and learned a lot. That very nearly resulted, in the fall of 1968, in my being promoted to the chairmanship of Princeton's Department of Music as an assistant professor, an idea derailed by the fact, as things turned out, that the president of the university wanted to return one of my senior colleagues to the department from broader administrative responsibilities, a move that necessarily terminated my more junior line. Moving from supreme elation to the nadir of depression over the course of a weekend wasn't easy, but I was told that the end of the world was not at hand. And it wasn't.

MIT

Early the following April I interviewed for an associate professorship in musicology at Ohio State and for an assistant professorship in music at the Massachusetts Institute of Technology and was offered both, at exactly the same salary. After several days of thinking about it, I decided to accept MIT's offer, reasoning that Greater Boston would offer a broader array of professional possibilities for a generalist like myself. And I turned out to be right. In Klaus Liepmann, Gregory Tucker (my former piano teacher at the Longy School), David Epstein, John Harbison, John Buttrick, Jeanne Bamberger, John Oliver, and Barry Vercoe, I had superb colleagues who worked well and cooperatively together. Though most of our work was with young men and women on their way to becoming the nation's leading scientists and engineers, I enjoyed doing something that I thought important. I formed and played oboe in a woodwind quintet composed otherwise of MIT students, called the Clean Wind Quintet; our group appeared in white suits and shoes and played only at women's colleges, claiming to exhale pure oxygen. I was invited to teach a graduate seminar at Harvard in eighteenth-century Italian opera, and I became the chairman of the New England Chapter of the American Musicological Society. And I met a wonderfully energetic young cellist from the Boston Symphony named Luis Leguia, with whom I began to play recitals, at first in Boston, then all over New England, finally making our Town Hall debut together in the winter of 1970–1971, playing at the Place des Arts in Montreal and coast to coast on the CBC Network, and in September 1972 on a monthlong tour of Europe that began with three concerts at the Berlin Festival and ended with a Wigmore Hall debut in London. From the outset of our collaboration, Leguia, always eager to play the Kodaly Sonata for Cello Alone, agreed to the idea of splitting the fees and the investment when necessary, with the Kodaly Sonata concluding the first half and with myself playing a solo piano piece of ten to fifteen minutes to begin the second half. Our Town Hall debut, built on this model, began with Beethoven's Opus 69 and concluded with Elliott Carter's Sonata for

Cello and Piano, with the inevitable Kodaly Sonata after the Beethoven and Schubert's beautiful little three-movement Piano Sonata in A Minor, D 537, beginning the second half. This assured me, as I imagined it would, of a good return on my investment: equal billing and some excellent reviews. Luis even persuaded Walter Piston to write for us a duo for cello and piano, one of Piston's last works, which we later premiered together at the Library of Congress.

While teaching at MIT was fun, my salary barely covered our expenses. I published the professional papers and gave the talks at professional meetings required of junior faculty, for I was eager to make tenure. With Donald Grout, a friend from meetings of the Visiting Committee at Princeton, I established at MIT a data bank for eighteenth-century Italian aria incipits aimed at straightening out the endless problems of attribution and dating that still beleaguer a field in which too many scholars work as individuals, without the spirit of cooperation that in the long term would bring about better understanding of a repertory that Professor Grout and I estimated at about ten million pieces of music. The necessary computer programming had already been accomplished, it turned out, in MIT's Department of Electrical Engineering, and the only problem appeared to be the collection of relevant data, with all cooperating scholars adopting a uniform cataloguing format. To encourage this, MIT's development people set up an appointment for me with the president of the Presser Foundation in Philadelphia, where, in the spring of 1972, I spent a whole afternoon describing the problem and proposing its solution to an executive in his eighties who appeared to be enjoying himself a lot. But as the clock neared five, knowing that I had a plane to catch at 6:30, I finally asked my new friend for one million dollars. He smiled cordially and asked how many people, in addition to my wife and mother, would be pleased were the foundation to provide one million dollars for my project at MIT. Counting as fast as I could, I said, "About a dozen people would at present be delighted, worldwide." He responded that, while he had enjoyed our afternoon, the world had not yet been blessed with anything approaching adequate resources for all the problems humanity faces, and that the sort of money I was talking about could easily be used, in music alone, for a multitude of worthy causes of potential use to a much larger number of people. Though I was disappointed, the Presser president had given me a lot to think about.

In preparing for my trip to Philadelphia, I had been provided with access to MIT's development archives, where I chanced upon the documents that in 1912 had helped turn Boston Tech (on Clarendon Street in Boston) into the Massachusetts Institute of Technology (on the Cambridge shore of the Charles River). James McLauren, president of Boston Tech during the early years of the twentieth century, had developed a cordial relationship with George Eastman, the founder of Eastman-Kodak, while working together on emulsion problems that Eastman had been unable to solve with his own people in Rochester. After the death of his mother, Maria Kilbourn Eastman, Eastman had apparently given some thought to marrying, at the age of fifty-eight. The alternative, or so it seemed to Eastman, was to give away something between five hundred million and one billion dollars, a process that seems to have begun in 1912 with his anonymous gift of three million dollars to establish the new campus and the initial buildings of MIT.

It was six months later, when visiting my parents' home in Stockbridge, that I chanced upon an article from Rochester's *Democrat and Chronicle* announcing that Walter Hendl had resigned from the directorship of the Eastman School of Music. The music school was George Eastman's second great philanthropic enterprise, founded in Rochester in 1919. I had come to think of myself as a generalist: a good professional oboist, a capable professional pianist, a productive musicologist with a recent PhD from an institution of distinction, and a capable conductor of student orchestras. I hoped to make tenure at MIT in the fall, having just submitted the appropriate papers to the dean's office. Weighing the situation at hand, I thought I could make a positive contribution to solving the problems that afflicted the Eastman School of 1972, especially as a judge of talent from the performing, the scholarly, and the compositional worlds of music. I spent two days writing and rewriting a carefully crafted two-page letter to Samuel Adler, chair of the search committee. There I suggested a couple of areas where I thought the school might improve, making it clear that my résumé was one of a generalist, and that while I had not attended Eastman's collegiate division, my parents had met as freshmen there. I assumed that the search committee would know that George Eastman had funded MIT as well as the Eastman School of Music.

EASTMAN

Having heard nothing from Rochester by the time I was to leave for Europe, I exercised what I tell current students is the patience necessary to land an important position. While in Europe, I learned that I had in fact made tenure at MIT. Arriving back in Cambridge on October 1, I found a callback slip on my desk from Samuel Adler, asking that I call him if I were still interested in the Eastman directorship. After two trips to Rochester, I was offered the position, together with a tenured professorship in musicology, a challenge I accepted by November 20, ironically reversing the ground covered by my parents twenty-seven years earlier. In resigning from my post at MIT, I visited Jerome Wiesner, then president of the institute, who complimented me on becoming the head of what he called "the music branch of MIT in the West." My response was something along the lines of, "Dr. Wiesner, I hope you won't think it improper, but because Mr. Eastman gave us his name, I should let you know that in Rochester we consider MIT the scientific and engineering branch of the Eastman School, in the East!"

Accepting the directorship of the Eastman School was the greatest challenge of my life, undertaken with almost no administrative experience. I simply had a broad musical background, a special personal relationship to the school, and dreams of what needed to be done in the education of musicians, while making music of all kinds a more integral part of American life, a dream I shared with George Eastman. My twenty-four years at Eastman, and time spent later at the New England Conservatory and at the University of Texas at Austin, have all been part of my continuing education.

NOTE

1. My grandfather's professional papers, together with those of my parents, are part of the Ruth Watanabe Collection of the Eastman School's Sibley Music Library.

FOUR

Advice for Parents

Should Your Child Learn to Play the Cello?

In Howard Gardner's influential book of 1983, *Frames of Mind*, the author postulates seven distinctly different kinds of human intelligence: linguistic (the ability to manipulate words to express ideas), mathematical (the ability to manipulate quantitative constructs), musical (the ability to manipulate pitches, silence, and rhythms to produce coherence), spatial (the ability to perceive in three dimensions), bodily-kinesthetic (the ability to deal in a coordinated fashion with one's body), and the abilities to control one's own ego and to deal productively with the personal needs of other human beings. More recently Gardner has added two further intelligences: naturalist (the ability to discriminate between things that are living and those that are not) and existential (the ability to pose fundamental questions on life, death, and ultimate realities). It is Gardner's thesis that, while we deal in American schooling with the first two of these as matters basic to the future of our democracy, we normally pay inadequate attention to the other seven.

Not surprisingly, I concur with Gardner that music should be a much more central matter, particularly in view of what positron emissions tomography shows us about how the plastic human brain of childhood and adolescence construes and processes music.[1] As a person who has thought about how to make musicians work together as productive teams, I also believe that we give much too little attention in the entire educational process to the teaching of numbers six and seven of Gardner's nine intelligences, skills that Daniel Goleman summarizes in his best-selling book of 1995, *Emotional Intelligence*.[2] Reflection on the latter during the past six years, since returning to teaching as a member of the faculty of the Butler School of Music at the University of Texas at Austin, has led me repeatedly to the conclusion that a major lack in the education and training of musicians lies in musicians' too frequent failure to understand the motives of those they work with. Had Mozart been better able to understand why people like Salieri were intimidated by his awesome musical ability, Mozart might have dealt more productively with his employer's jealousy and, as a result, might have lived seventy years instead of thirty-five. Had Toscanini been able to grasp in the fashion of Bruno Walter that orchestral musicians play at least as well under more empathetic leadership, who knows how many premature strokes and heart attacks might have been avoided among the players whom Toscanini's uncontrolled temper too easily terrorized?[3]

We know that babies bond with their mothers at birth for several reasons, among them the fact that, in utero, they learn to recognize the sound of their mothers' voices. Imagine what might be achieved were expectant mothers normally offered not only the exercises of the Lamaze Technique, for example, but were trained in the singing of a small repertory of lullabies. A year or two ago, I had a visit from the chief pediatric nurse of the North Austin Medical Center, a local venture capitalist, and the grieving father of a recently deceased baby girl born three months premature, the whole of whose three-month life had taken place in an incubator. The nurse and the grieving father agreed that, in a situation where it had been impossible for anyone to comfort the baby through touch, in a situation where it had been difficult for her to breathe and to take nourishment, the only positive thing in her brief little life had been her unfailingly positive response to music of all kinds. The nurse came to me because she understood that for several years I have had the privilege of serving as board chair of Dr. Mark Tramo's Institute for Music and Brain Science, now at UCLA, where among other research projects, Dr. Tramo and his associates have been working on a musical approach to lessen pain and stress caused by the necessity of regular heel pricks administered to prematurely born infants. Though anecdotal reports on music's health-related benefits date back to ancient times, scientific study of these benefits is just beginning to take shape. There is a wealth of anecdotal evidence that surrounding infants and small children with music is both psychologically beneficial and a sound basis for a lifelong interest in music, especially if the children are rewarded for listening heedfully for five minutes at a time.

Over the course of the past century, four distinctly different though related methods for introducing small children to music have been developed, all with professional associations and certified teachers, available in community music schools all over the country. The first was the work of Emile Dalcroze (1865–1950), a Swiss musician who developed a school in Geneva that focused on eurhythmics, a method of experiencing music through bodily movement, in order to develop an integrated and natural response for musical expression in children. The second is the Kodaly

Method, developed in Hungary at the behest of the great Hungarian composer Zoltan Kodaly (1882–1967), stressing the importance for composers of working on music of high quality that could be sung and played by schoolchildren, implemented in Hungary after World War II on a national basis. The third is the Orff Schulwerk, developed by the German composer Carl Orff (1895–1982), combining music, movement, drama, and speech into lessons that are similar to a child's world of play, stressing the centrality of active participation, a physical activity that Orff considered preintellectual, working with simple acoustical instruments played by children to produce simple sequential structures, ostinatos, and miniature rondos. The fourth was developed by Shinichi Suzuki (1898–1998), conceived in Japan shortly after World War II by a violinist eager to bring beauty to the lives of children in a country that had just experienced horrific devastation. Wrote Suzuki, "I want to make good citizens. If a child hears fine music from the day of his birth and learns to play it himself, he develops sensitivity, discipline, and endurance, developing a beautiful heart." Suzuki had noticed that the smallest children learn their mother tongues with much greater ease than is possible when a human being is twenty years old and reasoned that similar sensitivities might accrue to people who begin musical studies early. First developed in Japan, the method spread to other Pacific Rim countries, then to Europe, and is now taught all over the world, including in Africa. Formal instruction is begun as early as age three and emphasizes early saturation in music, including concert attendance, friendship with other music students, and listening to music performed daily in the home on recordings. In the beginning, learning music by ear is emphasized, as is playing in ensembles, retaining and reviewing every piece of music learned on a regular basis, the attendance at instruction of one or both parents, as well as frequent public performance, making the experience of doing so nonthreatening and enjoyable.[4] Relevant to the methods just summarized is the work of Kenneth Wendrich, an Eastman graduate who during the 1970s directed the Neighborhood Music School in New Haven and wrote a University of Connecticut dissertation demonstrating that, while children of eighteen months are capable of matching pitches, the ability to do so atrophies after the age of five if it is not addressed by that point in a child's life.

While the ability to match pitches by the age of five is an excellent test of musicality, the acquisition of absolute pitch—the ability to remember specific pitches and to recreate them from memory—is not, I think. The work of Gottfried Schlaug will determine whether infants born with an unusually large left frontal cortex are apt to have absolute pitch or whether early work on acquiring absolute pitch develops a larger-than-usual left frontal cortex. When I was about five, my mother succeeded in inducing absolute pitch through a series of brief age-appropriate games in which I won prizes by identifying pitches, one at a time to begin with, then in increasingly complex combinations. Parents who are eager to try this with their own children may cheerfully do so if they wish, especially since failure to do so has no negative results I know of. Later in life, I have learned that the "absoluteness" of my pitch sense varies by 10–20 cents at times, apparently depending on whether I am spending more time processing notes or words.

Eventually, a child apparently interested in music whose parents are eager that formal musical instruction begin should be entrusted to an able and dedicated teacher who provides age-appropriate instruction. Such a teacher should be more dedicated to the developing musical skills of the student than to his or her reputation as a teacher. He or she should be a good and enthusiastic musician, a person willing when the time comes to pass the student along to another person better able to provide age-appropriate instruction for the next step of the journey. There are no hard-and-fast rules about this, though advice from other parents whose sons and daughters are studying music nearby will inevitably be helpful. Parental attendance for at least some of the instruction will ensure that the teacher does not have the same physical and emotional impact on the student that Joe Jackson seems to have had on the King of Pop. The development of discipline in a young human being is a valuable asset, but only if the human wish to excel in a self-critical fashion can be developed in a healthy and loving way.

Although there are clear advantages to learning how to sing at an early age, our young musician will find it advantageous to develop some facility, early on, at a keyboard instrument. Though the current musical literature developed for children leaves a lot to be desired—composers, take note!—the music for children by composers like Bach, Mozart, Schumann, and Bartok provides an attractive potential repertory. While I recall piano practice between the ages five and ten without great pleasure, my mother had no qualms about imposing a sense of expectant responsibility in those days, and later. I knew that I was supposed to keep my room neat, to listen carefully to what others were saying, to eat vegetables whether I wanted to or not, and to practice the piano for at least an hour in the morning before going outside. I learned I had better proceed as my mother required and thus began to learn the value of deferred gratification. "By the time you get to be ten, you will find that learning new music on an instrument you control better will be a lot more fun." It *was* fun during my eighth and ninth years to study theory and basic musicianship with that wonderful British lady in the Eastman Preparatory Department, Marjorie Truelove MacKown, who clearly loved both music and teaching children, and whose ear-training dictation exercises sounded beautiful, challenges on which I did well and to which I looked forward each week. (We all look forward to what we know we do well.) I remember, too, my first encounter with "Oh What a Beautiful Morning!" from *Oklahoma*, then brand new. I made a point of buying the sheet music with savings from my twenty-five cents of weekly allowance, for I wanted better to understand and to reproduce the beautiful affect produced by the melodic rise from a low B-natural to a high B-flat at the beginning of the third bar, where there occurred what I later learned to think of as an unprepared appoggiatura on "morning" but was taken in by my eight-year-old brain as an event of wonderful expressiveness. My mother was right. Daily piano practice, weekly theory lessons, and an occasional concert to attend with my parents—a special privilege at the age of eight or nine—became much more pleasurable as I approached my teens. I learned that practice improved the aural result, and that the pleasure of making it better and better was a process in which I could take pride, not for the sake of the applause but for the feeling that I was actually competent to accomplish something that was both beautiful and difficult, the sort of thing that adults achieved.

From the perspective of a parent, music study can be very supportive to a young person's development as a human being. From the perspective of the society of which we are all part, what UCLA's James Catterall has taught us in the past twenty years makes much sense for public policy development. His research shows that music study, by good teachers, encourages cognitive achievement while raising young people's willingness to complete high school, an impact that, strikingly, is independent of the student's socioeconomic background.[5] The concomitant work of MIT's Jeanne Bamberger, a disciple of Jean Piaget in relating music learning to childhood cognitive development, is a gold mine of inspiration yet to be integrated into the outlook of those who teach music in our public schools.[6]

There is a lot to be said for the musical training and education of children and adolescents, especially in the hands of teachers who care in each case about the long-term happiness and fulfillment of each student as an individual. For this to be possible, however, parents are well advised to see to it that equally adequate attention be given to our young student's general education—to his or her development in Howard Gardner's skills in literacy and numerosity, the backbone of the skills that colleges and universities require for admission, and in computer literacy, areas of traditional importance in American education for careers vital to the continuing success of the nation. Taken together with musical training, a strong general education can provide our young person with skills in time management, with the habit of working toward the perfection of artistic outcomes, and with the abilities to listen carefully and pay attention to the world around him. Important, too, is learning how to collaborate with one's peers in a small ensemble situation and understanding when and why the subordinatio of one's musical wishes as an individual is important to the work of an orchestra or a chorus. The student should begin working, too, on the lifelong goal of any musician, to hear in his inner ear the music he sees on paper and to be able to write down,

if he wishes, whatever he hears, skills known as score reading, the basis
for any long-term professional achievement in music. Ongoing study
should provide him or her, too, with a sense of what Eric Booth calls the
importance of art, including music, as a means toward making one's own
life and the lives of others interesting, exciting, and meaningful, and of
being able to discuss with anyone even a little interested why music is
important.[7]

But, as my grandfather said, music is both beautiful and seductive,
easily drawing a young person who does it well into imagining a professional future in a field for which professional opportunities have been
increasingly hard to attain, even for those who play and sing at very high
levels. A high-school-age clarinetist, performing the clarinet solo in the
slow movement of Rachmaninoff's very moving Second Symphony, articulated those feelings very well in an interview broadcast several years
ago as part of an NPR broadcast. She said,

> During the dress rehearsal I had been nervous, but played decently.
> For several hours before the concert I had a terrible feeling in the pit of
> my stomach. But the concert was phenomenal, and I wasn't as nervous
> in performing as I had been in the dress rehearsal. I played very well,
> and what seemed like a million people came up afterwards to tell me
> how amazing it sounded. The conductor gave me a hug and kiss on the
> cheek. It felt so good that so many people liked it. I was able to hear
> myself in the hall, for the sound reflected off the back of the room. I
> could experience my sound as though I were not just a performer but a
> listener as well. I just played my heart out, and really enjoyed myself. I
> think that was the best the orchestra had ever played. When the piece
> finished I couldn't stop myself from smiling. The most important thing
> for me was not how I sounded. The important thing [was] that playing
> the third movement of the Rachmaninoff was like experiencing pure
> fulfillment. How could I go into any career other than music? I enjoy
> myself so much with this stuff. I think I'm ready to make my decision
> on what I would like to spend my life devoted to. Well, maybe I've
> been ready for a while now. It's just that now it's impossible for me to
> see my future in any other way.

Shouldn't any self-respecting parents, interested in their daughter's
long-term personal and professional fulfillment, opt enthusiastically for
her happiness? Yes, of course. But, looking ahead, perhaps no. Though I
had had similar experiences as a teenager, my father reminded me often
of how unhappy too many of his Boston Symphony colleagues were,
though playing in one of the world's greatest orchestras. As he and my
mother, herself a fine professional violinist, saw things, a fine musical
education was important for their sons, but not at the price of a strong
general education.

Though Blair Tindall had not yet been born at the time I was an
undergraduate, I already understood in my undergraduate years the

principal thesis of her book, *Mozart in the Jungle: Sex, Drugs, and Classical Music*, a tell-all memoir of her frustrating days as a freelance oboist during her twenties and thirties in New York City. Tindall's final chapter includes thoughts relevant to any seventeen-year-old considering forgoing a good general education in order to become a professional musician.

> Why are so many young people still planning to be professional musicians? Why is musicianship regarded so highly that young people are encouraged to train exclusively for a career in an industry that is clearly failing? A little girl wearing pink hair bows and playing a quarter-sized violin is adorable. A sixty-year-old fiddler who can't afford health insurance, has no retirement accounts or savings, and is virtually unemployable is not. Music schools, teachers, parents, and students need to ask themselves hard questions about the true value of their craft and how it might best serve their interests, the future of its students, and the community around them.
>
> The young person who dreamily "wants to go to Juilliard" or "be a concert pianist" should research the reality of those statements. Seek out a variety of professional musicians: soloists, teachers, and orchestral, theatrical, and freelance musicians. Tag along for an afternoon or evening. See where they live. Ask what their days are really like and how they pay their living expenses. Ask if they like what they do and why. Most important, ask yourself if you are willing to sacrifice hours to tedious practice and nights, weekends, and holidays to playing concerts at times friends and relatives are socializing and relaxing with one another. How do you feel about long periods of sub-standard pay, lack of health insurance, and possible unemployment? Do you love music, or are you just hooked by the attention your performances bring? Somebody else is paying the bills now, but that won't always be the case. If you truly have a passion for classical music, by all means pursue your dreams. You are one of the lucky ones.
>
> Parents of talented children should ask plenty of questions. Is your child receiving a scholarship to music school because he or she is a budding Heifetz or because the school is desperate to recruit new students to fill its empty classrooms? Perhaps the music student could gain a more valuable education by applying to a liberal arts college that needs musicians to fill its orchestra. Is your child receiving an adequate general education? Is he or she genuinely enjoying the music? Is it possible to receive both quality music training and a well-rounded academic education by enrolling in a conservatory that is part of a larger university?[8]

In the days when the United States was so wealthy and powerful that we could afford lavishly to waste the futures of our young people, allowing the market to adjust the supply and demand for human talent without much regard to the fact that young people too often lack the experience of their elders, we could perhaps continue to proceed as we have for the past century. But at a time when we are running huge budget deficits in the midst of a major recession that pushed the national unemployment rate to double digits, it would make a lot of sense for the government or for a major foundation annually to publish ongoing information about the relationship of supply to demand in employment generally. We are presently preparing too many attorneys, too many medical specialists, too many performing artists, too many narrowly trained PhDs in the humanities and social sciences, and too many professional athletes. At the same time, we are developing too few nurses, too few scientists and engineers, too few general medical practitioners, too few computer programmers, and too few Americans who can speak such crucially needed languages as Arabic, Urdu, and Chinese.

Parents who compare a recording of a Beethoven symphony made just after World War I with a compact disc of the same work recorded by any major music school orchestra in America during the past decade will note without difficulty the unbelievable distance we have come in the performance of classical music. Bach, Beethoven, and Brahms would all be amazed to find how wonderfully well their music is played these days. But when five hundred young people present themselves for an opening in a major orchestra, the decision about who plays best of all is bound to be made on a partly quixotic basis, especially since none of the candidates is interviewed.

The reasons why young people who are candidates for admission to Bachelor of Music programs do not recognize this are well explained by Robert H. Frank and Philip J. Cook in their persuasive book, *The Winner Take All Society*.

> The winner-take-all payoff structure of the entertainment industry has increasingly permeated other sectors of the economy. Our claim is that, as in the entertainment industry, this pay-off structure has led too many people to abandon productive alternatives in pursuit of the top prizes.
>
> Our claim is that, in comparison to an optimal mix, market incentives typically lure too many contestants into winner-take-all markets, and too few into other careers. One reason involves a well-known human frailty—namely, our tendency to overestimate our chances of prevailing against our competitors. As we go on to show, too many contestants would enter winner-take-all markets even if everyone were perfectly informed about the odds of winning. Worst of all, for present purposes, overconfidence seems to peak at precisely that point in the life cycle when it does the most harm. As Adam Smith put it, "The contempt of risk and the presumptive hope of success are in no period of life more active than at the age at which young people choose their professions." Psychologist Tom Gihourch has called this "the Lake Wobegon Effect," after Garrison Keillor's mythical Minnesota town "where all the men are strong, all the women are good-looking, and all the children are above average."

The invisible hand theory says that we get socially optimal career choices where people make well-informed, self-serving decisions on the basis of market incentives. But it also says, by implication at least, that if people generally overestimate their prospects in winner-tale-all markets, the resulting career choices will not be socially (or even individually) optimal. Whatever its ultimate source, the Lake Wobegon effect describes such a bias, for it makes participation in winner-take-all markets seem incredibly attractive.[9]

Here, as in all other aspects of my own education, I had the supreme advantage of parents knowledgeable about music as a profession, filled at the same time with the conviction that a good general education ought to be basic for us all. They understood that time is precious for every young person, and that each of us ought at the outset to be as well informed as possible about the nature of our professional competition. During my own undergraduate years, I thought of myself as a budding Rudolf Serkin. As a result, my father suggested that I spend the summer after my junior year at Harvard as a student at Marlboro, studying with Serkin. While in my own view I was at least as good as half of the dozen pianists enrolled at Marlboro that summer, I recognized that my piano playing was not in the same league as that of Malcolm Frager, Van Cliburn, Lee Luvisi, Anton Kuerti, Gilbert Kalish, or James Levine (who at the time was but twelve years old), among the other dozen pianists that summer at Marlboro. It was a good idea, in retrospect, that I spent one summer practicing the piano ten hours a day. But when Mr. Serkin announced in the middle of August that, as the result of the generous gift of a trustee, we would be able to continue our work for an extra three weeks, through Labor Day, I knew that that was not the way I wanted to spend the rest of my life. Parents who are not themselves professional musicians like my own are herewith advised to seek similar advice from trusted friends and associates who know the profession and its perils. In doing so, they should be aware of Howard Reich's *Chicago Tribune* article of March 8, 2009, which begins:

> With the economy in free-fall and unemployment taking off, it's no wonder college students these days are clamoring to study—music? Yes, music. As in symphony, opera, and jazz. Applications are soaring at music schools across the country, often mirroring the overall rise in college enrollment but in many cases surpassing the interest in other disciplines. Never mind that the chances of landing a playing job in a decent-size symphony orchestra have diminished, with many ensembles going out of business in recent years. Never mind that jazz clubs are becoming an endangered species.
>
> More students want to stake their futures on the seemingly rarified art of music. And parents are not only letting them—they're paying for it. "I hear parents all the time saying, 'I don't know if my son or daughter can make a living at this, but I want to support their dream,'" said

Joan Warren, associate dean at the Juilliard School in New York. "Whereas 20 years ago, you had to study what was practical."[10]

Because parents are eager to see their sons and daughters succeed, and because music teachers are understandably eager to make a living, it often happens that continuing music study is urged after high school for young people whose innate talent and subsequent preparation ought not to encourage matriculation as a college music major. But because each of the 638 NASM music schools will try to fill its enrollment, based in each case on an already determined number of largely tenured faculty, practice rooms, and ensemble slots, too many young people proceed at the age of eighteen to entertain dreams of a future as a professional musician. According to AOL.com, music in the spring of 2009 was the ninth most attractive undergraduate collegiate major in America, following sociology, English, computer science, communications, business, political science, journalism, and biology![11] Since none of us knows the future, my best advice to the parents of young people who insist on becoming undergraduate music majors is to urge a double major: music and entrepreneurial studies, music and business, music and pre-med, music and pre-law, music and computer science, music and Arabic.

A principal problem for the University of Texas at Austin is that the average length to an undergraduate degree here already amounts to six years. A distinguished faculty, our unusually low tuition, an abundance of sunshine, the availability of almost every conceivable subject, and the fact that Austin is so attractive a place to live all make their contributions. Many colleges and universities will go out of their way to accommodate student interest in double majors, for each such student makes the university of which he is part a more coherent institution. The existence of a double focus on the undergraduate level also makes each such student of special interest to graduate schools and to most potential employers.

Finally, the current design for undergraduate musical education, based as it is on the winner-take-all model, aims at placing each of our graduates in New York, Chicago, or Los Angeles. As I tell many of my Texas students, if you are both an accredited brain surgeon and a fine oboist and you move to Boston, the community will insist that you decide whether to work full-time at Massachusetts General Hospital or at Symphony Hall. If, on the other hand, you decide you would rather live in Harrisburg, Fort Wayne, Amarillo, or Sacramento—and there are many, many such communities in the United States—there will be general rejoicing if you will agree to do both brain surgery and oboe playing. The local symphony—and there is bound to be a pretty good one—only plays half a dozen concerts a year, and the local hospital normally has real difficulty finding good brain surgeons. Lisa Wong's *Scales to Scalpels* shows what a practical idea this is for young people who love to play orchestral instruments but would like to work in a field like medicine, where salaries are high and dependable because demand greatly exceeds supply, especially for general practitioners.

Of critical importance to parents considering an undergraduate future in music for their sons and daughters is the fact that the acoustic instruments in which one majors—piano and organ, violin, viola, cello, double bass, the wind and brass instruments, percussion, and voice—have wildly disparate musical repertories. While the repertory for the piano is rich, difficult, and endless, the repertories for the double bass and tuba are not. Thus, while practicing the piano for four hours a day is important for anyone who wants to be a professional pianist, it is hard to understand how or why one could possibly practice each day on the tuba for that much time. That notwithstanding, NASM-mandated undergraduate curricula for piano and tuba plan for the same intensive focus for both instruments. As I have pointed out earlier, parents should remember that too much practice produces two really negative outcomes: (1) the possibility of disabling physiological injury and (2) serious educational opportunity costs that can limit long-term happiness and productivity. The problem is that the amount of needed practice time appears to vary by individual, and to be impacted by stage fright, an important phenomenon addressed later.[12]

If, however, parents and students are reconciled on the idea of an undergraduate music major, the question becomes where to go to school. By the outset of our student's junior year in high school, I strongly urge parents and students to read *Higher Education?: How Colleges Are Wasting Our Money and Failing Our Kids—and What We Can Do About It* by Andrew Hacker and Claudia Dreyfus (New York: Holt, 2010), a readable outline of basic issues affecting collegiate study in America with a major in *any* discipline. The following issues are of special relevance to those considering matriculation at a professional music school.

THE REPUTATION AND QUALITY OF THE TEACHER OF OUR STUDENTS' PRIMARY INSTRUMENT

Consultation with one's high school teacher; with one's high school orchestra, band, or (as relevant) choral conductors; and with others who have studied that instrument in college are all worthwhile ways of collecting information. It is to be expected that networks of interpersonal and institutional loyalty exist all over the world to facilitate potential study with a leading teacher, and the most successful teachers, understanding that poor quality in implies poor quality out, work hard to see to it that they attract the best. The selection of the principal teacher is a central matter, for an unhappy relationship with one's primary teacher, especially in a school where that teacher is the only person available on the instrument in question, necessitates transferring to another college if there is a lack of interpersonal congruence between teacher and student to begin with.

THE QUALITY OF THE REST OF THE FACULTY AT THE SCHOOL OR COLLEGE CHOSEN

Some schools will spend the preponderance of their salary funds maintaining a splendid faculty in areas they wish to emphasize, without dedicating comparable resources to other parts of the faculty. If the school or department is part of a larger college or university, students of oboe or violin will study history or philosophy with faculty expert in those disciplines. If, however, the school is freestanding, one can easily understand that those teaching extramusical subjects may be given less support than those teaching music. At the Eastman School during my directorship, all students and faculty understood that, if a student's violin recital took place on Friday evening while her economics paper was due Thursday morning, the institution would expect her to do well in both areas, as scheduled. In questions of musical ensembles, success is very much like that in a sport where teamwork is vital. Just as one cannot make double plays effectively with a superior second baseman if all of the shortstops are mediocre, one cannot play a Brahms symphony at its best if the oboes are fine but the horns are always out of tune. While some of the faculty may have left professional work to focus on teaching, it is important that a considerable part of the faculty continue to be actively involved in the professional worlds of composition, performance, and scholarship. And it is equally important that at least some of the faculty be generalists.[13]

NET COST

Parents will notice that music schools—like colleges and universities—do not charge equivalent tuition and fees. That the list price for tuition at Harvard or Stanford may amount to fifty thousand dollars a year and that at Curtis or Colburn to nothing at all implies neither that the former are infinitely more valuable than the latter nor that the latter are not wonderful schools. And all four institutions are very well endowed! What is going on here has become a normal matter for higher education all over America in the past half century. For highly sought-after students, the school is willing to extend itself financially in order to see to it that the student comes to Texas instead of Rice, for example. What makes the student especially sought after may be her superior level of achievement as bassoonist, understandably important to a wonderful bassoon teacher, but it may relate as well to her high intelligence and imagination and thus to her longer-term potential as a conductor or composer, say.

The principal point for the parent to remember is that it is *net* cost that counts, the sticker price listed on the school's website minus the value of scholarship grants, guaranteed work-study funds, and loans. Which would our student rather have, a $5,000 scholarship or a $20,000 one? Not so fast! A $45,000 annual tuition bill discounted by $20,000 amounts to $25,000 due from the parents and the student each year; whereas a $15,000 annual tuition bill discounted by $5,000 amounts to only $10,000 a year out of pocket. If the educational value received is equivalent—and by this time in American history I believe it *is* equivalent in our leading public universities—I would be hard pressed to invest in the high price spread, simply for bragging rights with the neighbors. Doriot Anthony Dwyer, a distinguished Eastman alumna who in 1952 became the first woman to hold a principal chair in a major orchestra, once complained to me that, when she was an Eastman student in the early forties, she had been given no scholarship to study flute with the legendary Joseph Mariano. I told her, once I looked into the matter, that she had received no scholarship because her father had earned too high a salary for Eastman to justify such a discount. Understanding her point, I quickly established honorary scholarships, awards of psychological value perhaps but without any fiscal consequence.

This raises the question of varying income and expense streams for American music schools. If the faculty is largely part-time, they will be paid on an hourly basis, without tenure, and certainly without medical and retirement benefits. If the faculty is largely full-time, the cost will be a lot higher, but the faculty will be willing to spend a lot more time and energy, not only with our student but with his or her colleagues, thus facilitating the existence of a real school rather than just a building in which various experts are assigned space for two or three hours a week each. Some institutions try to keep the net price low by minimizing salaries, the quality of pianos, the richness of libraries, or the number of practice rooms. Others have advantages in income streams that flow from generous endowments, state funding, successful fundraising, federal research grants, and large numbers of dedicated graduates.

LOCATION

There are students and parents who are drawn by large cities, for there is a lot going on there. But there are also people who would prefer that their children be educated where there are trees and grass, and especially where there are students and faculty interested in other disciplines.

In Rochester, where winter lasts a long time, we used to brag that our advantages included a wintertime climate "ideally conducive to cultural and intellectual activity." In Austin, where we have at least three hundred days of sunshine a year and a snowy day once every three years, we stress the psychological benefits of living in an environment that is unusually open and friendly. Curtis is a music school where one can get to know all of the students, an impossible matter on campuses like those of Indiana or North Texas, at each of which there are 1,600 other music students. Musicians can be a clannish lot, even on campuses where other students work on other disciplines. The UT dean of engineering and I worked together on a dormitory that was to house only artists and engineers. Distance from home may be a consideration. Part of the reason I went to Harvard instead of Yale was so that I could get home for weekends without trouble. For some students, the possibility of living away from home may have advantages. All kinds of possibilities are out there. It is only a matter for careful investigation.

DORMITORIES, COMPUTER LABS, GYMNASIA, LIBRARIES, AND PRACTICE ROOMS

All of these cost money, and in every music school that exists, someone has made the decision to invest in these as a matter of course, or not to. While the NASM standard is no more than four enrolled music students for a practice room, practice-room availability makes a real difference for a student's time management, especially in a situation where the library is substandard. If students are allowed to practice in the dormitory, no one gets to sleep when he wants to. If informal areas are not provided for student discussion, too few get the benefit of a regular exchange of views with their peer groups, some of whom will inevitably go on to become the CEO of General Electric, the president of the United States, or the executive director of the Boston Symphony.

SEXUAL HARASSMENT

Does the institution have legislation on its books formally prohibiting inappropriately personal relationships between faculty and staff members on the one hand and students on the other? Especially dependent in music on their faculty mentors' candor and judgment, music students have, it has always seemed to me, a special right to being assured that the faculty member has no ulterior motives in passing artistic judgment. For more on this vital subject, see chapter 6.

GRADUATES

Does the school care what its alumni are doing? Are there regular reunions and are they well attended? In what proportion do the alumni contribute funding to the school, and do they send their best students as recommended candidates for matriculation? Does the school know whether its graduates regard the work of their student years with affection, whether they are happy in their current professional activities, and whether they think their school provided them with the tools they needed to succeed?

Once your eighteen-year-old has picked out his or her favorite half-dozen schools, I would strongly urge the scheduling of a family trip to visit each institution, spending at least a day on each campus, talking to the principal teacher (make sure in advance that she will not be on tour in Europe when you get there), sitting in on ensemble rehearsals, inspecting dormitory, library, and practice rooms, and talking to as many of the current students as possible.

Living away from home is a valuable experience at the age of eighteen for most teenagers, but there is every reason for parents to stay appropriately in touch with their offspring during college—by email, telephone, and in person. How are things going? How do you like your teachers and the other students? Is the administration open to questions and suggestions? Are you still confident that this is the field for you and that we have made the right choice of school? While it makes sense not to transfer to another institution as the result of ill-considered whims, there is every reason at the age of eighteen or twenty carefully to examine a variety of alternatives. Like Leonard Bernstein at thirty, I still haven't decided at the age of seventy-eight what I want to do when I grow up.

NOTES

1. Howard Gardner, *Frames of Mind: The Theory of Multiple Intelligences* (New York: Basic Books, 1981). See also Lisa Wong, *Scales to Scalpels: Doctors Who Practice the Healing Arts of Music and Medicine* (New York: Pegasus Books, 2012).

2. Daniel Goleman, *Emotional Intelligence* (New York: Bantam Dell, 1995).

3. At an Eisenhart House dinner in the 1980s, the late Philip Farkas, then a distinguished professor of horn at Indiana University, earlier principal horn of the Boston Symphony, the Cleveland Orchestra, and the Chicago Symphony Orchestra, was seated at my left. He spoke about a major heart attack he had suffered in Bloomington. In a consultation at the hospital, the cardiologist had said, "Mr. Farkas, I just don't understand why you had a major heart attack last night. You are not overweight, you have never smoked, you exercise regularly, and you eat a well-balanced diet." Farkas said he had replied, "Doctor, have you ever heard of Koussevitzky, Szell, and Reiner?"

4. On September 30, 2003, at my request, Doris Preucil laid out her views on the relationship of Suzuki violin pedagogy to more traditional violin studies:

> The question is often asked, "When does a child finish Suzuki and go on to a real violin teacher?" However, as the student grows in age and ability, the Suzuki books contain the sonatas and concertos universally studied, and [the method] evolves into actual concert repertoire. Along with the Suzuki books, most Suzuki teachers in North America follow the same sequence of reading sonatas, etudes, and scales used by "traditional" teachers.
>
> Some Suzuki teachers do not feel confident in the advanced levels and pass their students on to other teachers at this point. Yet many have the

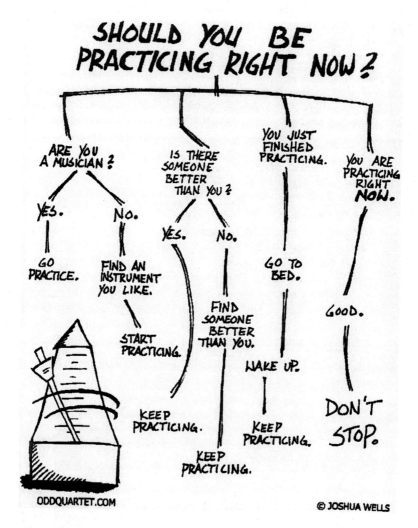

Figure 4.1.   As Robert Schumann said, there is no point in practicing when you feel tired and are not able to listen carefully. Good time management suggests that that may be an appropriate time to read or to exercise. © *Josh Wells*

training, ability, and performance experience to remain with the student until high school graduation and beyond, when the students are very advanced. What remains important about Suzuki training in advanced levels is the continuous concentration on tone development and sequential learning with success at every step—in other words, working for perfection. Suzuki writes, "To teach your child to perfect something means to improve his/her brain activity to the utmost; eventually this outstanding ability will enable him/her to handle other things well." This kind of superior training can also be found in many "traditional" teachers but is deeply ingrained in Suzuki teaching from the beginning. I consider my students "Suzuki students" even when studying the Sibelius Concerto, because the Suzuki pedagogical philosophy carries over into all teaching. Being this kind of teacher has given me a beautiful and fulfilling life.

Because Doris Preucil developed both a wonderful community music school in Iowa City and a musical family of professional all-stars that includes the present concertmaster of the Cleveland Orchestra, it is obvious that she knows what she's talking about.

5. James S. Catterall, *The Arts and Learning: New Opportunities for Research* (Washington, DC: American Educational Research Association / Arts Education, 2004); *Critical Links: The Arts and Academic and Social Development* (Washington, DC: Arts Education Partnership / National Endowment for the Arts, 2003); *Champions of Change: The Impact of the Arts on Human Development* (Washington, DC: National Endowment for the Arts, MacArthur Foundation, GE Fund, and Arts Education Partnership, 1999); "Does Experience in the Arts Boost Academic Achievement? A Response to Eisner," *Art Education*, July 1998; "Different Ways of Knowing: 1991–94 National Longitudinal Study Final Report," in *Schools, Communities, and the Arts: A Research Compendium* (Tempe, AZ: Morrison Institute of Public Policy / National Endowment for the Arts, 1994). Lisa Wong's *Scales and Scalpels* tells the history of Boston's amazing Longwood Symphony Orchestra, an "amateur" orchestra of professional physicians. It is also full of very positive suggestions for future studies on the scientific relationship of music to medicine.

6. Important works by Jeanne Bamberger include her books *Developing Musical Intuition: A Project-Based Introduction to Making and Understanding Music* (New York: Oxford University Press, 2000); *The Mind Behind the Musical Ear: How Small Children Learn Music* (Cambridge, MA: Harvard University Press, 1991); and, with Howard Brofsky, *The Art of Listening: Developing Musical Perception* (New York: Harper and Row, 1988); and her book chapters "How the Conventions of Music Symbol Systems Shape Musical Perception," in *Musical Communication*, ed. D. Mieli, R. MacDonald, and D. Hargreaves, 143–70 (Oxford: Oxford University Press, 2005); "Changing Musical Perception through Reflective Communication," in *Talking Texts: How Speech and Writing Interact in School Learning*, ed. R. Horowitz (Mahwah, NJ: Lawrence Erlbaum Associates, 2007); "Learning from the Children We Teach," in *Proceedings of the Third International Congress on Rhythm* (Geneva: Dalcroze Institute, 2001); "Action Knowledge and Symbolic Knowledge: The Computer as Mediator," in *High Technology and Low Income Communities: Prospects for the Positive Use of Advanced Information Technology*, ed. D. Schön, B. Sanyal, and W. J. Mitchell, 235–60 (Cambridge, MA: Massachusetts Institute of Technology Press, 1998); and recent papers in refereed journals: with A. Di Sessa, "Music as Embodied Mathematics: A Study of a Mutually Affirming Affinity," *International Journal of Computers for Mathematical Learning* 8, no. 2 (May 2003): 126–60; "The Development of Intuitive Musical Understanding," *Psychology of Music* 30, no. 1 (2002): 7–36; "On Making Distinctions Permeable: A Review of Creativity as Learning," *Israel Studies in Musicology Online* 2 (2002); "Music, Math, and Science: Toward an Integrated Curriculum," *Journal of Learning through Music* (Spring 2000); "Turning Music Theory on Its Ear: Do We Hear What We See?" *International Journal of Computers and Mathematical Education* 1, no. 1 (1996): 33–55.

7. Eric Booth, *The Music Teaching Artist's Bible: Becoming a Virtuoso Educator* (Oxford: Oxford University Press, 2009).

8. Blair Tindall, *Mozart in the Jungle: Sex, Drugs, and Classical Music* (New York: Atlantic Monthly Press, 2005), 304.

9. Robert H. Frank and Philip J. Cook, *The Winner Take All Society: Why the Few at the Top Get So Much More Than the Rest of Us* (New York: Penguin, 1996), 101–5, 126.

10. Howard Reich, "High Note for Music Studies," *Chicago Tribune*, March 8, 2009.

11. "What Is Your College Major?" AOL.com, January 23, 2009.

12. While piano teachers differ in recommended amounts of practice, my competition at Marlboro in the summer of 1956 used to aim for ten daily hours. Josef and Rhosina Lhevinne in *Basic Principles of Pianoforte Playing* (New York: Dover, 1972) recommended four hours.

13. One of my proudest moments as Eastman director came in the late 1980s with the visit to my office of a young woman about to graduate from the studio of a faculty member who was the only person in the institution responsible for instruction on a particular instrument. The professor had taught at Eastman for nearly sixty years, an unmarried lady in her eighties whose only relationship to humanity came through her students and who was very eager to set a new record by having taught at Eastman for sixty years. I knew that her studio was in trouble, and, with great sadness, saw to it that she retired after fifty-nine years on the job. Said her student to me, "As you know, I have not been very happy with the instruction from my principal teacher. But this is a wonderful school. I have had a lesson at one time or another with every single member of your instrumental and vocal faculties. Each of them was eager to try to help me become a better musician, and I feel as though I owe an enormous debt of gratitude to Eastman."

FIVE

Advice for Collegiate Music Students

How Best to Fulfill Your Dreams

Now that you have enrolled in a good music school, it is important to optimize what can be a wonderful educational and musical experience. In the summer before you start study, continue the kind of practice regimen that you have probably been following for several years, developing the kind of happiness in the regularity of your work that is characteristic of any serious person. Music is not a good field to get into if you are not serious! Too many older musicians practice too little during the summer before freshman year, then practice too much for ten days before school begins, arriving on campus with painfully sore backs, arms, wrists, and lips, and thus not ready for the beginning of school. Too little practicing is not good. But so is too much. Get to know your limits. Pay special attention to the cartoon from *Odd Quartet* reprinted as figure 5.1, "Shouldn't You Be Practicing Now?," an idea that has haunted too many music students for the past two hundred years, suggesting that one should feel guilty if one fails to spend all of one's time practicing.

Get used to listening carefully to your own playing, correcting what sounds wrong or awkward, carefully comparing what you are producing with your best idea of how you want the music to sound. Begin with scales and arpeggios. On wind, brass, and string instruments, work at beginning very softly and getting progressively louder, on a single note. Then try the opposite, beginning loudly and make a long, long diminuendo. Work on three or four pieces over the summer, all at a level of difficulty that you can handle with distinction. As Robert Schumann says, it is a lot better to play an easy piece well than a difficult piece poorly. Your new teacher will want to hear these in the fall, and it is always a good idea to make a positive first impression. Compare your performance with

63

those of several others, available these days on compact discs and on YouTube. Since some performances will be much better than others, try to determine what makes the really good ones superior to those that don't excite you. In any case, do your best to follow the composer's apparent intentions. Try to learn solo repertory so that you can perform what you study without the printed text in front of you. If you can write out the piece from memory, you know it well. That, however, is a goal that may be a long way ahead as you begin your freshman year. Begin to become familiar with a broad range of musical literature, whatever your instrument. We hope you will be trained as a musician, not just as a virtuoso kazoo player.[1] If you have not already heard a Mozart opera, *The Marriage of Figaro* is a wonderful place to begin. Get to know some Monteverdi madrigals. Compare the Berg Violin Concerto with Bartok's Second Violin Concerto and with the Barber Violin Concerto. All three are wonderful pieces. The excitement of learning new works that you have probably never heard before, listening to each at least half a dozen times with the score in front of you, will remind you why you want to become a musician. Try to explain to your friends and parents what makes each of these musical experiences so moving to you.

Schools may use slightly different ways of teaching so-called music theory. At your level, this is not at all theoretical. It is really just the development of basic music literacy, the abilities to write down what you hear and to hear internally what is written on the printed page. You do not need orally to pronounce everything you read in the morning newspaper. A musician should learn, as soon as possible, to acquire the same skills with respect to music.[2] If you have not already done so, buy a copy of Paul Hindemith's *Elementary Training for Musicians*. While only the first several pages are elementary, the whole of the book is full of the kinds of exercises that will strengthen your fundamental musicianship. Make as much progress as you can during the summer with *Elementary Training*, working, if possible, with a trusted friend or high school teacher. The exercises will be fun once you begin to perform them skillfully.

If in high school you have been persuaded that you could work at the music you love while leaving the abilities to think, read, write, and speak to others, you have been poorly advised. Musicians of the future will need to understand the changing role of music in the new millennium, help develop new institutions, and understand how to manage their own careers.

During the summer before you go to college, read Malcolm Gladwell's recent book *Outliers*, an assessment of the qualities that help a human being succeed.[3] Though you may well have been the greatest adolescent cellist that Helena, Montana, has ever heard, it may be that, at Eastman or Texas, a tour of corridors outside the practice rooms will suggest that you are for the moment only twenty-third best on the local totem pole. In Gladwell's view, relatively high intelligence is a sine qua non, though he cites the examples of several people who turned out to be fools despite their very high IQs. A willingness to work hard, the ability to relate positively to other human beings, and resilience in the face of adversity are all-important, too. Reading *Outliers* can help you develop the balanced point of view you will need in order to survive in your first year in music school. Each of us has his or her own special combination of strengths and weaknesses. Allowing time in college, and in the rest of your life, to read widely will make you a human being with broad interests, the kind of person who is impressive in an interview and gets hired over the competition. There will be those who tell you that music as a profession is so difficult that you have no time to read. But just as some pieces of music are much better than others, carefully chosen reading will in the long run make you a better musician. A broad regimen of reading, about music and about other areas that interest you, will make you a more interesting human being. In the Internet age, it is especially important to learn *how* to find the information you are looking for, while testing its reliability. Too much time in front of a television set, on the other hand, will provide relatively little added value.

Adjust yourself at the outset to the fact that the faculty are older than you, that they are there to guide you, and that they are entitled to a degree of respect that comes from their greater experience. It goes without saying that their experience goes back to a world of music dominant during the second half of the twentieth century, and that you will need skills to succeed in 2035 that were altogether undreamed of during the 1980s. In my student days, I disagreed a lot with some of my teachers, but I decided it would be imprudent to do so too vigorously, that someday I might get to teach my own students or to direct my own school, and that at that point, I would try to put into practice some of what I thought important when I was younger. Similar options are open to the next generations of musicians, supporting an aural skill base with visually oriented technologies now still in their infancy. And in the meantime, I have decided that some of my teachers were really good.[4]

CHANGING REPERTORIES, MIXING TRADITIONS

Here is a single example of the sometimes seismic shift between generations that I have in mind. When I was a college student, in the middle 1950s, the other students and I focused on the music of Bach, Beethoven, and Brahms, a repertory central to the whole of my life. It came from Europe and was called "serious music" or "concert music," deserving the attention of scholars who spent their careers answering questions of attribution, dating, and performance practice as accurately as musicologists could. Plaster of Paris busts of the great figures graced the pianos of the teachers who introduced us when young to such repertory. They were emblazoned around Paine Hall at Harvard and around the Hatch Shell on the Charles River. A statue of Beethoven stood in the lobby of the New England Conservatory, and a golden bust of Beethoven surmounted the stage of Symphony Hall. We learned how to be quiet until the whole of a masterpiece had been finished. I was told, as a boy, that it was a privilege to go to a concert in Symphony Hall and that listening to Brahms would make me a better human being. Because important people attended such concerts, a knowledge of Bach, Beethoven, and Brahms had presumably contributed to their success. This music was treated as a sacred relic of the past.

Music by such composers as Scott Joplin, Louis Armstrong, Fats Waller, Duke Ellington, and Art Tatum, on the other hand, came from bars and bordellos in New Orleans. Though of great interest in Europe during the 1920s, jazz was a four-letter word in American music schools during the first half of the twentieth century. It was excoriated by Henry Ford, and Eastman students found performing jazz in the 1920s or 1930s were summarily dismissed from the school. The earliest jazz program in an American university was founded in 1947 at North Texas University by Wilfred Bain (1908–1997), a young Canadian dean, though it was called the "One O'Clock Lab Band" to mollify a board of regents not yet ready in a public southern university for the use of the word "jazz" in a printed curriculum. The development of something actually *called* a jazz curriculum in American music schools took place only in the late 1960s, after Lyndon Johnson had passed civil rights legislation in 1965. This occurred first at Indiana University, established by the same Wilfred Bain and David Baker; at the New England Conservatory by Gunther Schuller; and at the Eastman School by Jack End, Chuck Mangione, and Rayburn Wright. Such music, we were told when I was a student, had a much shorter half-life than classical music. It was visceral and appealed to the mob, and the whole of its sociology was entirely different from that of the music we studied in school. I was the first dean to appoint a black man to the jazz faculty of the University of Texas at Austin, early in the twenty-first century, at about the time that the Juilliard jazz program was first established. Austin's program stemmed from the 1970s, but like a great many other American jazz programs of the last quarter of the twentieth century, it had been taught entirely by white men.

Important material for understanding the split between the study of European and American repertories in American music schools can be found in Laurence Levine's inspiring book of 1989, *Highbrow, Lowbrow*, while Bill Ivey's recent *Arts, Inc.: How Greed and Neglect Have Destroyed Our Cultural Rights* describes how these two repertories—the first needing to be subsidized while the second produces huge amounts of fiscal profit—were intentionally separated in the United States, sociologically and legally, from the middle of the nineteenth century.[5] While the 638 NASM schools focus on the first of the two repertories, only Boston's

Berklee School of Music concentrates on the second. It is a principal thesis of this book that musicianship of the twenty-first century will necessarily include both bodies of music, now assimilating, in addition, new influences from Asia, Eastern Europe, the Caribbean, Latin America, and Africa.

I have seen firsthand the power on an audience of mixing these repertories. During the 1980s, Eastman's faculty of conducting and ensembles came up with a terrific idea that always packed the 3,094-seat Eastman Theatre, though the idea was too expensive to produce more than once a year. A Prism Concert used six performing venues in the theater—the main stage, the apron of the main stage (which could be raised and lowered into an orchestral pit with a pneumatic elevator), two back balconies, and two side stages located at ten o'clock and two o'clock (with the center of the main stage at twelve). In the program notes and in a preliminary announcement from the stage, the audience was informed that the program of seventy-five minutes would comprise several six- or seven-minute pieces of music, broadly different from one another, performed from all over the theater in such a way that the last note of the first piece coincided with the first note of the second piece. All repertory for the evening was under a common thematic umbrella. The first Prism Concert was called "A Taste of the Twenties," comprising the climactic scene of Stravinsky's "Oedipus Rex," a movement of Bartok's Fourth String Quartet, Varèse's *Octandre*, and the finale of the Hindemith Wind Quintet, mixed with music by Victor Herbert, George Gershwin, Louis Armstrong, Duke Ellington, and Jerome Kern, concluding with a twenty-minute, orchestrally accompanied silent film called *Teddy at the Throttle*, about a dog driving a railroad train. We got wonderful reviews, too, for a concert produced at the Lincoln Center's Alice Tully Hall during the late 1980s entitled "New Music and All That Jazz." The first half of the evening comprised "serious" music written during the 1980s and led by Sydney Hodkinson, director of Eastman's Musica Nova Ensemble, with the second half comprising contemporary jazz, led by Rayburn Wright. The same students performed in both halves of the concert, dressed during the first half in full dress suits and after intermission in sweatshirts, jeans, and sneakers. The implied point of the program was that versatility is a good thing for young musicians. In January 2009, we did something similar in the University of Texas's Bass Concert Hall, seating three thousand. But while the hall was sold out, a lot of us faded before the three-hour event reached its conclusion, though the students, I'm told, stayed on till the end in anticipation of a well-known rock group in the finale. What I learned from the first Texas Prism event is that it is important, if at all possible, to eliminate all the time required for resetting the stage and for the inevitable applause-accompanied processions and recessions of the performers, from all of which the audience loses focus. Starbucks has by now gotten the idea that lots of people, the musical omnivores, like lots of different repertory, artfully juxtaposed, selling, with café au lait and mocha, compact discs featuring the favorite music of Tony Bennett, Yo Yo Ma, or Paul McCartney, all of whom, it develops, have remarkably eclectic tastes.

On the eve of Barack Obama's inauguration as our forty-fourth president, there took place a wonderful concert in front of the Lincoln Memorial in which Stevie Wonder and Aretha Franklin shared the stage with Renée Fleming, Yo Yo Ma, and Itzhak Perlman, instantly creating a whole new status for music that really matters, and of the long-term possibilities of American music as the new millennium unfolds in an entirely new world. At a time when the authority of classical music is now in question in the United States, young musicians will do well, I believe, not only to cherish the music of the European masters but to explore as well all sorts of American music—past, present, and future, building a repertory and a skill set that encompasses a much broader array of musics than most members of my generation considered relevant. Steve Mayer, a fine pianist who teaches at the Manhattan School and at the University of Denver, is a contemporary model of the kind of artist I have in mind here, having recorded not only the complete piano music of Charles Ives but the virtuosic arrangements of Art Tatum. Alan Feinberg, whose appointment I managed at Eastman, is an equally fine role model for young pianists. His four CDs for Argo—*The American Innovator* (Ornstein, Adams, Cowell, Babbitt, Nancarrow, Cage, Ives, Thelonious Monk), *Fascinatin' Rhythm* (Gershwin, Waller, Ellington, Joplin, Jelly Roll Morton, Zez Confrey), *The American Romantic* (Beach, Gottschalk, Helps), and *The American Virtuoso* (Gottschalk, Beach, MacDowell, Gershwin) are an admirably broad repertory for the kind of piano professor I would be looking for these days were I a forty-year-old music school director. (These days one can admire without embarrassment the similarly eclectic musical interests of such leaders as Leonard Bernstein, André Previn, and Gunther Schuller in a fashion that was not possible in 1950!)

Another essential aspect of the ways music will inevitably change relates to technology and the Internet. This is an area wherein those born before the Vietnam War have an inevitable disadvantage compared with younger people, though I expect that the speed of technological change will continue to challenge many young musicians for generations to come. By now the means of music's distribution has changed, as have the ways we compose, record, share, and perceive music. And they will go on changing even more rapidly. All of this would persuade me, were I an undergraduate music major in the current decade, to make friends of those on campus interested in music who are currently majoring in the liberal arts, business, law, communications, and the studies that lead to medical school. Conversations with such people will lead, inevitably, to questions about who our audience is, who it will be in the years to come, and the means of exploring, while still an undergraduate, what the non-music majors perceive as coherence and excitement in the musics that move *them*. I have always thought that my musical education facilitates my perception of the unfolding of musical coherence in longer time spans, and my ability to teach others often focuses on how to emulate those skills. Now I dream, in the years ahead, especially with the new technologies increasingly available, of using visual information and images to help an audience anticipate the arrival of a climax, the establishment of a new tonal area, or the simultaneous use of diminution and augmentation, in the fashion that professional sports in America has used to expand their fan bases. What do nonmusicians perceive in listening to a piece of music? What would they *like* to perceive? What might it be *possible* for them to perceive, given proper education and training, in fashions that they perceive as fun? What are the most effective means, using present and future technology, to provide music with an instructional base that might use the eye as a crutch to the ear? These are all questions I hope you will take seriously as an undergraduate music major. They were unanswerable a generation or two ago, but they will not be for your generation of professionals.

During my days as a music school dean, I tried to begin every new student's work with two very basic contributions to his or her education, thinking of both as excellent foundations for the work to follow. The first is a careful reading of Robert Schumann's aphorisms and maxims for young musicians, first published in his *Album für die Jugend*, Opus 68 (1848), printed in English translation by Konrad Wolff in *On Music and Musicians*.[6] A French edition was arranged by Liszt, who obviously agreed with Schumann that these were ideas worth thinking about. While some are a bit dated 160 years later, most of them still hit the mark. Among my personal favorites are:

- You must practice scales and other finger exercises industriously. There are people, however, who think they may achieve great ends by doing this, up to an advanced age. For many hours daily, they practice mechanical exercises. That is as reasonable as trying to recite the alphabet faster and faster every day. Find a better use for your time.
- Never strum. Always play energetically and never fail to finish the piece you have begun. Try to play easy pieces well; it is better than to play difficult ones poorly. Always play as though a master were present. You must reach the point where you can hear the music from the printed page.
- If you have finished your daily musical work and feel tired, do not force yourself to labor further. It is better to rest than to practice without joy or freshness.

- Look upon alterations or omissions, or the introduction of modern embellishments, in the works of good composers as something detestable. They are possibly the greatest insults that can be offered art.
- Lose no opportunity for making music in company with others, in duos and trios, for example. This will render your playing more fluent and sweeping. Accompany singers oftentimes. Much is to be learned from singers, male and female. But do not believe everything they tell you!
- If all were determined to play the first violin, we should never have complete orchestras. Therefore respect every musician in his proper field.
- Seek out among your comrades those who know more than you do.
- The study of the history of music and the hearing of masterworks of different epochs will speediest of all cure you of vanity and self-adoration.
- Do not judge a composition on a first hearing. That which pleases most at first is not always the best. Masters call for study. Many things will only become clear to you when you are old.
- Have an open eye for life as well as for the other arts and sciences.

Nothing worthwhile can be accomplished without enthusiasm. I urge you to become familiar with all of Schumann's aphorisms and maxims, as valuable today as they were in Schumann's time.

My second introductory contribution involved a ninety-minute annual exercise I led at which attendance was mandatory for all new students. This exercise was called "A Budget for the Chicago Symphony Orchestra." For the first half hour the students enjoyed developing an expense budget, the sum of money needed to run the CSO for a year. A student scribe recorded our work at a blackboard in front. The point of the exercise was to get Eastman students to think at the outset about problems of supply and demand for classical music, reminding them that the CSO could not spend money it did not have, that unplanned raids on endowment would undermine an orchestra altogether, and that an introductory course in business is an important investment for anyone planning to play in an orchestra. I would close the class by telling Eastman students what I repeat for the reader. While you may think that you have matriculated at a music school in order to learn how to play the piano or the oboe, you have in fact undertaken much broader responsibilities, including making Americans and their elected representatives more sensitive to the importance of music. Our review of the CSO budget of fifty million dollars revealed that, except in the event of exorbitant ticket prices of several hundred dollars each, we could not dream of breaking even in our effort to pay 105 players six-figure salaries on a fifty-two-week base. This presentation ended with a discussion of how to fill a 45 percent budget gap through endowment income and by raising funds from the private, the corporate, and the governmental sectors.

Besides needing to play and sing really well, you are going to need to be able to analyze complex situations and to think, read, write, and speak on behalf of music in ways that other people understand and are moved by. If you don't know why the Mahler Fifth excites you—apart from the fact that the principal trumpet part can be dangerous for the player—you cannot expect taxpaying nonmusicians to care enough about music to support it. And in the long run, the United States, pressed for expenditures on health care, education, defense, the environment, and interest payments on previous budget deficits, is going to continue to accord a very low priority to the arts. Every course that you take as a student in an institution where faculty are carefully appointed to help educate you, and where libraries, computer labs, and other bright young people are assembled to help stimulate your imagination, can help prepare you for this future advocacy role, on music's (and your own) behalf. Every educational opportunity needs to be taken seriously, for you will never again have so rich a learning environment, so easily available and with so much leisure time at your disposal. In my view, it is the inescapable responsibility of your generation to think and to act on these issues, if classical music is to survive.

As I write these words, in the summer of 2011, our federal budget includes $150 million for our National Endowment for the Arts, fifty cents a year for each man, woman, and child in America. Though much stronger support comes, to be sure, from tax-deductible contributions connected with voluntary gifts to our not-for-profit sector, of which the arts are but a part, it is taken for granted that such contributions will come from Americans who can afford such generosity, though certainly not as a central aspect of our national life. I believe that the United States is a truly great country in which to take great pride, but at least to this point in our history we have not been able to come to terms artistically with the values that the great majority of Americans think of as truly exceptional: except for winning and making large amounts of money.

CONTINUING ADVICE ON MAKING THE MOST OF YOUR MUSICAL EDUCATION

As Robert Schumann suggested 160 years ago, it is not by repeating a difficult passage ad nauseam that you will learn how to play that passage reliably and beautifully. It is rather by listening, very carefully, to the music you are producing, analytically inventing fingerings, phrasings, and exercises better to attain the artistic result you conceived in the first place. Frank Davidoff, in an article in the *Annals of Internal Medicine*,

"What Musicians Can Teach Doctors," describes well what seem to me the essentials of good practicing:

> The key here is the nature and quality of the practicing, not just the hours spent; its essential element is mindfulness, being really present while practicing, rather than mechanically repeating the motions. The single most important piece of advice on practicing is to "listen" (made easier these days by easy access to high-quality recording equipment), but to "slow it down" and to "break it into parts" are close runners-up. At its best, practicing includes learning how to practice; it involves both reinforcing what is already known and pushing the envelope into what has not yet been mastered.
>
> In his article "Deep into Sleep," summarizing some of the results of Harvard's program on sleep research, Craig Lambert, associate editor of the *Harvard Magazine*, writes, "Not only mental and emotional clarification, but the improvement of motor skills can occur while asleep. 'Suppose you are trying to learn a passage in a Chopin piano etude, and you just can't get it,' says Robert Strickgold (associate professor of psychiatry at Harvard). You walk away and the next day, the first try, you've got it perfectly. We see this with musicians and with gymnasts. There's something about learning motor-activity patterns, complex movements; they seem to get better by themselves, overnight."[7]

I was once told by Michael Charness, a fine pianist who teaches and researches at Brigham Women's Hospital in Boston, that, if he practices the piano thoughtfully in the morning, briefly in the afternoon, and then very thoughtfully and slowly in the evening, his brain will teach his fingers how to solve important musical and technical problems while he is asleep. While Dr. Charness was not prescribing this regimen for all young musicians, I believe it is well worth experimenting with for many of us. This idea is very much in line with recent results of sleep research.

HOW IMPORTANT IS COMPENSATION?

While it is easy to be idealistic so long as someone else pays your bills, you might consider marrying well (as some important conductors have done), developing skills and interests as a teacher (as most of us do), or staying single until you have discovered a bridge between your skills as a musician and the development of other skill sets that America appears to covet. The alternative, as in the case of Robert Schumann, for example, may entail the necessity of sending a pregnant wife out on the concert circuit. Someone needs to raise the children, and the more of them an artist has, the greater the burden for the support of his family. As I read the correspondence of Brahms and Clara Schumann, the two of them came very close in the summer of 1856, after Robert's death, to getting married. I believe that Brahms, who admired and cared for Clara deeply, walked away from marriage to her as the result of an acknowledgment that he wanted to live the only life he had the way he wanted to, writing and perfecting the music he knew was within him. To promise to live forever with the same spouse, "till death do us part," is an important commitment, not sensibly made before one understands one's own priorities. A commitment to a relationship with another human being demands time, a very difficult promise to fulfill with so scant a time commitment as too many young musicians are able to make, especially given the additional educational demands on young musicians outlined in this book.

As the old adage goes, "Too soon old, too late smart." Schubert, for example, who died at the age of thirty-one of syphilis, a disease he appears to have contracted in his midtwenties, regretted deeply that he had not been able to come to terms better with the idea of deferred gratification. So do the rest of us, bereft of Schubert's musical contribution had he lived to forty-five, say.[8] That Robert Schumann, Biedrich Smetana, and Hugo Wolf all suffered similar fates should remind us all to take care of ourselves. My continuing advice to young musicians is to take the long-term view of deferred gratification. Avoid tobacco, recreational drugs, promiscuous and unprotected sex, and too much alcohol. Get plenty of sleep, eat a balanced diet, and exercise not only the fingers but the arms and legs!

REFLECT ON YOUR OWN SPECIAL STRENGTHS

Most college music schools and departments will typecast you in the beginning of your studies as a composer, a performer, a historian, a theorist, or a public school music teacher, because it is less expensive for them to do so. I would urge, however, even from the very beginning of your college studies, that you imagine yourself in the fashion of a musical hero of *yours* from days gone by. J. S. Bach would not have known how to answer a census form which insisted that he declare himself as a composer, an organist, a string player, or a teacher, for from his point of view he not only did all of those things but thought that all of them informed one another in his work. The same could be said of Brahms as pianist, composer, conductor, administrator, historian, and editor. While he decided as he grew older that he didn't want to spend much time practicing the piano or to be a husband or teacher, to the end of his life he led a richly complex musical existence. Was Rachmaninoff a composer, a pianist, or a conductor? (He was offered and turned down the music directorships of the Boston Symphony Orchestra and of the Cincinnati Orchestra just after World War I.) Was Leonard Bernstein a conductor, a pianist, a teacher (he lectured on CBS-TV during the 1950s and at Harvard as Charles Eliot Norton Lecturer during the early 1970s), or a composer? Did he write classical music or Broadway shows?

Though some of my graduate student classmates have gone on to the kinds of positions for which we were prepared—as specialists, teaching musicology in major research universities to graduate students—my own first position was at MIT, where in addition to teaching undergraduate music history and theory, I performed regularly in Boston as a freelance oboist and pianist, and substituted regularly for David Epstein as conductor of the MIT Symphony. While I was involved in all of these activities on reasonably high professional levels, it took until my midthirties till I decided that my real métier lay in the leadership of music schools, a mission I did not give up even when offered a couple of provost positions at the University of California and the presidency of a major university. While it is impossible for you to determine at the age of eighteen who you will really turn out to be, it is not too early to begin dreaming about the possibilities, especially in view of the educational doors that you may knock on while in college or afterward, with a view to creating for yourself new and exciting synergistic possibilities still undreamed of in 2014. My late father used to tell me, "If you are afraid to knock on the door, you can be sure that it will not open."

EXPLORE APPARENTLY TANGENTIAL POSSIBILITIES

While change in college curricula is glacial, you always have the possibility of a year off, a junior year abroad, complete with the possibility of exposure to a new culture and learning a new language, and the possibility of summer music schools and working at professional internships. In my own case, the privilege of assisting Artur Balsam at Blue Hill during the summer of 1955, of studying with Rudolf Serkin at Marlboro during the summer of 1956, and of a musicological Fulbright to Vienna for two years in the early 1960s all opened new connections, new synergisms, and new ways of looking at a world that degree candidacy, even in such splendid institutions as Harvard and Princeton, would not alone have facilitated. The opportunity to view my own country from Vienna for three years inspired all sorts of new ideas. Most American colleges now offer lots of guidance on foreign fellowships and internships to students who take the initiative of seeking out such opportunities. During the past these have been concentrated in our own country and in Europe. But in the future I expect they will expand in Latin America, in Asia, in the Mideast, and in Africa. The idea of a brilliant young American musician who can speak fluent Chinese and English, for example, will open all sorts of possibilities in the years ahead. If you are a valued member of your teacher's studio, that person may not like the idea of your going abroad before you graduate, advice that you should weigh carefully, bearing in mind your own long-term best interests.

EXPLORE ARTISTIC RESIDENCIES IN YOUR HOMETOWN

There is a lot to be said, especially in a public university, for undertaking a weeklong residency in your hometown, especially in one whose population is but several thousand, where you can become an instant celebrity. During my days as a UT dean I adopted a practice that Charles Webb, Indiana's distinguished music dean during my days at Eastman, once told me about. As a result, I sent a UT senior in choral conducting for a weeklong residency in his hometown, Rockport, Texas, a community of 7,500 just north of Corpus Christi. With a grant of $2,500 from the University Cooperative Society, Cory Reeves arranged that he conduct two thirds of a Christmas-Hanukah concert by the Corpus Christi Symphony, in memory of Cory's music teacher in Rockport High, who had recently passed away and in whose memory the town had just named a beautiful 1,200-seat auditorium. Working with the chorus of the Rockport High School, Cory conducted repertory of his own choice relevant to the season, setting a ticket price of sixty dollars a seat (which I was obliged to pay even as a principal sponsor!), the proceeds going to music scholarships for future Rockport students at the University of Texas. In the midst of the concert, he asked the town's three principal public school music teachers to rise for the audience's acclamation, each after an enthusiastic and articulate endorsement from Cory onstage. At the end of the concert, the mayor announced that, because the event had been so successful as a community enterprise, the town would sponsor it annually in the future, inviting Cory back as the first guest conductor. And at the reception in Cory's honor that followed, the mayor unveiled a wonderful oil portrait of Cory himself, painted during his week of residency by a local artist in her eighties, to hang in the foyer of the new auditorium. The state legislators from the area, whom the president of the university had invited at my urging, all attended and seemed well gratified by the result. When a private school headmaster in Princeton, New Jersey, called me the following April to discuss a position on his faculty for a choral conductor, he began by asking me whether I knew Cory Reeves. The reader won't be surprised to learn that it was Cory who got the job. Obviously, he had profited from his work under James Morrow in choral conducting at UT, but he had learned a great deal more besides. During my days as a UT dean, we annually received six thousand dollars from George Mitchell, the very entrepreneurial president of the UT Cooperative Society, for three annual residencies, awarded to young Texans from the state's smaller communities, which exist in great abundance.

DEVELOP YOUR OWN TEAM OF SUPPORTERS

During your days in college, it is worthwhile to develop a team of faculty and administrative supporters, men and women who, when the time comes, will be willing to write persuasive and articulate letters and to make phone calls on your behalf. This should begin with your primary teacher and with other faculty in whose courses you have excelled. While the conductor of an orchestra to which you might apply will be interested mainly in how well you play, the director of a music school will be interested not only in your abilities as a performer but also in the breadth of your knowledge and enthusiasm about music, its history, and its future, and about your breadth as a human being. The people who can write good letters about you are those who know your work well. You should take the initiative of introducing yourself to them during their office hours, so that they can get to know you.

When I began as Eastman director, I was taught by my principal administrative mentor, Robert Sproull, then president of the University of Rochester, how important it is to be able to read what he called "an art letter," a document that says something even though, often to avoid unpleasantness or litigation, it seems not to. Bob Sproull's chief example was of a man who, at age forty-five, had inherited an estate that had belonged to his parents for many years. Unfortunately, the staff included a terrible cook who had served there so long that her new employer feared she would not be able to get a job, especially in the same community, where she wanted to continue to live. His letter, famous for its brevity, comprised but three sentences, the last of which, said Sproull, was the most artistic: "I write in support of Mary Smith for the position of cook in your household. She has been a cook in this family for the past thirty-five years. A good meal from this cook is a rare treat." Shortly afterward, I received a letter of support for an open piano position at Eastman from my beloved teacher, the late Rudolf Serkin, then director of the Curtis Institute. Wrote Mr. Serkin, "I write in support of the candidacy for the open piano position at Eastman of John Jones. He has been a student of mine at the Curtis Institute for the past ten years. This splendid young man fully deserves whatever consideration you may decide to give him."

Because I knew that Mr. Serkin was not an academic, not a man given to writing comparative letters about his students, I doubted whether he knew how to read or write an art letter. But there were other candidates, and Jones was not among the finalists. While faculty members and deans learn how to write thoughtful letters, some of the world's greatest artists believe that anything that bears their signature will get the job done. Choose those who will write letters in your behalf with a view not only to who knows you well but with respect to people eager and able to write articulate and meaningful letters in your behalf. It should go without saying that those on your list of referees should know what you have been up to recently and should appreciate the value that you bring to the institution where the letter will be directed. Letters of recommendation written several years earlier will suggest to the reader that your best work was accomplished some time ago. Especially useful will be letters that compare you favorably with others. Had Mr. Serkin written, "John Jones is one of the three best pianists I have ever taught at Curtis, a person vitally interested in teaching and in music's future," Jones would certainly have been interviewed.

BEGIN EARLY TO THINK ABOUT YOUR FUTURE AUDIENCES

Whose responsibility is the development of that audience? Your understanding that many Americans see classical music as European, elitist, boring, nonparticipatory, long, and incomprehensible is important. According to Greg Sandow, who has spent a lot of time researching the question, the existing audience is in fact getting older. Further, there is so much competition for leisure time in America these days that it will be your responsibility to develop your own audiences, a subject that is almost never addressed among collegiate music schools but ought to be.

What, if anything, is to be done about this? To begin with, a refocus in our studies on what counts as good music and what does not. Schubert and Schumann songs are wonderful, as we all know, but so are those of Gershwin and Kern, though also not in the mainstream for the other fifty thousand students on the UT campus. Some American composers such as William Bolcom, Michael Daugherty, Donald Grantham, and Christopher Rouse, for example, are drawn to assimilate more populist repertories into their own "serious" music. But music faculties born half a century ago are too often as ignorant as I am about the rest of our musical universe. It is easy for me to remember how I was excoriated in the *New York Times* of the early 1980s by Donal Henahan, the result of my willingness to allow Christopher Rouse, then an Eastman faculty member in composition, to teach a course he had asked to teach about the history of rock on the River Campus!

Barbara Butler and Charles Geyer, in the 1980s and 1990s Eastman's distinguished trumpet faculty (now teaching at Rice), developed with my support what they called a new trumpet curriculum. At the beginning of each semester, they routinely announced to their twenty-five trumpet majors that, while the focus of their curriculum was playing the trumpet well (their graduates now account for three quarters of the trumpet section of the Chicago Symphony Orchestra), no one would get an A unless he or she, once a semester, invited a student from the River Campus who had never attended a concert of classical music to do so. The invitation included a postconcert date to discuss, over coffee and a sandwich, what the guest had liked most and least about the concert. The young trumpeters had to follow up with a two-page paper on audience development to their trumpet teachers. Butler and Geyer told their students, "If you join the Boston Symphony or the New York Philharmonic, what you will learn from our exercise, in addition to improving your writing, may not be central to your work as musicians. But if you have the good fortune of joining the orchestra of Buffalo, Toledo, Kansas City, or Denver, for example, whether the orchestra still exists when you are ready to put your children through college will be directly relevant to your education. This is a central aspect of the trumpet curriculum at Eastman, and if you do not participate in it, you will not get an A." The students participated.

WHO IS THE AUDIENCE? WHAT DOES IT PERCEIVE? AND WHAT DOES IT WANT?

Though Kevin McCarthy and his colleagues at the Rand Corporation have in the last decade done excellent work on the relationship of the performing arts to a potential new audience, few college curricula that I know of use this valuable material, and even fewer American orchestras take advantage of it. In my view, especially at a time of such rapid change, college music majors ought to own, read, and think about the Rand Corporation's books in question: *The Performing Arts in a New Era* (2001), *A New Framework for Building Participation in the Arts* (2001), *Gifts of the Muse: Reframing the Debate about the Benefits of the Arts* (2004), *Arts and Culture in the Metropolis: Strategies for Sustainability* (2007), and *Revitalizing Arts Education through Community-Wide Coordination* (2008). Bill Ivey's *Arts, Inc.* and *Engaging Art*, ed. by Steven Tepper and Bill Ivey, are equally important. I believe that many of those currently enrolled in undergraduate music programs would do well to use these books and the literature they are based on to stimulate new sociology and business courses in the institutions where they are enrolled. There is equally little information on who the audience is, what their own musical education has been like, what they perceive, and what they are looking for. New technologies and the Internet make possible all sorts of pedagogic pathways to answering these questions that were not available a decade ago.

As the result of my experience in Austin, where the community recently built a new seventy-seven-million-dollar auditorium for a seriously underendowed orchestra whose base pay for the musicians amounts to but fifteen thousand dollars a year, I have come to the conclusion that even well-educated Americans have much better eyes than ears. Even Henry Lee Higginson understood, when he founded the Boston Symphony in 1881, that an important aspect of the motivation of many members of the Symphony Hall audience was to be seen in public by other Boston leaders. In this vein, why don't orchestras and music schools give more attention to the development of events for school children that are followed up with studies of the effectiveness of such events, over and above the undoubted fiscal contribution they make through state, county, and city support they add to the orchestra's revenue budget? Why don't we work on events for parents and their children in the five- to ten-year-old age group, probably best held on Saturday afternoons, at a time in a child's life when we hope he can keep still for twenty minutes and when it still feels like a privilege to be out with Mom and Dad? How about weekday afternoon concerts for senior citizens, for whom nighttime driving and parking may seem risky experiences, especially in an inner city? How about musical events of the kind the Japanese are developing for young adults in their twenties and thirties who are seeking the kind of significant other not to be found at bars? Such events, instead of lasting two hours with a twenty-minute intermission, might comprise three hours, in which the outer thirds are an opportunities to drink, eat, and meet new friends in the lobby, while only the inner third comprises musical performance.

During the past several years at UT, I have given several courses that are partly music-historical and partly an investigation of the kinds of topics that might draw an audience closer to the music, using a technique that Eric Booth calls "points of entry." Together, the students and I put together a dozen musical events, four in on-campus dormitories (each one equipped with a very good grand piano in an attractive formal lounge), four in local retirement homes (always excellent venues for long-term fund-raising), and four in public and private schools. Next semester we plan to expand our offerings into two local reformatories for juvenile delinquents. Each event takes an hour, beginning with my two-minute introduction of the student presenter, a seven- or eight-minute oral introduction by the student to the repertory he is about to perform, the performance itself, and a question-and-answer period in which the audience takes an active part. In the dormitories, the events are billed as "What Makes Music So Sexy?" In the retirement homes, the billing changes to "What Makes Music so Inspiring?" But the idea is the same in both cases. Though our students are busy, I encourage them all to attend one another's presentations, all of which are rehearsed beforehand in class and reviewed in class afterward. You, as a music student on another campus, are urged to undertake similar projects.

INVENT THEMATIC PROGRAMMING

Does every musical event have to be a concert, with formal entrances, bows, and applause, followed by an endless repetition of stereotypical behavior? I remember with admiration an event that Rebecca Penneys staged twenty years ago at Chautauqua that began with Rebecca's performance of John Cage's famous work *4 Minutes and 33 Seconds*, in which a solo pianist sits at the instrument for more than four minutes without using either hand. There followed a piano work for one hand (such pieces are usually designed for beginners), two hands (a huge repertory, as every pianist knows), three hands (very limited, mostly pedagogical for the beginning pianist accompanied by her teacher), four hands (a lot better than for three but not as good as for two!), five hands (the only work I know is by Maurice Ravel), six, seven, and eight hands (here one needs the help of friendly composers!). Even if the players are thin, however, it is very hard to get more than four performers seated comfortably at a single keyboard. Even so, Rebecca's recital ended with a work for nine hands, for which four of us sat at the Steinway while David Effron, then head of orchestral activities at Chautauqua, stalked behind the four players, adding occasional notes at both ends of the keyboard, occasionally reaching inside the instrument for a bit of plucking and strumming!

On another occasion, in Kilbourn Hall, Eastman's beautiful world-class chamber auditorium, Nelita True organized an evening that was advertised as a "Hungarian Dance Round-Robin." Working with Brahms's wonderful Hungarian Dances for piano for four hands, Nelita assembled the whole of the Eastman piano faculty, a group of more than a dozen, counting both collegiate and community education teachers. Of this group, A, B, and C began at the piano, with A performing the primo part, B the secondo, and C serving as page turner. With the completion of the first Hungarian dance, A moved to a row of people deployed behind the backs of the performers, while B became the primo pianist, and the page turner for the first dance moved into the secondo slot, with a new page turner coming from the back row, all of whose members moved one seat to the right with each successive piece. In Rochester, the pianists in the bleachers kibitzed in dumb show the performances of those at the piano, much to the amusement of the audience. When Anton Nel put on a similar round-robin of UT piano faculty, graduate students, and townspeople at the local Headliners Club, one of the city's leading social clubs on the twenty-first floor of a local bank, Sarah Butler, who with her husband, Ernest, had just endowed the Butler School of Music at UT, wrote that she had never experienced a more moving evening of music.

During my first Texas year as a faculty member, 2007–2008, I put together an evening of the three Grieg sonatas for violin and piano, focusing on the fact that the occasion took place on the centenary of Grieg's death, but playing with the idea that, despite the fact that the Grieg family had emigrated in the eighteenth century from Scotland to Norway, changing their name from Greig to Grieg, Edvard Grieg had nonetheless gone on to become a Norwegian icon. The event was advertised as an immigration concert in which the program notes emphasized the idiosyncratic biographical backgrounds of each of the six performers, all of whose ancestors had come to the United States from all over the world, intermarrying other American immigrants, a quintessential American process. Many of the biographical sketches were really interesting: one involved a Polish Jew, harassed by the Cossacks, who had moved to Oklahoma and married there. My own involved my paternal grandfather, who had emigrated from England with his parents and siblings for Australia when the family tavern went belly up in 1875, a voyage during which their sailing ship got becalmed for a month, with the ship running out of food and water, necessitating the burial of three of the children at sea. I invited an important Austin attorney from Scotland named Greig to join us with his family as guests of honor at the Grieg concert and to take a bow from the audience at the close of intermission. And with the focus on immigration, a timely topic during the first decade of the new millennium in Texas, the *Austin American Statesman* produced a major article in advance of our "immigration concert," leading to a packed auditorium.

It ought to be your objective not simply to perform music for hundreds or thousands of people but to guide each of them, through stories they can understand, to a deepening of their experience with the work at hand. A goal for the conductor of any modern American orchestra ought to be the ability to give a good two-minute talk that draws the audience's interest to the music that follows. Anything much more than two minutes is probably too long, for the audience grows weary in anticipation of the music. But saying something meaningful in two minutes in a fashion that is both instructive and charming is not easy. Peter Bay, the fine music director of the Austin Symphony, gives excellent two-minute talks and is a fine role model for Texas music students. All students enrolled in current Texas courses of mine practice giving two-minute talks for one another. As you can imagine, I believe that this is a skill you should practice, even while giving recitals as an undergraduate.

Herewith two of the most effective two-minute talks I have heard to this point: The first took place in Woodstock, Vermont, where Carol and I attended a concert with good friends in the Unitarian Church given by the Ying Quartet. The program that evening comprised the Mozart G Major Quartet from the six dedicated to Joseph Haydn, the Bartok Fourth Quartet, and the Debussy Quartet. Said one of our guests before the concert began, "The Fourth Bartok Quartet in Vermont? What are you fellows smoking?" While nothing was said in advance of the Mozart, beautifully performed, just before the Bartok, David Ying, cellist of the quartet, said, "As history developed, neither Mozart nor Debussy ever visited America. Bartok, because of the Nazis, lived here from 1940 until his death in 1945, the most unhappy period of his life. He found it hard to get work, except for an occasional piano student. He thought New York City a dirty and crowded place, and he came down with leukemia, which eventually took his life. He missed his home, his friends, his family, and his native Hungary. There was but a single ray of sunshine in Bartok's

American life. He had a piano student in New York City whose family owned a farm in Vermont and who invited Bartok to spend the summers of 1943 and 1944 with them here. Friends, I am happy to tell you that Bela Bartok loved Vermont." As our friends subsequently agreed, the Fourth Quartet of Bela Bartok was the hit of the concert, for David Ying had found a way of relating Bartok's values to those of his audience.

A second such talk was given several years ago in Austin when John Largesse, violist of the just appointed Miro Quartet, introduced Beethoven's Opus 130 to a packed audience in Bates Recital Hall. Said John, "When Beethoven first composed Opus 130, he concluded it with a long and very difficult piece called the Grosse Fuge. Beethoven's publisher immediately suggested that because the Great Fugue was so long and so hard, both for the players and for the audience, Beethoven might write a shorter, simpler finale. And Beethoven, not given to suffering fools gladly, did so. It is in fact with the shorter, simpler finale that the work is normally performed these days. However that may be, *this* is Texas, and in making our formal Texas debut, we think it wholly inappropriate to begin with the shorter, simpler finale. Thus, we will end tonight's concert with the Great Fugue. We think you are up to it. You can pray for us, and we will pray for you, to be there with us till the end!" The performance was a smashing success, and the audience gave the quartet a standing ovation, followed by an encore, their own arrangement of "The Eyes of Texas." Seated next to me for the evening was Larry Faulkner, then president of the University of Texas at Austin. Commenting afterward on Largesse's two-minute talk, Faulkner told me, "That was about the most inspiring little speech I think I ever heard. It perfectly set the stage for what was to follow."

You should be working, too—undergraduates and graduate students, performers and composers—at learning to write your own program notes. If need be, the necessary editing can be done, as at the New England Conservatory, by graduate students in musicology. While such notes are especially important with unfamiliar repertory, you should understand that, to most Americans, the works of Beethoven are unfamiliar! Such notes should, in every case, provide historical context for the audience, focusing especially on aspects of the music that are most easily perceptible by an audience that has never previously thought of such matters.

DO YOU NEED TO BE TRAINED IN EVERYTHING YOU UNDERTAKE, OR CAN YOU LEARN HOW TO DO SOMETHING BY DOING IT?

As one who never was really trained to be a conductor but conducted the Princeton and MIT symphonies for several seasons, as one who never was trained to direct a music school but who has been responsible for the leadership of three of them, and as one who still knows relatively little about visual art, theater, and dance but served successfully for more than six years as the dean of fine arts at UT, I would vote enthusiastically for taking well-calculated risks. There are all sorts of things that you might usefully undertake, not as the result of individual ad hoc courses of study but as the result of the ability to synthesize learning experiences from childhood, formal study, and the workplace. A habit of reading in domains other than your area of PhD study does wonders. As you already know, I regularly recommend to my current students books on music, history, politics, and sociology from which they can draw in interview situations, making them more interesting potential colleagues than other candidates for the academic positions they seek.

PREPARE TO REINVENT YOURSELF: LEARN VERSATILITY

The most dedicated and accomplished musicians, especially as one grows older, are those who focus on music because music and its dissemination continue to mean something very special to them. We are now living a generation longer than was normally possible even half a century ago. The human gains this facilitates could be enormous were we all to use our added years for productive purposes, within music and beyond. That is why the Scandinavian countries have invested so heavily in recent years in making it possible for men and women in middle age to take time out for additional education and training, in the professional areas where people wish to upgrade their current skills, and in areas where people seek new beginnings. Each of us gets to live only once. Each of us should undertake the responsibility of making a long life in music as productive and exciting as possible, beginning while in college to acquire skills and attitudes that will make that goal possible, for ourselves and for those with whom we come into contact. The phenomenon represented by Rossini and Sibelius, where a composer says what he has to say, then retires to lassitude and too much alcohol, is on one end of the human spectrum. The phenomenon represented by Verdi and Stravinsky, where the composer goes on creating new worlds, through the very end of his life, lies at the opposite end. While we don't all get the chance to emulate Verdi and Stravinsky, thinking about how best to have a continuing impact by staying active is an art I enthusiastically recommend!

Remember that the future will not simply repeat the past, especially in the arts. Remain open to new opportunities. While music schools almost always produce curricula that are normative—the result of their discovering how to prepare some of their students for careers in chamber music and orchestral playing during the twentieth century—you should not be afraid to ask about increasing opportunities to develop careers that are better adapted to your interests and talents. Anthony Tommasini, in the *New York Times* of April 6, 2009, reports on a Carnegie Hall concert by the Saint Louis Symphony in which David Robertson, the orchestra's music director, surprised everyone by filling in at the last minute for the evening's guest composer and vocal soloist.

> That David Robertson conducted the Saint Louis Symphony Orchestra at Carnegie Hall on Saturday night in the most transparent and riveting account of Sibelius's elusive Fifth Symphony in memory would have been momentous enough. But for making news in the staid world of classical music, nothing topped Mr. Robertson's unplanned New York debut as a singer during the symphony's concert on Friday night at Zankel Hall, the first of two programs during this visit.
>
> As they applauded the boss after the Gruber piece, the musicians seemed impressed with Mr. Robertson's daring and versatility. How many conductors could gleefully sing the crazed words "Frankenstein is dancing with the test-tube lady" and then 24 hours later lead a serenely confident account of Wagner's most spiritual music?

That David Robertson and his Saint Louis Symphony, turning catastrophe into challenge and opportunity, drew so long and so appreciative a comment from Tommasini in the *Times* suggests that we have taught too many people that their optimized listening experiences should be completely anticipatable, devoid of participation by the audience.

The examples of two young Eastman graduates further support the idea that versatility is often a key to having a successful career in music. Allan Kozinn, writing in the *New York Times* of October 5, 2008, has similarly positive things to say about the career of Caleb Burhans, an Eastman violin graduate who plays in and composes for Alarm Will Sound and Signal (two New York–based new music groups), sings countertenor in New York's Trinity Church, conducts chamber choirs, and performs with itsnotyouitsme, his ambient rock duo:

> At 28, Mr. Burhans has pursued a career path so logical that it seems almost foolproof. Just sing, compose, and master several instruments (besides the violin he plays viola, guitar, bass, keyboards, and percussion) and the New York freelance world is your oyster. But this is a new development. Until recently, the conventional wisdom went, musicians with diverse talents should specialize: decide whether they are better suited to composing or performing, singing or playing an instrument, working in classical music or a variety of pop.
>
> There's no mistaking him. He's the one with the short, sometimes spiky hair, retro eyeglasses, black nail polish, and earring. As new as Mr. Burhans's career approach is, he is hardly an anomaly. Seven other musicians in Alarm Will Sound also compose. Several have rock bands as well. And the number of musicians with fingers in both classical and pop seems to be growing.

That Kozinn and his editors give so much enthusiastic coverage to Caleb Burhans has doubtless helped the development of his career, making as the article does the point that Burhans's career focus is much, much less narrow than those of many of his contemporaries, and that if the development of market niches is important, Burhans is following a road map quite unlike those recommended by most American music schools. Implicit in Burhans' success is that the mastery of one musical repertory is apt to provide a musician with all sorts of new insights into other repertories and opportunities that may come his way.

Daniel J. Wakin, in the *New York Times* of December 19, 2009, has similarly positive things to say about the multifaceted career of Kelly Hall-Tompkins, another Eastman graduate and a fine violinist who plays in the New Jersey Symphony. Wakin's article is entitled "For the Homeless, Music That Fills a Void."

> Just three blocks from Lincoln Center, they arrived at the concert on Thursday night by shelter bus, not taxi or limousine. They took their seats around scarred, round folding tables. The menu was chicken curry and rice, served on paper plates.
> These concertgoers were eight tired, homeless men who had been taken to the Holy Trinity Lutheran shelter for the night. They listened to the latest performance by Kelly Hall-Tompkins, a professional violinist who had been playing in shelters for five years under the banner of Music Kitchen. "I like sharing music with people, and they have zero access to it," Ms. Hall-Tompkins said of her homeless audiences. "It's very moving to me that I can find people in a place perhaps when they have a greater need for, and a heightened sensitivity to beauty."

Herewith a final boost for versatility, described by Hillel Kuttler in the sports section of the *New York Times* of November 23, 2013: There one reads of Justin Tucker, an exceptionally successful second-year placekicker for the NFL-champion Baltimore Ravens, who as a recent undergraduate at the University of Texas at Austin studied singing with Nikita Storojev at the Butler School of Music. Tucker, an aspiring baritone who has just recorded a serenade from *Don Giovanni* as part of an online soft drink commercial, has been invited by the Baltimore Symphony and the Peabody Conservatory to make his stage debut. In reflecting on a postfootball career for Tucker as a professional singer, Kuttler writes, "Examples abound of American athletes' musical avocations, slanting towards hiphop in recent times. Prominent exceptions include the former linebacker Dhani Jones, a known classical music lover and a guest conductor for the Philadelphia Pops, and Keith Miller, a former Colorado and Arena Football League halfback who played in the Fiesta and Cotton Bowls and now makes his living as a bass-baritone with the Metropolitan Opera."

The careers of David Robertson, Caleb Burhans, Kelly Hall-Tompkins, Justin Tucker, and Keith Miller, the multitude of whose talents are hinted at in the newspaper quotations just cited, stress versatility and a willingness to take risks after careful preparation, rather than the narrow focus of unending hours in practice rooms. Eastman's Arts Leadership Program and Juilliard's Academy, in collaboration with Carnegie Hall, represent the cutting edge of redirecting musicians' goals from often meaningless competition to broader goals informed by wider vision and versatility.

Openness to variety and change can be of benefit to more than the very young. The career of the late Metropolitan Opera basso Richard Gill demonstrates that new opportunities sometimes come along in midcareer. Mr. Gill outlined the remarkable story of his own professional career over breakfast together a decade ago at the Regency Hyatt of West Palm Beach.

Having deeply enjoyed his participation at Cambridge in the Harvard-Radcliffe Choral Society, he well understood the relationship of supply and demand for singers in the United States and thus went on at Harvard to take a doctoral degree in economics, eventually attaining the position of senior lecturer (and tenure) at Harvard in that field. In his late thirties, he was invited by the president of Harvard to take over the house mastership of Leverett, an undergraduate living center of five hundred students that has a long tradition of staging musicals. The students, hearing Gill sing "Happy Birthday" on ceremonial occasions, invited him to participate in a show. And when he did well, they asked whether he wanted to study voice, with a view toward singing Sarastro in the following season's production of Mozart's *Magic Flute*. Sarah Caldwell, Boston's great operatic director, came to hear him sing Sarastro and, impressed, cast him as the male lead for Roger Sessions's very difficult opera *Montezuma*. Responsible people from New York City came to hear him perform the Sessions and offered him solo appearances with the New York City Opera and the Met. Accordingly, in 1971 he left Harvard and moved to the Met for fifteen years, singing leading bass roles all over the world. During this second career, he performed in many of the world's great opera houses: Chicago, Houston, Dallas, Boston, Washington, Pittsburgh, Caracas, Toronto, Edinburgh, and Amsterdam, as well as appearances in important solo roles with the New York Philharmonic, the Boston Symphony, Pittsburgh, and St. Louis, among many others. There were, he said, only about fifteen really good roles for his vocal type that he enjoyed singing. "Once one has performed them several dozen times each, all over the world, why should one want to continue forever, living out of a suitcase?" he said. Thus, he was delighted to accept Harvard's invitation to return to Cambridge, where he went to work with some really interesting colleagues on a book about demographic questions in America's future. "Traveling is not all it's cracked up to be, especially as one gets older!"

A decade after this interview, Gill was the primary economic analyst on the Annenberg-CPB television series *Economics USA*. He wrote eleven textbooks, several short stories, and a novel, *The Taking of Farnham Hall: Searching for Reality in the 1960s.*

An equally moving biography is that of Dr. Jeffrey Tate, who, "inspired by the devotion his surgeons demonstrated in caring for his congenital spina bifida, went on to medical school and became a practicing eye surgeon for a time at St. Thomas's Hospital in London. But his main love was opera, and he eventually left medicine altogether to become one of the world's most respected conductors."[9]

LEARN TO THINK AND ACT LIKE AN ENTREPRENEUR

To summarize the advice offered in this chapter, you must learn to imagine apparently disparate connections between people and organizations before those directly involved have ever thought of the need for such connections. The possibilities of flying across America in five hours, of a cure for polio, or of a virtual link to the world's knowledge through personal computers were all undreamed of during the days of Wagner and Brahms, even in the days of Schönberg and Stravinsky. So, too, are all sorts of possibilities for music's future and for your own future in music, possibilities that await but the application of your own imagination. This is not simply a matter of inventing new technologies and new businesses, although some readers of this book will actually be involved in such activities. It is rather the development of a personal capacity for thinking outside the box about how to use your own talents and educational opportunities to imagine new worlds for music, and with the help of others, to accomplish those goals. It comes from a point of view which suggests that the phone will not ring unless you figure out a way of making it do so. If there is a problem, it is that too many of us have been trapped into obsessing about the ways it has always been done, instead of considering, while taking a shower or going for a walk, how music might become a more powerful force for humanity. There is nothing inartistic or inappropriate about thinking this way. I believe in fact that your future depends upon your developing the ability to proceed in this fashion.

Thus my continuing advice for all young musicians: Life is an adventure, and you only get to develop your interest in music once. While music schools normally stress the idea that it pays to specialize, there is a lot to be said, while in school, for pursuing as broad an education as is available to you. While in college, you will probably have the best chance to explore what humanity has learned and to recognize new opportunities for synthesis and discovery. You will need to know which balance of work and leisure works best for you, to develop outstanding skills in time management, and to take maximal advantage of the educational offerings available on your home campus, while, of course, practicing several hours a day! Then keep your eyes and your imagination open for the myriad opportunities that are bound to develop. I am told that the science fiction author Robert Heinlein once wrote, "Specialization is the work of insects."

NOTES

1. I am always inspired by the thought that Debussy asked that his tombstone read simply, "Claude Debussy, musicien français."

2. Yet more sophisticated is the ability, having heard a piece, to play it perfectly without any intervening musical notation, the skill known as "playing by ear."

3. Malcolm Gladwell, *Outliers: The Story of Success* (New York: Little, Brown, 2008). Equally recommended are Mr. Gladwell's other four books, *Blink: The Power of Thinking without Thinking* (New York: Back Bay Books, 2005), *The Tipping Point: How Little Things Can Make a Big Difference* (New York: Little, Brown, 2006), *What the Dog Saw: And Other Stories* (New York: Little, Brown, 2009), and *David and Goliath: Underdogs, Misfits, and the Art of Battling Giants* (New York: Little, Brown, 2013).

4. My Harvard and Princeton student colleague, the brilliant pianist-composer Frederic Rzewski, must have suffered greatly from this, as the result of his inability to observe such rules of decorum and protocol. Says he in his own memoir, "At Princeton I worked with both Sessions and Babbitt, and I enjoyed working with Sessions. Although, again, the lessons with Sessions consisted mostly of anecdotes, which were quite interesting, there wasn't a great deal of time to go into the actual technique of

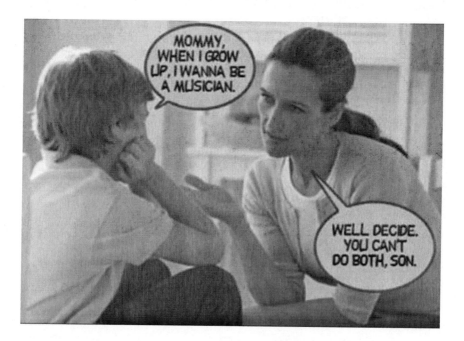

Figure 5.1. With the possible exceptions of violin, cello, and piano, I strongly recommend double majors: music and pre-med, music and pre-law, or music and business, for example.

composition. And with Babbitt I think this was even more the case. My lessons with Babbitt consisted often of discussions of baseball or Broadway. . . . I worked with Dallapiccola the year afterwards in 1960—I went to Italy with a Fulbright, and worked with him during the first part of the year. But with Dallapiccola I made a serious mistake. When I first showed up there he asked me what I wanted to do. And I made, I think, a fatal mistake, which was to say to him that what I wanted to do was orchestration. This was the area where I felt I was weakest, and I wanted to concentrate on orchestration rather than on composition. I think I gave the impression that I was not interested in what he had to say about composition. At first, he agreed, he said fine, we'll work on orchestration, and we did do several lessons on orchestration, but then one time I missed a lesson because I had gone to visit some friends in London, and when I came back from London I found a letter saying that Maestro Dallapiccola felt that I was not the kind of student that he wanted, needed to work with, and would I please go somewhere else. And I realized that I had made a serious mistake. I must have given the impression of arrogance, because I probably was rather arrogant at that time. And now, it's one thing I've always regretted, because I certainly could have gotten a lot from that man if I had approached him correctly." Frederic Rzewski, *Nonsequiturs: Writings and Lectures on Improvisation, Composition, and Interpretation* (Cologne: MusikTexte, 2007), 170.

5. Lawrence W. Levine, *Highbrow, Lowbrow: The Emergence of Cultural Hierarchy in America* (Cambridge, MA: Harvard University Press, 1988). See also Michael Broyles, *Music of the Highest Class: Elitism and Populism in Antebellum Boston* (New Haven, CT: Yale University Press, 1992); John Seabrook, *Nobrow: The Culture of Marketing, the Marketing of Culture* (New York: Vintage, 2000); Paul J. DiMaggio, "Cultural Entrepreneurship in Nineteenth-Century Boston," in *Nonprofit Enterprise in the Arts: Studies in Mission and Constraint*, ed. Paul J. DiMaggio, 41–61 (Oxford: Oxford University Press, 1986); Joseph Horowitz, *Classical Music in America: A History of Its Rise and Fall* (New York: W. W. Norton, 2005); Stephen J. Tepper and Bill Ivey, eds., *Engaging Art: The Next Great Transformation of America's Cultural Life* (New York: Routledge, 2008); Bill Ivey, *Arts, Inc.: How Greed and Neglect Have Destroyed Our Cultural Rights* (Berkeley: University of California Press, 2008); John Spitzer, ed., *American Orchestras in the Nineteenth Century* (Chicago: University of Chicago Press, 2012). As the result of arguments outlined in these books, I have begun in my own teaching to ask graduate students to consider a new taxonomy for music, listing Schubert's "An die Musik," Schumann's "Widmung," the Gershwins' "Summertime," and the Beatles' "Imagine" in one column and the Kalkbrenner piano concertos, the Saint-Saens Oboe Sonata, and much (though not all) of contemporary rock in another column. My thesis in doing so, both in Eastman Prism concerts and at the University of Texas, is that the younger people whose futures we seek to influence in the concert hall are a lot more willing to try to develop an interest in the music we care about if we do not begin by implying that the music *they* respond to isn't worth our time. I have come in the meantime to believe that the music that is easier for nonaficionados to perceive on first hearing is tonal, periodic, relatively brief, and texted. No wonder that the finale of Beethoven's "Hammerklavier Sonata" has a smaller audience than that for "Silent Night."

6. Robert Schumann, *On Music and Musicians*, ed. and trans. by Konrad Wolff (New York: McGraw Hill, 1964), 30–51.

7. Frank Davidoff, "Music Lessons: What Musicians Can Teach Doctors (and Other Health Professionals)," *Annals of Internal Medicine* 154, no. 6 (2011): 426–29; Craig Lambert, "Deep into Sleep," *Harvard Magazine*, July–August 2005.

8. An inspiring example of how differently this might have turned out comes from John Harbison's beautiful piano quartet "18 November 1828," in which Harbison, having just read Alfred Mann's *Theory and Practice*, composed a work inspired by what Schubert might have accomplished had he only had time to take advantage of what he was learning in his contrapuntal study with Simon Sechter.

9. Lisa Wong, *Scales to Scalpels: Doctors Who Practice the Healing Arts of Music and Medicine* (New York: Pegasus Books, 2012), 212.

SIX

Advice for Collegiate Music Faculty

Should All Your Students Aim at Carnegie Hall? Should All Your Students Teach at Harvard?

American colleges and universities are set up to follow a system of specialization developed in Germany during the nineteenth century, as the result of which an institution decides what it wants to teach, organizing its curriculum under the jurisdiction of schools and departments. Princeton, among the nation's wealthiest universities, is a relatively small, residential institution in which even the most senior faculty take undergraduate teaching very seriously, where the liberal arts and engineering are the only order of the day, and the focus is on individual branches of the liberal arts (literature, philosophy, art and music history), the social sciences (economics, history, sociology), and the natural sciences (biology, chemistry, physics). But if in Princeton there exists but a single college, in a large institution like the University of Texas at Austin one finds seventeen colleges (Texas includes architecture, business, communications, continuing education, earth sciences, education, engineering, fine arts, geo-engineering, government, information, law, liberal arts, natural sciences, nursing, pharmacy, and social work, for example), a method of organization that is both disciplinary and administrative, with each college responsible for studies in a series of smaller schools and departments. The College of Fine Arts at the University of Texas now comprises the Department of Art and Art History, the Butler School of Music, the Department of Theater and Dance, and Texas Performing Arts, UT's arts presenting wing, with seven auditoria ranging in capacity from three hundred to three thousand, all over campus. These schools and departments comprise in turn a variety of yet narrower disciplines, most of them with their own doctoral curricula. Music at Texas, for example, includes composition, performance, musicology and ethnomusicology, analytic and historical theory, music and human learning (known in many other institutions as music education), conducting and ensembles, jazz, and music business. And each of these areas is further divided into a series of subspecialties, the aggregate of which will provide coverage as broad as possible for what humanity has learned so far about itself and the world we live in. Because all universities have finite funding for doctoral students, almost all dissertations—which must present new material and analysis—are, like my own, of surpassing narrowness, a sensible means toward persuading the student to finish at least by the time he is in his midthirties.

This organization of the nation's higher educational domain thus aims at developing the next generation of faculty, through a system of research and publication that rewards the dissemination of material of interest to a very small number of people. (Only once in my career have I taught a course on eighteenth-century Italian opera; my dissertation had focused on Italian opera in Vienna during the period 1716–1736.) Though the system attracts talented young people to our shores from all over the world, it should be noted that only a single American president of the forty-four thus far elected has had a doctoral degree: Princeton's Woodrow Wilson, who advanced from the presidency of Princeton to the governorship of New Jersey on his way to the White House. One is reminded in this context of Harvard's Bill Gates, Texas's Michael Dell, and Reed's Steve Jobs, each of whom failed to finish college because, struck by really good ideas, they felt themselves hemmed in from accomplishing through college what they thought they could do off campus. It is a continuing concern of many of us that post-secondary education in America in this fashion develops specialists who too often are unable to deal with the larger societal questions of special interest to our students, especially the undergraduates.

It has always seemed to me that teaching—whether of children, adolescents, young adults, or senior citizens—is one of the most important missions a human being can embark on, synthesizing and passing on to the next generation what humanity has learned, in the hope of improving lives and developing a better world. But as the result of my thirty-four years as an educational administrator, I have come to believe that we have developed a world of higher education that makes it a lot harder than it should be for too many of our students to find what they are looking for. Thus, as a professor in his seventies, I find myself dividing my time in the classroom between what the syllabus says I am teaching in music-historical domains and what I think are skills and attitudes that my students had better learn toward making the music they study more central to the next generation than it has been to my own. Put another way, there is a lot of information and opportunity available on each of our campuses, but the way we have trained faculty too often makes them focus more on the future of their disciplines than on the futures of their students. We present our students with experts in a broad array of disciplines: piano playing, music history and theory, microeconomics, and eighteenth-century German literature, for example. Then we ask our students to make their own syntheses, failing while doing so to persuade them, while they are still in school, to think about answering larger questions most of them ask. For example: "Now that I am a really good cellist, how do I develop a career as a soloist if, in spite of what I can accomplish artistically, no management firm can make enough fiscal profit from my fees to be interested in trying to manage a solo career for me?" Or, "If everyone says I am a great artist, what's the sense of creating yet further great artists if I can't make a living myself?" Or, "If there are thousands of students on my campus who are excited by music but not by the kinds of repertory I have spent twenty years mastering, what can I do to reach what I dream of as a fertile potential market, but which for the moment seems not to be?" Or, "If I love the orchestral repertory and think of myself as an enthusiastic contributing member of a fine orchestra, how might I use my participation in an orchestra to help solve the structural problems that currently beset those groups?" In a course I teach regularly on the history and future of the orchestra, we read and discuss the recent papers of the Andrew W. Mellon Foundation on this issue, outlining the results of a series of thoughtful meetings attended by players, staff, and board members, but by relatively few music directors of the dozen orchestras involved. And we take Robert J. Flanagan's new book, *The Perilous Life of Symphony Orchestras,*[1] very seriously.

What would happen were tenured faculty to look at this problem from the other end of the telescope? With this in mind, I try to engage each of my students, privately, in conversations like these: "You will be graduating before you know it. Tell me what you think you have learned here. What are your professional strengths as *you* see them? How about your weaknesses? Now that you have a better idea of how your abilities compare with those of your contemporaries, on this campus and elsewhere, what do you dream of accomplishing by the time you're forty, say?" At the same time, I tell each of them, "If you imagine yourself an Eastman trombone alumnus (and I try to draw three circles of equal radius), you are already in trouble, because Eastman has done such a superb job for ninety years in training really good trombone players. There are now, in fact, two or three hundred of them, still active, practicing, performing, and competing with you. What I'd suggest instead is that you imagine yourself as a person with a completely idiosyncratic skill set." (Here I draw as weird a two-dimensional Rorschach blot as I can.) The point of the exercise is to get the student to think of who she is, who she might become, and the education available on the campus to help her achieve that goal. Though this can be practiced during master's degree candidacy, it is most helpful while the students are still undergraduates.

In the normal American university, tenure is awarded on the basis of research and publication, teaching, and service (normally defined as administrative work for the university, the college, the department, the community, or the discipline).[2] In those universities with whose work I am most familiar, 45 percent of the credit is awarded for research and publication, 45 percent for teaching of high quality, and 10 percent for service. As a dean, I have told many faculty over the years that it is not wise to commit oneself to too much time spent on service. When the tenure system began in the late 1930s, most American universities had no idea how to evaluate creative work in the arts. (The late Roger Sessions once told me, on a bus trip together from New York City to Princeton in the mid-1960s, that he had left Princeton for UC Berkeley in 1946 because the then president of Princeton "could not figure out how to evaluate my music." Sessions returned to Princeton in 1954 when a new administration there had figured out how to determine the value of his admittedly difficult music.) At the Eastman School, no faculty tenure was awarded until Howard Hanson retired as director in 1964, after which it took the school another eight years to determine how to operate the University of Rochester's system for promotion and tenure. (When I arrived as director in 1972, I was confronted with a situation where, at a school where rules for promotion and tenure mandated that assistant professors not serve longer than eleven years in that rank, half a dozen assistant professors had been serving for periods of between eleven and seventeen years.) At the New England Conservatory I tried to lead during the late 1990s, no faculty member had been awarded tenure, though by the time I left for Texas, the faculty, the board, and I had developed a system that ultimately provided faculty with one-, three-, and five-year contracts, together with a system for faculty evaluation and promotion. The bias against tenure at NEC came partly from board reluctance to install what they regarded as the intrusion of an "academic" system of evaluation into an artistic institution, partly from a fiscal unwillingness to commit funds in an environment that was endowment poor.

Subjected throughout my career to a variety of tenure and promotion systems and in my career as Eastman director to several five-year faculty reviews, I have come to think of academic review processes partly as an effective means to ensure that the institution is hiring and promoting the right people, partly as a means toward encouraging faculty and administrative growth and accountability. The most appropriate means in my view for music schools and departments to think about this involves a means for evaluating faculty whose professional reputations make it possible for them to recruit outstanding students, and an articulated basis for evaluating the quality of a faculty member's teaching. While until the

1990s it was normally thought easier to evaluate an ongoing record of publications—where deans were assisted by other professionals all over the world—later we made considerable progress in convincing ourselves that we knew a good deal about a faculty member's teaching. (The exemplary report on this subject of an Eastman faculty committee of the late 1970s, chaired by Jon Engberg, comprises appendix 1 of this book.) Sensibly, it involves a paper trail of peer evaluation, student evaluation, and self-evaluation.[3] One of the most important contributions of my administration of the Eastman School lies precisely in the area of faculty job security. I was able to convince the central administration of the university that, at a music school, it makes a lot of sense to advance the amount of credit given to excellent teaching from 45 percent to 55, with emphasis on professional work and reputation diminished from 45 percent to 35. (Since coming to the University of Texas, I have come to the conclusion, especially as the result of collaboration with Professor Richard Cherwitz, head of the university's deservedly well-known Intellectual Entrepreneurship Program, that American universities traditionally undervalue the contribution of "service," misdefining it as work in support of one's academic discipline instead of, as Cherwitz and I think vital, as support for the solution of major societal questions and thus as service to the nation. (How can we change the balance between the supply of artists and the demand for their work? How can we best serve Texas's growing reputation as a state where entrepreneurship is a vital part of our future? How can we best organize institutional thinking about the future of water policy in the state? How can we best deal with the problem of urbanization, retaining more of the Midwest's citizens in our smaller towns and cities rather than tacitly accepting the ever-growing numbers who leave the countryside for the metropolis? How should we decide as a nation when to undertake warfare in support of causes that support both the long-term interests of the United States and those of the rest of the world?)

While I have argued with many board members over the years about what is often perceived as the pernicious effect of "dead wood" in the academy, it has always seemed to me that an effective dean can undo tenure mistakes through careful mentoring of all faculty and through the judicious use of raises, teaching loads, time on leave, and location within the physical plant. (No one wants to have his office moved to the basement, next to the boiler, or to have her teaching load doubled.) At the University of Texas, I was deeply impressed that President Larry Faulkner read (and understood) all of the university's annual 150 cases for promotion and tenure, a responsibility delegated in most American universities to the provost, the deans, and carefully selected committees of already tenured faculty.

While the promotion system just reviewed does a lot for seeing to it that you, as a tenured faculty member, achieve a high level of professional expertise, it also helps persuade faculty that they have been appointed to help preserve the future of the status quo, thus making it difficult for institutions of higher education to be as flexible as I think desirable in helping students accomplish goals important to our national future. Put another way, it would be helpful in the tenure process if leading schools of music could give careful consideration to music's future in America, and then work toward a faculty that balances generalists and specialists. This is why, once a faculty member made tenure at Eastman or Texas, I took him or her aside for a talk that went something like, "Now that you have convinced the nation's leading musicologists (composers, theorists, violists) that you are good enough to teach here as one of us, you have demonstrated that you are a specialist of real accomplishment. It is important to our school, however, especially since we have just guaranteed you what amounts to a lifetime position, that you use that privilege for music's and for the university's best interests by thinking outside the box about your own future and music's." I sincerely hope that all faculty reading this will reflect seriously on how the perspective just summarized relates to the future of your career and especially to those of your junior colleagues.

In 2008 the Surdna Foundation of New York City announced a program I had been advocating for the past quarter century. Directed by George Kuh of Indiana University, Surdna's new program, the Strategic National Arts Alumni Project, conducts decennial surveys of arts graduates, asking them what they are doing professionally as the result of the instruction they experienced in college, and asking them to comment, for the benefit of the faculty, on what in retrospect they have found most and least helpful about their educations. While business, law, and medical schools have a close relationship with those offering professional employment to their graduates, schools in the arts have typically resisted such efforts, preferring simply to list in their public relations materials the names of celebrity graduates recognizable to the public. What I am advocating here is that future music faculty take a broader view of your responsibilities and potential than has been possible for many in the past.

SEXUAL HARASSMENT

Though the balance between male and female enrollment in most American music schools is now about fifty-fifty, it has long been the case, especially in Asian countries, that female students are in the preponderance. Unfortunately, as the result of the many hours of private instruction that take place for both undergraduates and graduate students in music schools, it happens much too often, at least since Liszt's time and probably before, that a male instructor is attracted to one of his students, most often in a sub-rosa situation where the administration of the school hears lots of unsubstantiated rumor but nothing on which a dismissal case might be built. The problem existed in all three of the institutions I led, at a time when the rapidly changing role of women in the world has led to increased sensitivity to sexual harassment and to wholly changed attitudes on inappropriate faculty conduct. At Eastman this led in the mid-1980s to the appointment of a faculty committee very ably chaired by David Roberts, which recommended that, were it proven that a faculty member had developed "an inappropriately personal relationship with a student," that faculty member might be asked to resign. Because a faculty member whom I had appointed and who had done splendid work for the school and for music was rumored to have been involved with his female students on several occasions, I warned him that the Roberts Committee report, adopted unanimously by the vote of the faculty, had to be taken seriously. And I went to the trouble of seeing to it that my boss, the university provost, took the faculty member out for lunch to issue a similar warning. But one Saturday afternoon the university intercessor and a young Japanese DMA candidate came to my home with a long list of allegations about what the faculty member had done. I took careful notes to be certain that I was not exaggerating the allegations. Then on Monday morning I met with the faculty member, who admitted that the allegations were true, adding that he had asked the young woman to marry him. It saddened me more than I can say to have to tell him that that was not why the young woman had come to Eastman; she wanted to study, not to marry, and that in any case she already had a fiancé her own age who was a law student at another university. She threatened to sue—the university, the school, the faculty member, and myself—if I failed to see to it that the faculty member left. Thus I saw no alternative but to ask him to choose between resignation and my bringing him up on charges to the faculty committee on tenure and privileges. As one would imagine, he resigned, thus concluding, sadly, a very distinguished academic career long before it should have ended.

At the University of Texas at Austin, something similar happened during my first year as dean. The university, like a great many other public universities, takes the position that human beings will fall in love without warning and that it is not the business of an academic institution to determine the course of true love, an interference with human freedom, though very problematic in the issuing of grades and of salary increases. But there was so much unfair damage done to more than one faculty career, the result of actions by the federal Department of Justice and of a very unfair article in the *Chronicle of Higher Education*, that I appointed another faculty committee, which came to the same conclusion as the Roberts Committee at the Eastman School. The result is that the faculty of the Butler School of Music, following an overwhelming vote of the faculty, now has much more restrictive legislation on its books in this area than any other unit of the university, a good thing from my perspective for the protection of the reputation of the music school, its faculty, its staff, and its students. Faculty members are urged that we all have a special trust, especially in a field where supply overwhelms demand, to see to it that our work with individual students be regarded as sacred, not allowing personal considerations of any kind to distract us from the teaching and mentoring role with which we have been entrusted. The issue, I think, is one that involves senior people who have more power than their almost inevitably younger students, and in its potential involves not only heterosexual but homosexual relationships. In deciding on a music school at which to matriculate, students and their parents would do well in my view to inquire at the outset about institutional policy in the area at hand. While the subject can be problematic whenever two human beings spend a lot of private time together, it is a more sensitive issue in music schools than elsewhere because the private time begins with undergraduate study (when the student may be more vulnerable) and because the methodology of teaching musical performance on some instruments may necessarily involve touching that can easily be perceived as inappropriate. (Zachar Bron, one of the world's most successful violin teachers, once commented while demonstrating better vibrato to a young woman he was teaching in a class I was observing in Lübeck, "Were this a lesson in the United States, it would be prudent for me to ask, before the demonstration, whether my student felt in the least uncomfortable about touching of the kind I think important here." To which I responded, "You are absolutely right, Professor.")

"THE OLD SCHOOL"

Some faculty will recognize the nineteenth-century severity of the Music Vale Academy for Young Women, cited earlier, in colleagues or teachers who went to school late in the nineteenth century and early in the twentieth. My own best friend among such teachers was the late Cecile Staub Genhart, a wonderful pianist, a fine teacher, and an extremely nice lady who had been born in Zurich in 1899 and had studied with Edwin Fischer. She taught piano from the 1920s at the Eastman School, where her students included John Perry and Barry Snyder, and had retired to Switzerland in the late 1960s. I was persuaded by Allen Wallis, chancellor of the University of Rochester, shortly after he had appointed me to the Eastman directorship, that it was worth inviting Mrs. G—for so she was known to all of her students—back to Rochester. And I did so. She was a most courtly lady, and she always treated me as though I were Beethoven. But she felt it her mission to provide personal guidance, like a sixteenth-century master with an apprentice, for the complete lives of her students. Understandably, she felt entitled to assign the repertory that she thought important, and in the order she determined. But she also felt it her role to insist on the other courses her students enrolled in, on the amount of time they divided between that work and piano practice, the amount of time her students spent in contact with their parents, whether they attended church, what they ate, and whom they dated. From Mrs. G's point of view, the role of the master piano teacher was all encompassing. I believe that the time for such proprietary use of one's students' time and energy passed some time ago.

FULL-TIME OR PART-TIME?

In my brief presidency of the New England Conservatory, I ran into three different though related problems, deriving from a music faculty's sense of ownership of each of the majoring students working with him or her. The first was my positive reaction to the report of an ad hoc committee of board members that recommended regular professional counseling for each student from someone other than his studio teacher at the end of each of the first two years of undergraduate study. The second came from my inaugural address, in which I recommended faculty consideration of what I called a three-track curriculum, with an intensive review for all students at the ends of their sophomore years, aiming to determine in each case how the student was doing with his private teacher and what he could tell about his dreams for the future, after having compared himself for two years to classmates of similar aspiration. It was my view that, following such a review, some of the students would continue in the track they had selected as freshmen, while others might wish to become performance minors, majoring in an academic aspect of music (history, theory, music education) or in the development of entrepreneurial and managerial skills. My objective was a curriculum that might optimize the welfare of each student as an individual, thus attracting an applicant pool that did not as a whole require as much financial aid as the faculty and I agreed we needed to spend but did not have. Thus my continuing plea to faculty reading these pages: you and I are here for the long-term benefit of each of the students who works with us.

Though I had imagined that the faculty would appreciate any moves that improved the quality of the student body as a whole and its success, I had not paid enough attention to the fact that, at schools where so much of the faculty is part-time, faculty compensation results from multiplying a unit rate of instruction (ranging during my days at NEC from one thousand to twelve thousand dollars) by the number of units taught. At a place like Eastman, this is the sort of thing that could be discussed with the faculty chairs and at the monthly meetings of the faculty itself. But at a place like NEC, where faculty expect to be paid separately for every individual act of participation in the school's work, it is hard to get many people to attend a faculty meeting.

My third problem resulted from a staff member who wanted to be president and by a faculty made nervous by the fact that the new president's plan might threaten a flow of continuous compensation by putting more pressure on the recruitment and review of additional students. This raises an obvious point for parents, students, and teachers to consider. Does the institution exist as a means of employment for the faculty and staff, or as a means of training and educating the next generation of musicians? I made the mistake at NEC of thinking it could do both. Colleges and universities where the faculty is salaried, where the risk of enrollment shortfalls belongs to the dean and to the institution rather than to the faculty member as an individual, perform an entirely different kind of educational role.

A related advantage of the university-based music school lies in the fact that the faculty, especially if preponderantly full-time, have the time and leisure to talk together about the institution's principal output, its graduates. I remember with nostalgia a prelude to an Eastman meeting I was chairing with a couple of dozen faculty. In the five minutes that preceded my calling the meeting to order, I had an informal conversation with my distinguished colleague violinist Sylvia Rosenberg. Sylvia, seated to my left, began by complaining about a freshman student of hers (for our current purposes, named Sue) whose violin practice, Sylvia said, was being undermined by a new assistant professor of musicology who was assigning Sue so many papers that there was no time for her to practice the violin. Since our newest assistant professor of musicology, Jessie Ann Owens, was sitting immediately to my right, I took the opportunity to introduce Sylvia to Jessie Ann, who in her turn complained that Sue had told *her* she had so much violin practicing to do that she was unable to write a single paper. Discovering that Sue was telling two different faculty members two different stories, I asked Sylvia and Jessie Ann to have lunch together on my tab and discover what Sue was up to. With a bit of research, Sylvia and Jessie Ann determined that Sue had met her first serious boyfriend and that a lot of practice and writing time was being expended at his apartment nearby. This persuaded me of the importance of faculty members getting to know one another on a social basis, the better to keep track of the evolving activities, talents, and aspirations of our students, a process that cannot possibly be encouraged to the same degree at an institution where the faculty are part-time and have often never met one another.

Further means of encouraging faculty friendship and interaction on behalf of the students include arranging for faculty studios and offices to be distributed all over the school's physical plant, in such a fashion that a musicologist looking for a date for lunch naturally meets in the hall the trombone professor, looking for new repertory. Effective maneuvers toward similar goals involved the idea of "affiliate faculty," recognizing the multiple musical accomplishments of performers like Russell Saunders and Abram Loft, both interested in the history of music, of cellist Steven Doane's interest in early music performance practice, and the pianistic achievement of the late Robert Bailey, the nation's leading Wagner scholar, during the seventies and eighties a professor in Eastman's Department of Musicology. While affiliate faculty did not get to vote on matters affecting departmental appointments and curricula, they were invited to departmental social functions and made to feel as though they had something worthwhile to contribute to the artistic and pedagogic lives of their colleagues. The composition faculty made a point of assigning each composition major to a different faculty mentor during each year of a student's residence in Rochester. And the cello faculty, at one point comprising Paul Katz, Steven Doane, and Robert Sylvester, regularly sent their private students for study with one another on repertory for which it was thought a colleague had special expertise. Regularly including faculty colleagues from other departments on faculty search committees had a similar affect, as did the annual awarding of the Rayburn Wright Award, a monetary prize for faculty who took a special interest in the interdisciplinary work of their Eastman colleagues. All of this, it will be found, greatly facilitates a faculty member's willingness to participate wholeheartedly in the governance of the school, attend faculty meetings, participate in faculty searches, and take an enthusiastic part in the necessary committee work. The idea of taking a single day or two each year to study as an institution the same piece of music is also excellent—for the students, for the faculty, and for the school—but is understandably difficult without the enthusiastic collaboration of a largely full-time faculty.

STAGE FRIGHT

All those studying musical performance, including many of international reputation, have suffered at one time or another from memory lapses, a terrifying and potentially disabling problem for a young performer. As a child, I was told repeatedly that the way to avoid stage fright was by practicing every memorized piece with such diligence that one could afford on stage to lose 50 percent of one's ability and still perform acceptably. Unfortunately, this leads to a Protestant ethic of unnecessary practice, producing, as indicated earlier, two unfortunate results already mentioned: physiological injury and hobbling educational opportunity costs. Clearly, anyone who performs without adequate practice is skating on thin ice. The question is how to measure the ice. My own advice to students is to prepare responsibly, relying not only on one's muscle memory but on cognitive control of what is going on musically in the piece. David Craighead and Russell Saunders, Eastman's two master organ teachers, used to teach Bach fugues by asking their students, in measure 127, say, to stop playing, while the Bach fugue continued in the student's musical imagination. At the end of forty-five seconds of silence, the professor would say, "Go on now," and the player was supposed to begin at exactly the place in the composition that she would have reached had she been playing the organ for the intervening forty-five seconds. Proper rest, exercise, and psychological conditioning, as the result of which one never imagines anything but really positive outcomes, are also important. The reader already knows of my experience with little white pills at Tanglewood when I was fifteen.

Once I became a music school director, twenty years after the little-white-pills incident, I wondered how much of this sort of thing goes on informally backstage, between teachers and students, or between students and other students, and at what medical risk. It seems to me that there is fertile ground here for a research project involving several leading music schools and proximate medical centers: New England Conservatory and Massachusetts General Hospital, Eastman and the University of Rochester's Medical Center, the Cleveland Institute and the Medical School of Case-Western Reserve, Northwestern's Medical School and its Bienen School of Music, the Shepherd School of Rice University and the Texas Medical Center at Houston, for example. At the University of Texas at Austin, I tried to put together a project of this kind involving the Butler School of Music, UT's outstanding College of Pharmacy, and our Phobia Avoidance Clinic in the Department of Psychology, but I retired from the deanship before I was able to get this project off the ground. While the amount of practice time required of individual students must vary from instrument to instrument, and while individual students certainly have varying degrees of willingness to spend their days devoted exclusively to their practice rooms, the careers of such musicians as Bach, Mozart, Beethoven, Schubert, Schumann, Brahms, Wagner, Debussy, Rachmaninoff, Charles Rosen, Robert Levin, Michael Steinberg, David Burge, Ralph Kirkpatrick, and Edward Cone all suggest that there is more to music study than keyboard practice. The faculty member is here urged to do your very best to stress to the student that the principal task of practice, on any instrument, is not to clock hours of practice on the instrument but to learn to listen very carefully, always comparing what comes out of the instrument with an evolving musical ideal stored in one's imagination. Occasional recording, even on an informal basis, of one's own playing can be extremely helpful in this area, the reason why Eastman used to have excellent recording equipment in every faculty studio.

OUR RESPONSIBILITY TO OUR STUDENTS

As stewards of humanity's future skills and knowledge, it is vital that we pass along to our students a sense of common contribution to the larger enterprise of human accomplishment and happiness. In my first class as a graduate student with Oliver Strunk, he dove in, as was his wont, to the solution of a real problem: the transcription of troubadour and trouvère melodies from the original Notre Dame manuscripts, projected with some difficulty in the fall of 1958 on the wall of our basement seminar room. There was no preliminary reading of the secondary literature on how to do this; we began in medias res, as though the six students in the room were all young professionals who knew what we were doing. This eventually led Professor Strunk to an exposition of the theory of modal rhythm and to a discussion of the contributions of Pierre Aubry, Jean Beck, and Friedrich Ludwig to that idea. It developed that Aubry and Beck had been students of Ludwig, that they had had a disagreement about who should receive credit for the development of the theory, which led to a duel from which Aubry died, after which Professor Ludwig himself claimed credit for the idea, an idea that a century later has been discredited in any case. The notion was typical of Oliver Strunk and a wonderful introduction to scholarship: a demonstration that the integrity of the enterprise could only be supported through collaboration and sharing.

While visiting Professor Strunk in Copenhagen, for work together on my dissertation in the summer of 1961, he learned that I was about to spend several days in Bayreuth on my way back to Vienna. Said he, "As you know, Richard Wagner normally began by writing a libretto, then publishing it, for he needed the income. I have noticed in the original libretto for *Tristan* that there are three or four hundred lines of text that appear in the original libretto but do not appear in the orchestral score. While you're in Bayreuth, you may as well go over to the Wahnfried Archive, where you'll find a copy of Wagner's composition sketch for *Tristan*. It would be interesting to know whether Wagner ever set the lines of text that eventually got omitted in the orchestral score: it would provide us with some pretty interesting information on Wagner's working methods." Of course, I did as asked, sending the material from the composition sketch back to Professor Strunk, whence it became the basis for the fine dissertation of Robert Bailey, another Strunk student just beginning his work on Wagner. This seemed to me a wonderful demonstration of a scholarly and entrepreneurial mind, responsible for team building among his graduate students. It went along with the philosophy, "If, in your investigation of an archive, you find information that would be of use to a colleague, by all means pass it along to him. To fail to do so diminishes you as it does him," the opposite of the attitude one encounters too often in some of our schools, where the idea is to try to diminish the self-confidence of the other students.

My other principal mentor in the Princeton Graduate School was Arthur Mendel, a fine conductor and leader of the Cantata Singers who became a major critic, editor, and the country's leading Bach scholar before his appointment to the Princeton faculty. From my perspective, Mendel was not only a very effective chair of music at Princeton for fifteen years but a master teacher who knew how to admit what he didn't know—a tricky problem at Princeton, where the students are unusually bright and knowledgeable—and who understood how to communicate to his students, in private, how a seminar paper or a response in a class discussion fell short of his own standard, and why. It was from Mendel that I learned not only the importance of communicating a clear and ongoing interest in one's students and their work but the importance of letting each of us learn how to improve his work, without destroying the psychological underpinning of self-confidence necessary for each of us. I was always disappointed by the fact that Mendel, having been appointed to the chairmanship of the Princeton Music Department, felt that he had to abandon his work as a musician, not so much because of considerations of time, I thought, but because he worried lest his Princeton colleagues view him as a jack-of-all-trades instead of as a serious scholar. I was able to watch him conduct but once in my ten years as a Princeton graduate student and junior faculty member, when he led a Bach cantata behind the scenes, in a rehearsal room invisible to the public, for the ceremonial opening of the Music Department's new Woolworth Center, in the spring of 1964.

THE ROLE OF JUNIOR FACULTY

A special faculty problem, I think, is the difference between institutions like Harvard and Princeton, which most often choose senior faculty from the outside, as a means of ensuring quality, and institutions like Texas and Michigan, where the promotion rate for assistant professors approximates two thirds. In the latter universities, senior faculty treat junior faculty as a human resource to be developed and nurtured, in the former as a temporary resource to be exploited. It makes no sense to turn a promising young colleague into a personal friend if he is about to be exiled to what one thinks of too easily as the minor leagues.

THE IMPORTANCE OF BALANCE IN THE LIFE OF A FACULTY MEMBER

Faculty members must learn how to balance their inevitably finite time among professional work, teaching, avocational interests, and their families, for there are but 168 hours in a week for any of us. I have always valued faculty who were absolutely dedicated to the interests of their students, and to junior faculty members for whom they served as mentors. Certainly, I valued many faculty for their compelling artistry, as I did others for the breadth and fertility of their avocational interests. Some of us have been married but once, to the same partner. Others have been married, as I have been, more than once, with inevitable damage to many of the people around us. Because there are lots of forces in contemporary America that destroy marriages, I believe it important for teachers to try to teach their students the value of developing skills in time management, for if one aspires to a career in music, there is not a lot of time to waste. Time spent with spouses, children, parents, students, and colleagues is always in short supply. Putting too much on one's plate ends up producing unhappiness for too many people. Because valuable faculty members present to the dean all sorts of professional and personal profiles, it is up to the dean's persuasiveness in negotiating colleagues' future with the provost to be able to represent the faculty, not only as individuals of outstanding commitment and ability but also as members of a team that works together seamlessly on behalf of the students, the alumni, and the institution.

KEEPING THE FLAME ALIVE: THE IMPORTANCE OF CONTINUING ENTHUSIASM FOR MUSIC

All those who teach music should work at remembering, as often as possible, why and how music became so important a motivating force, a slightly different story, I'm sure, for each of us. Read Eric Booth's terrific book *The Everyday Work of Art* and reflect at least once a year on the following theme:

> We must perceive reality with empathy, compassion, and a patient hunger to penetrate more deeply into its complexity. We need to seek the valuable in the unfamiliar, and allow ourselves daily doses of wonder. We must yearn to make things that make sense to us, developing an interest in the processes themselves and the balance that comes with a long-term view. We need to be amateurs to engage in the work of art throughout our lives. We need the serious play of flow to run through the life of every home.[4]

Teachers have a responsibility for staying professionally alive, writing new music, meeting new audiences, teaching new students, publishing new books, constantly seeking connections that will help make music an ever more important and valued part of our society. While we can't all be involved in all of these pursuits, meeting new people, forming new coalitions, and remembering that the future need not repeat the past are all valuable for us. So is staying in touch with and counseling former students, taking an active interest in their developing careers, and learning from mistakes we may have made in our own teaching. It is important, too, especially in a university music school where faculty colleagues are easy to meet over lunch at the Faculty Club, to take an active interest in the professional activities of others and to seek out opportunities for current and future students to be included in developing opportunities that relate to music. These include but are certainly not limited to evolving theories and practices of entrepreneurship, the relationship of non-hierarchical management to the ongoing work of a professional chamber ensemble, the relationship of evolving technology to teaching and understanding music, future methods of distributing music, the evolving law of intellectual property, and the relationship of medicine to brain plasticity and to the physiological problems of performing musicians. Martha Hilley, professor of class piano at the University of Texas at Austin, performs outstanding work on behalf of the university as a result of her ever-widening campus interests of this kind, a remarkable achievement in a university as big as Texas. (Professor Hilley has just chaired a national search for a new provost for our university.) Elizabeth Marvin West, a fine singer who turned into one of the country's leading music theorists, has had a similar role at Eastman, especially since her Bridging Fellowships in cognitive science and psychology.

HOW NARROW A FOCUS IS APPROPRIATE FOR AN UNDERGRADUATE?

Encouraging double majors whenever possible at the undergraduate level seems to me a good idea for music's future and for the futures of many of our students. As things stand, too many of our students begin in music later than they should, then spend their undergraduate years catching up by making the musical part of their studies more intensive than I think desirable for many of them. Certainly, there is no reason for encouraging substandard performance. But neither is there much reason to encourage undergraduate music students so to narrow their educations that, whether they like it or not, they turn into professionals frustrated by the overwhelming supply of talent that no one has told them about, simply as a way of balancing collegiate music enrollments. Those who perform at UT in the 360-member Longhorn Band have, I am told, a wonderful musical experience. Ninety percent of them are not music majors, for music majors would rather play inside and seated than marching with their clarinets and trombones in one-hundred-degree heat! The Alumni Band of the University of Texas is an awesome sight, comprising 1,200 players. And they all love music. Or just being together, performing music, through the nostalgia of reminiscence!

IS IT WRONG TO BE A MUSICAL AMATEUR?

Matthias Vogt, a musicologist who directs the Saxon Institute for Cultural Infrastructure in Görlitz, a friend of many years' standing, told me the first time we met that, since the founding of Germany in Bismarck's time, there has never been a single deutschmark (or euro) in the federal German budget for music. When questioned on the subject, Matthias quickly explained that there has been a lot of public money, during the days of the Second and Third Empires, during the Weimar Republic, and since Reunification, but never in the *federal budget*. It has all been in the budgets of the cities and the Länder, where the sum spent varies enormously on a per capita basis. It appears that the driving force that persuades some parts of Germany to support music more generously than others is neither higher education nor affluence, as in the United States, but an enthusiasm for participation in music as avocation. Those who sing in church choirs, who play in town bands, or who perform chamber music at home on weekends, with and for their friends, form the basis of a German avocational culture in music that goes back well before the days of the French Revolution. That something of this kind is badly needed in our own country is a principal argument of Robert Putnam's provocative book *Bowling Alone*, in which it is argued that the period 1960–2000 in the United States produced a degree of increasing social isolation all over the country, isolation that participation in amateur musical ensembles could help rectify in the national interest. Says Eric Booth in *The Everyday Work of Art*,

> The etymology of the word "amateur" suggests a lover, quite literally—one who does something for the love of it. But the love at the heart of the amateur does not require reciprocation. It is not sophisticated, or romantic, or self-conscious; it is grounded and irrepressible. It is the natural force that drives us towards the realization of our entelechy. Just as the opposite of love is not hate but apathy, the opposite of amateur is not professional, but perfunctory, grudging, boring, required.
>
> For a long time, I was uncomfortable with the connotative baggage that comes with the word amateur. I had no impulse to stand up and brag that I was an amateur—hey, I was a hot entrepreneur, or a Broadway actor, a professional something. I didn't want to be lumped in with old Aunt Sadie who makes Christmas baskets all year to fill with her dreaded fruitcake. But I feel honored to be linked to millions of inspiring amateurs throughout the country who quietly spend lifetimes discovering and making things of meaning; people who understand Kahlil Gibran's line in *The Prophet*: "Work is love made visible"; people who make work that they love, and make love in their work a fundamental part of their lives; people who transform the ordinariness of the everyday into valuable grist for growth's mill.[5]

These are the people who could go on to support America's professional music scene of the future, for these are the people who, when young, learn the language of music that, as Mendelssohn and Hanslick said, is not less communicative in its meaning than words but more so. These are the people who compete every year in the extremely valuable Van Cliburn Competition for Amateur Pianists. These are the people identified in Clay Shirky's wonderful recent book *Here Comes Everybody*. These are the people spotlighted in Chris Anderson's equally provocative *The Long Tail*, in which we learn that modern technology and the Internet have broken down the traditional method of producing stars and hits— the current focus of too many Juilliard wannabes—dividing what used to be a field in which a small number of celebrity stars earned humongous fees for compact discs that sold millions of copies into a world in which many amateur musicians appear on the net, promoting their own music and musical performances for much smaller audiences that aggregate to a huge long-term interest in music. Richard Florida's inspirational book of 2002, *The Rise of the Creative Class*, makes the same point with respect to Austin, a city whose best days are all ahead, a wonderful place in which to live and work at the beginning of the new millennium. Says Florida about a convention he attended in Austin in 2001:

> The usual drill at a convention is to endure a long day of stuffy presentations and working-group sessions, then head out to the local nightspots and cut loose. At the Austin 360 Summit it was work and play together all day long. When we filed into the noisy main meeting room in the morning we were issued plastic wiffle balls. If you didn't like what a speaker was saying, even Michael Dell, you could pelt him with one. The lunchtime keynote speech on the first day—typically given by a grey-headed pillar of the community—was a satiric monologue by performance artist Steve Tomlinson, who appeared only because Sandra Bullock, originally scheduled, was on location making a film. In interludes between conference sessions at the Austin 360 Summit, a rock band played—and not the kind of watered-down, easy-listening rock band you sometimes find at business functions. This was an excellent, hard-driving band, full of guys with real chops. Austin, after all, is the live music capital of the world, one reads at the local airport.
>
> After a full half-day of this, it was my turn. I was moderator of a panel of CEOs and venture capital types, addressing a question that I believed central to the region's future economic development. I had gotten the idea from a cab driver, who worried that the crush of high-tech industry and people threatened to drive out the ethnic and cultural diversity that had fueled Austin's creativity to begin with. So I organized the panel around the question: "Is Austin losing its soul?" After some predictable back and forth among the panelists about their investments in the music and cultural scene, I used the moderator's prerogative to interject, "It's not something you can keep in a box and trot out at work. You can't have high-tech innovation without art and music. All forms of creativity feed off each other."—and so on. Then a sudden inspiration struck me. "If you really want to know how important this is," I said, "don't ask your fellow high-tech CEOs or the mayor or the head of the Chamber of Commerce. Ask the guys in the band!" I gestured grandly to the musicians seated at the edge of the stage, who looked like the members of Conan O'Brien's late-night ensemble. Then one of the panelists cued me in. The guys in the band, now grinning

broadly at me, were not local grungers. They were high-tech CEOs and venture capitalists. Not only were they top-notch musicians on the side; they had felt perfectly comfortable bringing their instruments and playing for their peers at an economic summit. It was as if Jack Welch, George Soros and Warren Buffett had agreed to jam for the crowd at Davos![6]

The reader can imagine how I felt when arriving in Austin on August 31, 1999, for my first interview for the UT deanship and was confronted at the Bergstrom Airport with the sign at the end of the jet ramp that Richard Florida mentions, welcoming me to the "live music capital of the world." My first reaction resulted no doubt from my having come directly from "the Hub of the Universe," where the NEC faculty felt uncomfortable about even preliminary conversations on collaboration with the president of the Berklee School, which teaches jazz and other contemporary (if commercial) repertories. My reaction to the Bergstrom sign was that the University of Texas's School of Music—in the meantime generously endowed as the Sarah and Ernest Butler School of Music—could not afford to be thought of by our community as the moribund music section of the live music capital of the world, an implicit challenge for the future. With the election of our forty-fourth president, music lies near the center of the community's ambition to create a home where all sorts of art can live productively together, where the diversity that is America can be supported by an artistic scene that reflects the enthusiasm, optimism, and energy of this wonderful place, a productive melting pot for the professional and avocational communities of music, a turning point for the arts in America for many years to come.

I have always thought it a triumph of the Eastman School that its graduates include not only many fine composers, orchestral players, operatic singers, university professors, K–12 teachers, and maintainers of private music studios but many others who went on to undertake successful careers not directly related to classical music. Goddard Lieberson (a composer who became president of Columbia Records, where he introduced the long-playing record), Paul Ouncley (a church organist who during the work week was vice president of Boeing Aircraft, responsible for noise reduction!), Richard Ziter (a fine pianist who became a distinguished ophthalmologic surgeon), Leatrice Gochberg (a singer who became an important real estate developer in New York City), Mitch Miller (a legendary oboist who became a vice president of Columbia Records, the director of a popular nationally televised series called *Sing Along with Mitch*, and a successor to Arthur Fiedler as a superlative Pops conductor), Theodore Szulc (a bassoonist who became one of the country's leading experts in room acoustics), Max Conner (a public school music teacher who became head of physical security for the FBI), and Mary Ann Krupsak (a singer who became lieutenant governor of New York) were all among them. Clearly, these people have all had satisfying careers. It is up to you as a conscientious faculty member to produce not simply outstanding players and singers but successful and happy human beings.

Joanne Lipman's article in the *New York Times* of October 13, 2013, "Is Music the Key to Success?" should give each of us a lot to think about in this context. Ms. Lipman, having interviewed such nonmusical celebrities as Condoleezza Rice, Alan Greenspan, Bruce Kovner, Paul Allen, Woody Allen, Chuck Todd, Paula Zahn, Larry Page, Andrea Mitchell, Roger McNamee, Steven Spielberg, and James D. Wolfensohn about their serious studies in music, summarizes their several speculations about the important role each believes music to have played in his or her success. These include crediting music for opening pathways to creative thinking, sharpening the ability to collaborate, the power to focus on the present and the future simultaneously, to reinforce one's confidence in the ability to create, and to encourage a drive for perfection. Lipman quotes Alan Greenspan, former chair of the Federal Reserve, as having told her, "It's not a coincidence. I can tell you as a statistician that the probability that the connection between music study and creativity in other disciplines is mere chance is extremely small."

We think too narrowly about careers that involve music. All music school professors are aware that not all of their former students go on to careers in the areas of musical subspecialty for which they were so intensively trained while in music school. And we are aware, through our exposure to the history of music, that some great composers of the past either had trouble making a living in music (Mozart, Schubert, Schumann, Wolf), did not have to make a living (Prince Louis Ferdinand, Mendelssohn, Gordon Getty), or made a living doing something else in order to be able to write the music each wanted to produce — Alexander Borodin (1833–1887) as a PhD in chemistry; Cesar Cui (1835–1918) as an expert in fortification and military matters; Modest Mussorgsky (1839–81), at first independently wealthy, then a clerk in the czar's Ministry of Communications; and Charles Ives (1874–1954), a life insurance executive. The biographical sketch of Raoul Berger that follows, generously written at my request by his son, Carl, a psychiatrist, is a fascinating story of human accomplishment. It is included here as a reminder to music teachers, especially at the collegiate level, that because musical careers evolve in all sorts of unexpected fashions, it is vital for you as a faculty member to seek out in each student those qualities for future growth that may make each of them special and fulfilled.

Raoul Berger was born in 1901 in the town of Kahreminits, a small city not far from Odessa. His Jewish parents, harried repeatedly by Cossacks, brought their two children to America in 1905 and settled in a largely Catholic, multiethnic neighborhood on Chicago's west side. Raoul began to study the violin relatively late, at about age twelve, with a private teacher to whom he was referred by one of his teachers at Crane Tech, where Raoul took an engineering curriculum. His progress was such that in his last year of high school he ably performed the Saint-Saens B Minor Concerto with his high school orchestra.

Raoul Berger went to New York City shortly after graduation from high school to audition for the master class of Franz Kneisel, who, having resigned as concertmaster of the Boston Symphony, had become a faculty member at what was then called the Institute of Musical Art in New York City. The class numbered perhaps fifteen violin talents, chief among whom were Joseph Fuchs, Sasha Jacobsen, and Karl Kreuter. Only in retrospect and after several years of study did Raoul comprehend the significance of his decision to study with Kneisel, whose pupils, unlike those of his counterparts Leopold Auer and Carl Flesch, were not groomed to be nor catapulted to solo careers but were rather given a broad-based musical education in chamber music as well as the solo literature. During the summers, Kneisel and his class repaired to Kneisel's summer home in Blue Hill, Maine, in which idyllic setting and rarified musical climate lessons continued with an emphasis on chamber music. Everyone played quartets and was expected to learn not only violin parts but those for the viola as well. There were visits not only from former members of Kneisel's own quartet but from New England composers of the day, among them Charles Martin Loeffler, himself both a gifted composer and a fine string player, Arthur Foote, and George Chadwick. A typical day began early and included many hours of solitary practicing and chamber music every evening as well. Kneisel was an exacting teacher whose public ridicule of his students took its toll on all. However, Raoul's own steeliness sustained him, and at one point he was sufficiently dissatisfied with his own bowing (on which Kneisel hammered unceasingly) to make what was consensually deemed an unthinkable decision in its sheer rebelliousness: he would go to Berlin to study with Carl Flesch. In about 1922, Raoul and his sister journeyed to Berlin, she to study piano and he to join Flesch's own master class. However, he quickly found that Flesch's own concertizing allowed him little time to teach, and Raoul remained there only for the year it required for him to gain the confidence of "playing out" and establishing the rock-solid bowing he had sought. Thereafter, Raoul reapplied to rejoin the Kneisel master class and (to the astonishment of the class!) was permitted to return. He recalled on occasion Kneisel's sarcastic introduction of him to the class. No one, not even his personal favorite, Fuchs, was exempt from Kneisel's ridicule.

Shortly after his return to the class, Raoul completed his studies and secured a position in the first violin section of the Philadelphia Orchestra, where he remained for a year. During this time he regularly traveled by milk train to New York to visit his eventual wife, who was studying piano there. At that time, the Philadelphia Orchestra was conducted by Leopold Stokowski, whom Raoul viewed as supremely arrogant though possessed of genius. Not long thereafter, he auditioned for and was given the position of second concertmaster of the Cleveland Orchestra, at the time conducted by Artur Rodzinsky. The change also brought his reunion with Fuchs, then the orchestra's concertmaster and arguably Raoul's closest musical colleague, though the friendship was marred by Fuchs's own bitterness at his apparent inability to break through as a celebrated soloist.[7] Following perhaps two years in Cleveland, Raoul went to Cincinnati, where he became the associate concertmaster under Fritz Reiner, whom Raoul regarded as a martinet of limited gifts. A story from that period is both suggestive of what would follow and illustrative of Raoul's own granite self-belief and defiance of authoritarianism (of which, he was, of course, capable himself). Reiner had a practice of singling out individual players for criticism in rehearsal by shouting a stentorian "You!" On one such occasion when he was himself thus addressed, Raoul responded to Reiner before the entire audience that the maestro knew Raoul's name. Years later, Raoul was sought out by Désiré Defauw, music director of the Chicago Symphony, to become its concertmaster, only to find that Reiner would not release him from his contract in Cincinnati. I believe that this event may well have been the last straw in Raoul's disillusionment with his career in music.

During his years in Cincinnati, Raoul formed the Cincinnati String Quartet with members of the orchestra, and the group performed often, both in Cincinnati and elsewhere. On the afternoon of April 9, 1932, the quartet played at the Library of Congress, though Raoul could see the sheer impossibility, even then, of making a living by such means for all but a few, whether as soloist or quartet player. When an opportunity arose to take a teaching position at the University of Texas, he accepted the position (while breaking off his engagement to my mother for *her* sake). While he returned a year or two later to Cincinnati to rejoin the orchestra, he had decided to leave music for another profession.

Raoul's fiancée, with whom he had remained in contact, accepted his proposal of marriage, and he began college at the University of Cincinnati, carrying twenty weekly credit hours a semester while maintaining a full-time position with the orchestra. His wife believed that he had left music in part because he feared that to continue as a musician would expose her (who had all the advantages as the daughter of a distinguished Chicago surgeon with an international career) to a harsh life. Although he departed music as a profession, Raoul continued to play chamber music thereafter until he ceased to play at the age of sixty-two. In the period 1938–1940, he became close personal friends with Leonard Sorkin, first violin of the Fine Arts Quartet, and was in fact its coach as this quartet launched its own career. Raoul played concerts with Sorkin, Milton Preeves, its violist, and George Sopkin, the cellist.

In Washington, where Raoul worked in government as a lawyer after graduating from the Northwestern University Law School, he came to know the members of the Budapest Quartet personally, was an intimate friend of its first violinist, Josef Roisman, and played quartets on occasion with its violist, Boris Kroyt. His introduction to Paul Olefsky, later professor of cello at the University of Texas, took place in Washington, where the latter played with the U.S. Marine Band, and that gave rise to another lifelong friendship, leading to the formation of an outstanding quartet whose other members were the violinist Gordon Staples and the violist Richard Parnass. This group played together virtually yearlong at the Berger home, and in fact in 1951 played a concert at my school, Swarthmore College, in which the school newspaper opined that they had totally eclipsed the concert of the Roth Quartet, which preceded it by a week. From the time I was eight years old until my departure for college at the age of seventeen, Raoul took me as his only pupil. My weekly lessons with Raoul brought me from the earliest beginnings to much of the concerto literature, though I was too intimidated to join Raoul for quartets. Although Raoul brought me to a professional level of playing, he was always firm in his insistence that it be for the joy of music making and was not to be applied to making a living (as he feared I might end up doing), especially in an orchestra.

Raoul's last and perhaps most venturesome performances came during a year's stay in Copenhagen and Vienna, which allowed the closing of his private law practice to begin what he thought would be his retirement but which in fact preceded his accepting appointment to the Magruder Chair of Constitutional Law at the University of California, Berkeley. During his European sojourn, Raoul played recitals after a lapse of thirty years of public performance in Copenhagen and Vienna. He gave the first public performance in many years (with piano) of the difficult First Violin Concerto of Wienawski, to critical acclaim. He was proud to have programmed it and clearly set himself the task as characteristic of the boldness with which he faced challenges. Thereafter, dissatisfied with the (even limited) slowing of his vibrato, he sold his Stradivarius and his Tourte bow and never played thereafter. Although he eschewed modern music, Raoul was sufficiently intrigued with Heifetz's performance of the Prokofieff G Minor Concerto that in 1951 he arduously undertook learning it.

After serving as professor at the University of California, Berkeley, Raoul Berger was appointed Charles Warren Senior Fellow in American Legal History at Harvard Law School during the period 1971–1976. Following his retirement from Harvard at the age of seventy-five, he continued to publish as a legal scholar, even in his nineties. His major books include *Congress vs. the Supreme Court* (1969); *Impeachment, the Constitutional Problems* (1973); *Government by Judiciary: The Transformation of the 14th Amendment* (1975); *Death Penalties: The Supreme Court's Obstacle Course* (1982); *Federalism: The Founders' Design* (1987); and *The 14th Amendment and the Bill of Rights* (1989). He died in 2000.[8]

To quote, finally, from the Wikipedia entry on Berger: "Berger was a popular academic critic of the doctrine of executive privilege and is viewed as having played a significant role in undermining President Richard Nixon's constitutional arguments during the impeachment process." Quite an accomplishment for a graduate of the class of Franz Kneisel! Clearly, Raoul Berger had three different careers: as professional violinist, as attorney, and as professor of constitutional law, with such solid accomplishment in each that he was motivated to live very fully, for a life that spanned nearly a century. I hope the amazing story of those three distinguished careers will persuade teachers of young musicians that there is more in life than being frustrated by Stokowski, Rodzinski, and Reiner.

Now that I am once more a college professor of music, let me conclude this chapter to my fellow professors with a brief description of several of my own students, from Princeton in the middle 1960s, at Eastman, and at the University of Texas since 2007, for each of them represents a vocational outcome that included but was not limited to strong pre-professional musical training.[9]

1. A Princeton freshman who asked in the fall of 1964 whether it would be possible for him to undertake a double major in English and music. I told him that I thought his idea eminently reasonable, so long as he was willing to work hard. He went on to take a Princeton AB in English with a summa cum laude while playing principal flute in the Princeton University Orchestra, enrolling successfully in a fistful of music courses and serving as music director of an undergraduate a cappella group called the Footnotes. He went on to take a PhD in English at Yale, studying flute with the late Samuel Baron, taught at Yale and at the University of Michigan (where he was professor of English *and* music), and served for a decade as founding director of the University of Michigan's Institute for the Humanities. He has made several fine CDs as solo flutist, has written two superb books on music, both published by Yale University Press, and half a dozen books and a slew of articles on seventeenth- and eighteenth-century English literature. Chairman of English at Boston University for the past several years, he is now William Fairfield Warren Professor at BU, that institution's most generous faculty honor, and is married to the chair of the string faculty at the New England Conservatory. His name is James A. Winn.
2. The principal oboe of the Princeton University Orchestra was a candidate for a master's degree in government at Princeton in the middle 1960s. When his principal professor in the Woodrow Wilson School called to tell me about the student's apparent lack of interest in government, evidenced by "working with a knife and a bunch of pieces of wood" while the professor was lecturing, I suggested that Joseph Robinson, a very gifted oboist who had studied with John Mack, might do well as a professional oboist. When Joe told me that he had not been to music school and had no idea what a dominant seventh chord might be, I told him that he really didn't need to understand music theory as long as he enjoyed making

good reeds. Several years later, when turned down by a search committee for the principal oboe chair of the New York Philharmonic as a result of what the committee thought too little professional experience, Robinson wrote a legendary letter to Zubin Mehta suggesting it important that the maestro hear him play the oboe in person. The letter was so persuasive that Mehta auditioned Robinson, who then spent more than thirty years as the New York Philharmonic's very distinguished principal oboist. Though it was Joe's oboe playing that impressed Mehta, had it not been for his liberal arts education at Davidson College I doubt Joe would ever have gotten past the New York Philharmonic's search committee.

3. The Princeton University Orchestra's timpanist was a talented young percussionist whose family wanted him to become a professor. It fell my lot to persuade him that I thought he had managerial ability and entrepreneurial vision, and I helped him find a Ford Foundation internship to work on the staff of the Cincinnati Symphony. He did well in Cincinnati, followed up with an MBA at Wharton, and by age thirty had become the general manager of the Boston Symphony. Having served in that position with real distinction for seventeen years, he moved west in the late 1980s to become the equally successful executive director of the Cleveland Orchestra, a position that he filled with high distinction for another seventeen years, when he became artistic director of the Ojai Festival. In that position, he is better able to have the fun he always dreamed of as a percussionist. His name is Thomas W. Morris.

4. In the late 1970s, I had a visit in the director's office from a Yale graduate who was successfully finishing an Eastman master's degree in music theory. He said that he was considering staying on for a doctoral degree in theory but had come to the tentative conclusion that professors of music theory speak mostly to other professors of music theory—like professors of inorganic chemistry and of medieval French literature—that he wanted to teach music to the uninitiated adult public, and that he wondered whether he really needed a doctoral degree to do that. When he said he was a good pianist, a capable conductor, and an able composer, he asked whether I thought he might be able to combine his various skills and interests in music as a presenter to general audiences. Impressed both by his candor and his enthusiasm, I simply indicated that I thought he had an excellent idea and that I would be happy in the following year to stake him to three performances in Kilbourn Hall, in each of which he explored his long-term dream as a charismatic speaker who simultaneously exploited his several musical abilities. He decided to call his new miniseries in Kilbourn "What Makes It Great?" using the first half of the evening incandescently to explore with the audience several salient points of

each work, following intermission with an uninterrupted performance of the entire work. Thirty years later, he is a very active member of the roster of IMG Artists; has published two terrific books, *What Makes It Great?* and *All You Have to Do Is Listen*; and is a regular guest on National Public Radio. All I did to facilitate his career was to encourage his dream, investing minimal institutional resources in the development of his idea. His name is Rob Kapilow.

And at the University of Texas:

1. A wonderful young Czech pianist in her midtwenties who speaks English with a charming European accent and who can play the virtuosic nineteenth-century literature for the piano as well as anyone now active. With a script I drafted in which Clara Schumann meets Hillary Clinton and the two of them compare notes on the roles of women in the nineteenth and twenty-first centuries, Karolina Syrovatkova is now preparing two musical evenings as Clara Schumann, the first immediately after the death of Robert Schumann and her breakup with Brahms in the late 1850s, the second in the early 1890s, just before her retirement from the concert stage.

2. A fine young violinist in his midtwenties who was hired when he graduated by the Austin Guitar Society and the Miro Quartet to do administrative work for both groups. A friend of the late Michael Steinberg and Jorja Flezanis, he writes well and is deeply interested in what seems to me the dysfunctional administrative situation of American orchestras. His interest is in building chamber music and orchestral festivals through thematic programming and through preconcert events that draw the audience better into the music they are about to hear. Two years ago he was appointed senior artistic advisor and project manager at Artist Led, the group responsible for the Lincoln Center Chamber Players and Music at Menlo. In the summer of 2012, he was appointed artistic administrator of the Milwaukee Symphony Orchestra. His name is Isaac Thompson.

3. A fine young pianist who has just taken a senior lectureship in a new university on the island of Macau, forty-five minutes by hovercraft from the home of her mother in Hong Kong. While Anton Nel was wholly responsible for the development of her piano playing, I have been responsible for helping her think about how to prepare the first music course ever given on Macau, teaching musical coherence in western music to nonconcentrators, an opportunity she would not have had, I think, without the help of someone who has spent much of his life thinking about how to do this.

4. A terrific Texan pianist in his midthirties who has just come back from a week of recitals at the Liszt Academy in Budapest. In his

native San Angelo, he has put together a wonderfully entrepreneurial piano festival that draws musicians from all over the state and which he has now replicated in Austin. An especially imaginative aspect of his piano festival has become a request concert of repertory that concert attendees consult with him on, planning what he will perform a month hence, as the result of activity he undertakes beforehand with his potential audience on the Internet. During the past year, he has had several major successes playing piano recitals of music by Franz Liszt, which he plays magnificently while impersonating Liszt in his seventies. His name is Michael Schneider.

5. A very attractive soprano from Connecticut whose voice, though lovely, would never project in the vast confines of the Metropolitan Opera. After taking a master's degree in voice, she has founded a new Austin business called Princess for Parties. For a price, she caters receptions and dinners in the homes of Austin's affluent, each of which comes with a thirty-minute voice recital by the caterer, from repertory chosen in advance by the customer. When I suggested that that was a good idea for the next fifteen or twenty years, she responded, "I was thinking about that. By the time I'm fifty, I'd like to be living in Chicago, franchising Princess for Parties to attractive young women of 2035 who operate from Boston, Atlanta, Los Angeles, and Seattle. I'm taking a couple of courses in the Red McCombs Business School at UT to learn how optimally to accomplish this goal."

6. A fine Texan pianist in his late forties named John Ferguson. He is now making a decent living, he reports, performing American music in Islamic countries, where he and several other American musicians collaborate with Afghan and Iraqi musicians, for example. During each of the past two summers, he has helped run a summer music camp in Kurdistan and Lebanon for enrollments of about 750 Iraqi teenagers. When one of my students asked John whether it isn't dangerous to teach music in Iraq, an activity sponsored by the Department of State, Ferguson responded, "Not particularly, especially if you compare it with work in Detroit or Cleveland!" In my view and his, it would be worthwhile for him to spend one semester each season passing along his highly unusual skills at one major university after another. His website is www.americanvoices.org.

The bottom line is that, while these men and women are all fine musicians, what each of them is working on involves skills special to him- or herself, skills that can be developed and nurtured by a variety of people at so large a university as Texas, skills that I hope you, as a music professor of the future, will be alert to in your own students as the new century unfolds, remembering that what even an assistant professor encourages an undergraduate to consider may have a profound effect on the outcome of his life. Any of these careers seems to me every bit as rewarding as working in the already existing musical institutions for which we now prepare our students. And each of them came simply as the result of a mentor's positive response to a student inquiry.

NOTES

1. Robert J. Flanagan, *The Perilous Life of Symphony Orchestras: Artistic Triumphs and Economic Challenges* (New Haven, CT: Yale University Press, 2012).

2. For a wonderfully comedic parody of the academic promotion and tenure process, see Richard Russo's novel *Straight Man* (New York: Vintage, 1997).

3. Mary Vaughn, in an essay on her website (www.eventsmusic.com) under "Teacher Mentors," tells about the studies of her teacher, Roy McAllister, with the late Isabella Vengerova, the famous Russian piano teacher about whom Indiana professor Joseph Rezits wrote a book entitled *Beloved Tyranna*. A demanding pedagogue of the old school, Mme. Vengerova was famous not only for her high musical standards but for the intimidating manner she used on her students to attain those standards. The following passages from Harry Neal's chapter in Professor Rezits's book gives an idea of what was involved here.

> Vengerova was hardly a believer in progressive education. Her word was law, and to fall short of her expectations was to welcome disaster. She was a tyrannical disciplinarian. For someone accustomed to America's let-the-little-darlings-express-themselves educational methods, entering her studio could be like waking up in a Spanish Inquisition. Her great weapon was fear. And fear works: the records are full of people who have performed impossible feats while motivated by great fear. . . .
>
> After a period in which Neal was one of Vengerova's special pets, "the day came when Vengerova asked no further questions. She had made up her mind; I was to be wrenched from one way of life, and forcibly implanted in another one. Even after her announcement that the honeymoon was over, I remained unworried. However, the whole of Harry Neal was a mass of bad habits. In order to build a new structure which could withstand any storm, it would be necessary to destroy the old one. She then set about to destroy the Harry Neal who had been. . . . One of her comments to me was, '. . . I had a gifted student once and mentioned his name to Rachmaninoff. . . . You have heard of Rachmaninoff? . . . His only answer was, "Yes, so God gave the boy talent, but does he practice? You do not practice, and without practice you have nothing."'
>
> "Suddenly, brutally, as no one had ever done before, she was laying out my character for open inspection. I was lazy. I was spoiled. I was conceited. I felt sorry for myself. While admitting my ignorance, I was seeking to trade on the sympathy it aroused at Curtis, rather than producing great quantities of superior work." On and on she swept. "You have a frightful tendency toward amateurishness. In all your life you have never realized your possibilities. You never will, as long as you live, unless you completely change your way of thinking and living. And if you don't, neither I nor this institution will have any use for you. . . ."
>
> Isabella Vengerova was another of those who told her students that nothing was ever ready for performance. When a performance loomed, a lesson could go on until way past midnight. Her temper increased as the days before the concert diminished. Insults raged; sarcasm stung; furniture was thrown. She predicted doom and disgrace for everyone, herself in-

Why Complicate Life?
A Musician's Guide

	Go practice
Missing Somebody	~~Call~~
	Go practice
Wanna meet up?	~~Invite~~
	Go practice
Wanna be understood?	~~Explain~~
	Go practice
Don't like something?	~~Say it~~
	Go practice
Like something?	~~State it~~
	Go practice
Want something?	~~Ask for it~~
	Go practice
Love someone?	~~Tell it~~
Have questions?	Go practice

Figure 6.1. Would your students really be better off in the long run without the opportunities for friendship, love, and curiosity?

cluded. In gentler movements, however, she could become quite rational, giving advice like, "You must always be 200% prepared because as soon as you go out on stage you will absolutely forget 100% of what you know."

Reminiscences of my parents and of Koussevitzky! For an over-the-top comedic parody of this kind of instruction, see the YouTube video "Piano Lesson" by igudesma-nandjoo, https://www.youtube.com/watch?v=ZHyYGD33MyQ&list=PL86F70924F618C849.

The reader will not be surprised that, as a person with but a single life to live, I have always rejected such a philosophy as this one to be imposed, for any reason, on human beings of any age. If the world has changed in the past half century, this outlook on dealing with young people should, I believe, have died with humanity's willingness to use poison gas and nuclear weapons.

4. Eric Booth, *The Everyday Work of Art: Awakening the Extraordinary in Your Daily Life* (Lincoln, NE: Sourcebooks, 1999), 270.

5. Booth, *Everyday Work of Art*, 248.

6. Richard Florida, *The Rise of the Creative Class* (New York: Basic Books, 2002), 199–200.

7. Even in the summer of 1955, when I had the privilege of playing sonatas on a practically daily basis with Fuchs's students, I had the repeated experience that, as great a teacher and artist as Fuchs was, he never recovered from the frustration that he somehow deserved to be the soloist of celebrity he felt he had never become.

8. Materials here summarized on the remarkable career(s) of Raoul Berger are quoted from a letter to the author by Berger's son, Karl Berger, MD, of Philadelphia, dated October 27, 2002. See also Berger's own account, "A Fiddler Turned Lawyer," *Harvard Law School Bulletin*, October 1962, 1–7. There Berger summarizes the respective joys of the two quite different professions, including the fact that musicians are often reviewed by people who know little if anything about music, while attorneys get reviewed by their peers.

9. What was accomplished at Eastman during my administration was reinforced by an article in *Newsweek's College Guide 2008* on the nation's twenty-five "hottest" schools, including Cornell as "the hottest Ivy," the University of Florida as "hottest for sports fans," Cal Tech as "hottest for science and engineering," Harvard as "hottest for rejecting you," Tulane as "hottest on the rebound," Cooper Union as "hottest for free tuition," Johns Hopkins as "hottest for pre-meds," Princeton as "hottest for liberal arts," Smith as "hottest women's college," and the University of Texas at Austin as "hottest for saving America's schools." Eastman is there listed as "hottest music school," with the following comment: "Eastman is heaven for instrumentalists, but students also get to study at the University of Rochester, of which it is a part. It's perfect for aspiring musicians who don't want to sacrifice academics. That's why bassist Erin McPeck of Aurora, Colorado, chose Eastman; she's now planning a scholarly career in music research while working as a physics teaching intern at Rochester and participating in Eastman's Institute for Music Leadership. Applications were up 10 percent this year, more than the national average." I was delighted to read what *Newsweek* had printed, more than a decade after my leaving Eastman, excellent evidence that the brand I had tried to establish there was long lasting.

The *Newsweek* guide is relevant to an event that took place in Boston, on the Green Line, where, during the summer of 1999, the chairman of NEC's Board of Overseers had treated me to a wonderful dinner in Park Square, followed by attendance with him at baseball's All-Star game, held that season in Fenway Park. A young Eastman graduate got on at Arlington Street and greeted me warmly. "What are you doing these days?" I asked. She responded, "I play principal double bass in the Boston Philharmonia," a fine group that performs on a per-service basis. "That's fine," said I, "but what do you do to make a living?" "I manage the commercial properties at Logan Airport, a pretty time-consuming job, as you can imagine, but fun." My host followed up with an incredulous question of his own: "Did you get that job right out of East-man?" "No," she said, "my first job was to be in charge of the commercial properties at the Prudential Center."

SEVEN

Advice for Music Deans

Building Educational Programs for the New Century

This chapter is addressed to current and prospective music deans. I'd like to begin by sharing some of my experiences as a tyro dean, a new leader entirely unused to the territory.

As related in chapter 3, my parents helped provide me with an excellent general education, with a fine musical education, and with plenty of professional performing experience as oboist, pianist, and conductor. I had gone on to earn a Princeton PhD in musicology because I had decided on a career as a college professor and knew that a doctoral degree had become a necessity for admission to the dance. By the time I had reached my midthirties, I saw myself as a jack-of-all-musical-trades, the fifteenth-best in the country in a broad array of musical subdisciplines, but nowhere close to being the national leader in any of them. Then, one day in the summer of 1972, I read in a Rochester newspaper that the University of Rochester was looking for a new director for its very well-endowed music school. Although my father warned me that Howard Hanson, a formidable force regarding all things Eastman, would never think kindly of a Harvard-Princeton graduate as director of the Eastman School, I thought that the two key figures were Samuel Adler as search committee chair and W. Allen Wallis, an economist from the University of Chicago who was chancellor of the University of Rochester.[1] I sat down to learn what I could about the outlooks of Adler and Wallis, imagining that, because Eastman had such a reputation for inbreeding, those men might have a favorable reaction to the candidacy of someone whose parents had graduated from Eastman but who had himself gone to Ivy League schools. I spent two days and many iterations writing a letter of application, partly to explain my background as an Eastman descendent from the outside. In two paragraphs among half a dozen, I hinted at how Eastman had been missing the mark, but in a fashion designed to offend as few as possible. The first had to do with my view that Princeton had had a stronger composition faculty in the days of Roger Sessions, Milton Babbitt, Edward T. Cone, and Earl Kim. But I suggested that, with Sessions retired, Cone retired from active teaching, and Kim at Harvard, the appointment of new faculty who followed Milton Babbitt's in-and-of-itself excellent philosophy had weakened the diversity of Princeton's compositional offerings, a point of view especially relevant at the time to the Eastman School as a whole, though I was careful to imply that without stating it. My second paragraph had to do with defining the Eastman School as something radically different from a Juilliard imitator in the Snowbelt. Here I argued that the Eastman School had a huge sunk asset of already-committed funds in the Sibley Library, then by far the largest collection of any music school in the world and the third largest music collection in America, exceeded in size only by the music collections of the Library of Congress and the New York Public Library. I suggested that, if the Eastman School really wanted to compete with Juilliard on its own Lincoln Center turf, one ought to cut the Sibley Library budget by three quarters, putting the funds saved into faculty salaries and student financial aid. As an alternative, I proposed the strengthening of the musicology and theory faculties with men and women better able to exploit Sibley for the good of the school as a whole. Though the ad for the position not surprisingly indicated the importance of several years of previous administrative experience, my letter made it clear that I had had almost none.

I told the committee that I could be reached in Boston through the end of July, after which I was off for Europe to deliver a paper at the triennial meeting of the International Musicological Society in Copenhagen, followed by a monthlong tour of Europe with Luis Leguia, beginning with three concerts at the Berlin Festival. Hearing nothing by July 31, I successfully resisted the temptation to call Rochester.

During the summer, the committee and Allen Wallis offered the Eastman directorship to Grant Beglarian, a distinguished composer who had served the University of Southern California very successfully for several years as dean of the College of Fine Arts there. But Beglarian, a wonderful man, ended up by turning Rochester down. The committee, not able to recruit their first-choice candidate, began to think of younger people who might well accept the position if offered. And, fortunately for me, they thought of my candidacy.

When I returned from Europe in early October, I found a telephone message from Samuel Adler indicating that, were I still interested in the Eastman position, I might call him. I did so immediately, of course. After preliminary interviews with the search committee and Allen Wallis—the latter of which went on for six hours—I was visited in Boston for a morning by Robert Sproull, then UR president and a physicist, who spent his afternoon at MIT, I later learned, checking with my engineering and scientific colleagues on what sort of person Freeman might be. When my family and I were invited in early November for a three-day interview in Rochester, I knew from my first look at the agenda for my visit that I had the position if I did not mess up, for the itinerary ended with lunch on Sunday at the Country Club of Rochester with Sproull and Wallis, an invitation that followed half-hour meetings with a broad array of Eastman faculty and staff.

The moment I decided I really had won the Eastman directorship was in my Saturday interview with the late Everett Gates, then chairman of music education at Eastman. I thought it pretty clear, during the half-hour interview, that Professor Gates, a good violist, did not think much of the candidacy of someone from the Ivy League—until he remembered that, in the summer of 1935, he had played the Mozart duos for violin and viola on the radio with a pretty young violinist named Freeman who, he said, was eight months pregnant at the time. Then looking down at my résumé, for the first time, I thought, and noting that I had been born in August 1935, he looked up to say, incredulously, "That was you!" On the instant, we became friends. It is only partly a matter of what you know. Success depends, in equal measure, on one's resilience, on one's emotional intelligence, on one's ability to get outside of one's own culture, and on whom you know, as Malcolm Gladwell points out in *Outliers*. With that almost completely accidental connection of Professor Gates between Mozart duos in the summer of 1935 and the date of my own birth, I had made a friend.

I had at the time of my Eastman appointment almost no administrative experience. I was saved from my complete greenness by the fortune of reporting to Robert Sproull, a former Cornell provost, who went on in 1974 to serve a ten-year term as CEO of the University of Rochester. Said he, "Freeman, Allen Wallis, the faculty, and I think you know quite a lot about music. But we know that you have practically no experience in business and finance, and in administration for that matter. Thus, it will be important for you to remember that we are here to help you. If you don't know what to do, don't fake. Just call, and we will help." And, until his retirement from UR in June of 1984, he did exactly that. It was also Bob Sproull's idea that I divide the secondary line of direct reporting to the director between Dan Patrylak, Walter Hendl's chief deputy, and a new person, whom Sproull suggested should be "someone who loves music, is a friend of yours, and has an MBA." That person turned out to be Wendell Brase, a twenty-five-year-old MBA from MIT who had played tuba in the MIT Symphony and had four years of experience as the chief administrative aide of the CEO of J.C. Penney. I learned as much from Brase as I did from Sproull, though several members of the Eastman staff, people in their fifties, bridled at the idea of reporting to a man as young as Wendell, who in the meantime has gone on to serve, very successfully, as the vice chancellor for business and administration at the Santa Cruz and Irvine campuses of the University of California.

The first time I met as a tyro dean with the Eastman faculty chairs, I proposed cutting sixty thousand dollars from half a dozen annual concerts with the Rochester Philharmonic, in which all twenty or so of Eastman's annual performance certificate winners got to play full concertos with the RPO, conducted by Howard Hanson and Walter Hendl. In my reasoning, the school would be a lot better off were those funds transferred to faculty salaries and to student financial aid. But when I proposed the idea to the faculty chairs, I was told by all hands that beginning with such a radical change in policy would be dangerous. I went home, wondering what I had to do to try to get the faculty chairs behind what I considered an important opening initiative. I waited a couple of months before asking whether student financial aid was adequate to our needs. When told that it was not, I distributed a copy of a skeletal budget, asking each of the chairs to report back at our next meeting on their recommendations about where to find the needed money. They proposed all sorts of things two weeks later, among them the cut in Philharmonic services, which was implemented for the following season. It all depends, I decided, on investing the faculty with the director's willingness to listen carefully to their ideas and to finding ways of acting on the most important ones. (This is an idea that seems obvious in the new millennium but was something of a novelty in an institution that had been led rather autocratically for its first half century.) While Howard Hanson never listened much to his faculty, that time in American history had clearly passed. (The problem just sketched is also relevant to the relationship of the well-endowed Eastman School to the rest of the Rochester community, almost all of which feels that the generous endowment left by Mr. Eastman for his music school should be shared with the rest of the Rochester community, explicitly against the terms of George Eastman's will.)

But as we approached the winter holidays of my first full year in office, 1973–1974, the ceiling fell in, with all hell breaking loose. Allen Wallis desperately wanted to move the Eastman School to the university's River Campus, an attractive place on the banks of the Genesee River, three miles south of Eastman, itself located in the midst of a badly decaying downtown. In February 1973, he invited me for lunch to discuss the school's future geographic location—whether to renovate downtown or to move, abandoning the 3,094-seat Eastman Theatre (just renovated by Kodak with a grant of two million dollars) and beautiful Kilbourn Hall, one of the world's great chamber auditoria and building an entirely new facility on the River Campus, where we could begin developing future audiences, a move vehemently opposed by the faculty, the students, the alumni, and the community. At my lunch with Chancellor Wallis, I tried to present both sides of the argument: on the one hand, the strong opportunity for closer integration of the school within the university, of which it had been a part since its founding in 1921; on the other hand, the historical roots of the institution in a beautiful facility of which George Eastman and Rochester had been very proud. I worried, too, I said, about the enormous incremental expense of building anew, of raising the necessary funds for such a facility in the midst of a major public controversy, and about the fact that to that point no reasonable location had been uncovered on the River Campus for a new Eastman School. I led with the arguments for moving, and closed with the rationale for staying put and renovating—only to be told by the chancellor that my closing arguments were the most fatuous he had ever heard. (Those were his very words!) I pled for time for consultation with the faculty, students, and alumni, though it was clear that if I wanted to hold on to a very promising new position, I was in no position to buck a determined chancellor. This was profoundly depressing, for it immediately suggested that I had been selected not for my abilities or background but, at least in part, because the chancellor thought I was green enough not to be able to withstand in the school's possible interest what he was convinced was in the overriding interests of the university. It may be important, I have decided in the meantime, to come to an at least preliminary understanding with one's potential employer, before accepting a position, on *why* one is being appointed to an important position.

After lots of public haranguing now recalled by the tea party assaults on health care reform of August 2009, we presented a proposal to the trustees for a move to the main campus at a specially convened meeting in Toronto, the confidential result of which was immediately leaked by one of the trustees to the local papers. These, not surprisingly, exploded with rants against the chancellor and myself, further inflaming the Eastman community.[2] I was booed at the annual Christmas Sing, usually a warm and happy conclusion for the fall semester; faculty and students produced bumper stickers urging that the school not be moved; and signs appeared in the men's rooms urging that the new director be flushed. As a result, I consulted privately with Howard W. Johnson, my former boss at MIT, where I had made tenure just before leaving for Rochester. He offered me my old job back but suggested that I stall in Rochester, and I proceeded to try to do so, from the departure of Chancellor Wallis in the winter of 1974–1975 till the appointment of Sproull as his successor in May of 1974. That I ultimately stayed in Rochester for nearly a quarter century as Eastman director is a gift I owe primarily to three people: my second wife, Carol, who has always sustained me through the heaviest going; Jon Engberg, associate director of the school between 1975 and his retirement in 1994, a hardworking, highly intelligent, and very loyal deputy; and Robert Sproull, the second UR CEO to whom I reported.

Shortly after taking office, Bob Sproull asked for my advice on the location of the Eastman School for the next quarter century. I responded in a white paper that the issue of the school's location had become such a contentious one that I thought it would ruin his presidency, especially in the midst of a serious recession, were we to try to move. As a result, he accepted the idea of staying downtown, provided Eastman with $5.5 million for what we called a short-term renovation, ably directed by Wendell Brase, in which we reduced the number of gross square feet while raising the number of usable square feet, thereby freeing up nearly a million dollars a year for increased faculty salaries and student financial aid on a budget base of $8 million. Bob Sproull and I worked collaboratively and positively together for the balance of his administration, and we have remained close friends ever since. I consider him in every way my principal administrative mentor. The fact that I did not resign in the winter of 1973–1974, as I came close to doing out of sheer despair, has always suggested to me that resilience is an important mark for any leader. The path is not always downhill with the wind at your back, but if the enterprise is an important one, courage and good advice from those one can trust and who know the turf are important.

Our "short-term" renovation of the downtown facility that was and is Eastman was so announced, partly to mollify the outgoing chancellor, who went on to become one of Ronald Reagan's undersecretaries of state for eight additional years of very productive work, partly to produce pressure on the City of Rochester and the County of Monroe to invest in the area immediately around the Eastman School. This strategy worked, though I was at first attacked in the press and by the ACLU for the new "cultural district" legislation that banned strip bars, porno shops, and massage parlors from the school's neighborhood. The university's investment of $5.5 million produced an additional investment of $18 million, split evenly by the city and the county, leading to a marked upgrading of the entire neighborhood and to a good deal of additional private investment for the area. This was a project notably supported by the work of my able stepson, Scott Henry, who produced a moving computer-driven multi-image show called "George Eastman's Vision," shown for a critical year at locations all over Greater Rochester. The project of remaining downtown took so much of my time that in 1983 I won the Chamber of Commerce's annual civic medal for my contribution to keeping downtown Rochester alive.

Whether Bob Sproull's decision to follow my recommendation was the right one or not, we will learn, I suppose, in another half century, for the forces undermining the future of Northeastern cities of Rochester's size are powerful, and the lack of contact between the education of musicians and of those who will ultimately be their audiences is now more problematic than ever. The most important lesson I learned from all this includes protecting beginning deans from too heavy an emotional load and the importance for the leaders of all colleges to focus with equal zeal on short-, mid-, and long-term futures. As dean, one gets nowhere without understanding that the school one heads is part of a living, breathing community that includes students, parents, staff, alumni, community, and leaders of the discipline itself, all of whose sometimes conflicting interests must be carefully balanced.

I was almost immediately confronted with an equally unhappy personnel situation. Eastman's Department of Music Education recommended a man in his midfifties for promotion to a tenured associate professorship with a dossier so weak that I did not see how it could possibly sustain scrutiny by the provost and the anonymous ad hoc faculty committee appointed in Rochester to advise the provost on each tenure case put forward by one of the deans. As a result, it was my unhappy responsibility, as I saw it, to tell the man, early on a Friday afternoon, that I felt unable to recommend him for tenure and, as a result, that the following academic year would be his last at Eastman. Later the same afternoon, he was admitted to a local hospital. And before twenty-four hours passed, he had died, a terrible shock to us all, for there was no previous medical history that I had known of. On Monday morning, I telephoned the man's widow to extend personal and institutional condolences and to let her know how deeply sorry I was about what had happened. Understandably, she was very upset and let me know about that in no uncertain terms, in a conversation that lasted half an hour but seemed eternal. When I spoke with Bob Sproull, he described academic administration as a voyage between Scylla and Charybdis. Scylla, he suggested, represented the problem of hemorrhaging psychologically to the degree that one went home and beat his wife while kicking his dog. Charybdis, in Sproull's metaphor, stood for getting so good at annealing one's emotions that one became an excellent candidate for commandant at Auschwitz. "The problem," said Sproull, "is that the distance between the rock and the whirlpool is very short, and that the rate of hourly pay in such positions is relatively low. The fun," said he, "is in having a role in making the institution stronger and more competitive, a happy and productive place for the faculty and staff to work, and a place in which students of real promise go on to discover careers ideally suited to each of them," a proposition that I believe my twenty-four-year stay as Eastman director made possible. I am afraid, too, that though the federal government forbids us all from discriminating on the basis of age, I have ever afterward looked for faculty whose accomplishments already earned them tenure, or for faculty young enough that failure to make tenure would not preclude further happy career development at another institution.

From the early history of music schools in the United States, leadership was normally chosen from the ranks of composers and outstanding performers: George Chadwick, Quincy Porter, and Gunther Schuller at the New England Conservatory; Antonin Dvorak at Jeanette Thurber's New York Conservatory; Howard Hanson and Walter Hendl at Eastman;

Josef Hofmann, Randall Thompson, Efrem Zimbalist, and Rudolf Serkin at Curtis; Ernest Hutchison, William Schuman, and Peter Mennin at Juilliard. My appointment represented, I believe, the beginning of a new model, an effort to select leadership from those who have had a broad education in music and were willing, like the presidents of colleges and universities, to devote large amounts of time raising money, while developing, with the support of the faculty, a vision for the institution that would differentiate it from its competition. After thirty-four years as a director, president, and dean, I have come to think that the list of attributes that follows is important for those of you who seek posts of leadership in this area.

CHARACTERISTICS OF A GOOD MUSIC DEAN

- Intelligence. But, as Malcolm Gladwell points out in *Outliers,* there are people with very high IQs who are fools.
- A broad experience in music. But because of how higher education is structured and tenure is achieved, musical breadth of the kind I was able to attain is hard to come by, inevitably putting at risk, in a way I did not adequately appreciate when I was young, the further development of a meaningful relationship with one's spouse.
- Good listening skills. Though these ought to be relatively easy for a musician to develop, it is surprising how much some of us like to talk. I consider my own listening skills both vital and at the same time the weakest part of my armamentarium. I remind myself daily to listen more attentively.
- Judgment. I'm not sure how to acquire this except by doing a lot of reading, asking hard questions, and learning from the judgment of mentors, inevitably older men and women who have already passed over the course.
- Good synthesizing abilities. The ability to connect people with one another by seeing in others abilities that can profit from new relationships among them—and to connect ideas in the same fashion. My own best synthesis to date I consider to be Joseph Schwantner's *New Morning for the World.* In that work, Joe's moving music supports the equally moving words of Dr. Martin Luther King Jr. By connecting the project with the interests of the NAACP and the Urban League, the impressive skill set of the late Willie Stargell (whose voice and presence had impressed me through his interaction with the media immediately after the Pittsburgh Pirates won the 1979 World Series), David Effron's superb leadership of the Eastman Philharmonia, the dedication of our Eastman students, and the work of a very effective staff, working together as a team, we had a real winner. All this led to superb national press, a White

House reception given by President and Mrs. Reagan, and a national NPR broadcast of the premiere performance from a packed Kennedy Center on Dr. King's first publicly celebrated birthday.

- Abilities in reading, writing, and speaking English. You are called on as dean to produce an unending stream of letters, memoranda, reports, papers, and five-minute speeches. A prospective dean who finds it difficult to do this will have no time to accomplish the other myriad details of the job, even with a fine professional staff.
- A willingness to spend lots of time raising money. Helpful to me was the idea that the worst thing that could happen was that the potential donor might say no. I once learned from a vice president for fund-raising at Stanford that no is not really no until the client has declined to give on six occasions! "I'd give you one million dollars were it not for the recent drop in the stock market" may be an invitation to return for a second visit a month after the market recovers.
- Resilience, emotional intelligence, and courage. The human problems you deal with as an administrator are sometimes difficult. Having trusted associates with whom you can consult in absolute confidence greatly helps in keeping your moral and emotional compass pointed true north. Jon Engberg and Douglas Dempster were both enormously important to my success, in Rochester and at Texas. In my second year at Eastman, I began to feel a lot better when Francis Tursi, then chair of the faculty's Committee on Committees, visited me with the news that the faculty had decided they could trust me. As a result, he had come to present me with a check for $250,000 that the faculty had saved as a reserve against what they feared might eventually necessitate a faculty strike. Naturally, I put the funds they had entrusted to me into improved faculty salaries.
- Integrity and trust. Without a reputation for truth telling, the game is lost. In fact, without this, there is no game. That does not require you to say only nice things. It means that the truth is always the truth. It is vital for all hands to be able to trust the head of the institution. The dean, of course, must be able to trust those reporting to him to follow through on what has been discussed and agreed upon. The passive aggression of a deputy who says he agrees on matters of policy but then tries to misrepresent his boss by misrepresenting the truth must be stopped, by termination if necessary. In all such matters, a dependable paper trail, summarizing what has been agreed to, is vital.
- An understanding of the institution's table of organization and a respect for it. In some schools you report to a provost, in others to a lay board of trustees, and in still others to a dean of fine arts. That Texas has a more complicated table of organization than Oberlin results from the fact that Texas is forty times Oberlin's size, requir-

ing an intermediate layer of management by deans. Each institution has a different mission and a different history. At Eastman, I used to point out that it was a provost's job to extract money, as painlessly as possible, from the director, for Eastman, by any order of measurement, is a much more affluent institution than any other part of the University of Rochester. At Texas, on the other hand, the dean gets money from the provost, a more traditional modus operandi. In either case, a trusting relationship with the person to whom you report and with the people who report to you is simply indispensable.

- The development of a thick Rolodex. The more good and imaginative people you know, the easier it is to ask them to do favors for one another, thereby strengthening the institution and developing the dean's reputation for helpfulness.
- Ego control. The mission of the dean is to help strengthen the institution and its people, not to project one's own personality and beliefs onto others. This means taking great pride in the composing, conducting, performing, and scholarship of your colleagues, and in a willingness to accept the ideas of others.
- A sense of humor. This does not mean the necessity of endlessly telling jokes, though Abraham Lincoln often found joke telling a useful way of getting through painful meetings. It means the necessity of not taking yourself more seriously than necessary.
- A willingness to hire people smarter and more talented than yourself. The role of the dean is to help make the institution stronger, a mission that can be fulfilled only by appointing the most able people available and listening hard to their ideas. There was a time in the history of the Eastman School when Bartok, Hindemith, Schönberg, and Stravinsky could all have joined Eastman's composition faculty. To be sure, none of them had been born in the United States, and music by American composers was a central aspect of Howard Hanson's creed. I believe, however, that a potential role for any of them in Rochester would have strengthened the whole fabric of music in America, an opportunity missed.
- A willingness to forgive and forget. If a disagreement results in a genuine misunderstanding, there is no reason why you should not apologize and move on. Learning new truths is a valuable exercise for all of us, so long as trust is not impaired.
- A willingness to work hard in behalf of many other people. While the annual pay rate for a dean is not bad, the hourly rate is terrible, as Bob Sproull once said. This means attending not only lots of meetings you might prefer not to undertake but also lots and lots of recitals and concerts. Thus you must be prepared to work at any hour of the day or night. While the general public can walk out after the performance of a third of a program, the dean may not, at

least not without offending and undermining the self-confidence of faculty and students. My good friend Charles Webb, the distinguished dean of what is now the Jacobs School of Music at Indiana University, once installed in his kitchen a listening system that allowed him sensibly to monitor recital activities in his school's several auditoria. Negative reaction from the faculty, which didn't want the dean to listen without their being able to see him, persuaded Charles quickly that this was not a wise policy.

- Knowing when it is time to step down. Though we are all living longer than we used to, none of us lives forever, and none of us can anticipate when his time will come. While it is sometimes hard to give up piloting a school or university, especially if one is still in good health, it always concerned me that Howard Hanson found it so difficult to let go. Thus, when I came to Texas, I told Provost Sheldon Ekland-Olson that I would love to work as dean for one final six-year term, through my seventy-first birthday. When that event took place, I was provided with a year of paid leave and a generously endowed professorship, through which, on Tuesdays and Thursdays, I get to teach future musicians what I have learned to this point from fifty years of teaching and administration, while enjoying the opportunity to spend more time with my wife and do more reading, more writing, and more playing than is possible as a dean or director.

CONFLICTS OF INTEREST

Though I was honored in 1972 to succeed Howard Hanson and Walter Hendl in the directorship of the Eastman School of Music, I quickly learned that, in the final third of the twentieth century, different kinds of skills were needed for positions of the kind at hand. If the dean or director (it really doesn't matter what the person is called so long as the table of organization makes it clear to whom he or she reports) thinks of himself as a conductor or a pianist, you are apt to develop a toxic tug-of-war with the faculty. The chief orchestral conductor is the person on whom one must count for the highest musical-performance standards, even if additional rehearsal is necessary. While the wind, brass, and percussion faculty can be counted on to take a strong interest in the large ensemble performances of their students—for that is where most successful wind and brass players will find work—you must understand from the outset that most of the string faculty do not feel the same way. As the result, I decided, nearly from the beginning of my years at Eastman, that I would abjure conducting.

To keep the peace between conductor and the faculty relevant to an orchestra, I required the orchestra conductor, in a meeting with myself as director, to negotiate each season with the string, wind, brass, and percussion faculties. As a result, the conductor decided out front what the repertory for the following seasons would comprise, an arrangement that required him to accomplish performances of that repertory at a high artistic level, within time limits already agreed upon. The scheduling of additional rehearsal time, especially at the last minute, could be accomplished only with my sign-off. Our exceedingly fine orchestral conductor learned to consult with the faculty on the seating of principal players and to confer with them privately on the work of students whom he felt were unable to meet his high technical and artistic standards. There was, I stressed, in an educational environment, no room for acting like Toscanini or Reiner. While I could have conducted from time to time, I suppose, I decided I did not want to risk undermining the regimen I had established in this area for the faculty. With the future of the American orchestra now in such severe jeopardy, future deans of at least some of the nation's 638 professional music schools should be questioning the centrality of the symphony orchestra to institutional planning and enrollment.

Piano playing is, of course, something entirely different. If you play too well, the faculty believes you have been practicing too much, and if you don't play well enough, the faculty is justifiably embarrassed. I raise this issue because I believe that, if the administrative head of the organization likes to make music, he or she should be encouraged occasionally to do so. The alternative is the development in a successful dean of further administrative ambition, for provosts and presidents are inevitably better compensated than are deans and directors. During my own career at Eastman, I was offered three other major-league deanships, two University of California executive vice chancellor positions and the presidency of a major university. All these paid better than my Eastman position, and all were turned down, for a variety of reasons, of which the most important was a continuing dedication to changing the world of musical education in America, the subject of this book. The fact that I did so inevitably had a positive effect on Presidents Robert Sproull and Dennis O'Brien, for while I never tried to negotiate a higher salary through an outside offer, I was always eager that the people to whom I reported understood that I could move if I felt I needed to, at least during my forties and fifties.

FACULTY DEVELOPMENT

Your most important asset is the excellence and loyalty of the faculty. And the most important quality of any faculty is its conviction that tomorrow will be better than today, that they have a vital say in the institution's evolving policies, and that their role is to recruit, teach, and place in the profession of music young people of excellence and promise. At

Rochester I set to work improving an already excellent faculty. Working largely with faculty search committees, I was able to add some very attractive new people, while reserving for myself the authority to make occasional appointments that did not initially enjoy broad popular support. The first of these was of the late Jan DeGaetani,[3] with whom I had recorded for Desto a song cycle by my MIT colleague and friend David Epstein. Jan, a Juilliard mezzo then in her early forties, was known not only for her superb work in music of the twentieth century but for a spectacularly broad range of other musical interests, ranging from the Middle Ages (she had been part of Noah Greenberg's Pro Musica Antiqua) to the giants of the nineteenth century. She was at the same time a gifted and dedicated teacher. Though in 1973 Jan's appointment produced local controversy at Eastman, for she excelled in a repertory not then generally popular with other voice faculty, it provided me with instant national credibility as a music school director. That other might think, "If Jan DeGaetani wants to move to Rochester, someone must be looking to the future there; perhaps I ought to accept Freeman's invitation," was a powerful force on my behalf at a time when no one knew my name. Bob Sproull, who had to sign off on such matters, understood this well and agreed without difficulty. (There are some advantages to working in a private institution!) Other important Eastman appointments made without the support of search committees included the pianist David Burge (a specialist in twentieth-century repertory and an unusually thoughtful and broadly based musician), the Cleveland Quartet (one of the two or three most important international string quartets of their time), and David Higgs, now the school's brilliant chair of Eastman's organ program.

But a great many other strong appointments were made as a result of the work of a long series of faculty search committees. Unless the director listens carefully to such committees, it is hard to get good faculty members to serve on committees, and the school's integrity and morale are undermined. I believe that, while each new faculty member must meet or surpass institutional standards, the goal of the most successful dean or director, with the support of provost and president, is team building. While professional distinction is important as a means of drawing good students, the faculty members who teach heavy loads with dedication and accomplishment are as important as the DeGaetanis, the stars who teach necessarily lower loads. Just as Michael Lewis tells us in *Money Ball*, the team that wins the World Series includes pitching, balanced offence and defense, those who can run like the wind and veterans who know what it feels like to win big games, those who are just beginning their professional careers and others who are capable of mentoring their junior colleagues in moments of crisis. In the competition among music schools, the prize goes to the faculty that works together as a team, focusing in every case on what consultative judgment can accomplish on behalf of each student. In what follows, I shall attempt to show how this was accomplished in each department at Eastman.

Composition

Chaired by Samuel Adler, still a force of nature in his eighties and now teaching at Juilliard, the Eastman composition faculty I met in 1972 also included Warren Benson, Wayne Barlow, and Joseph Schwantner. To that group, over the twenty-four years that followed, we added Sydney Hodkinson (the very able director of Eastman's Music Nova Ensemble), Christopher Rouse (one of Eastman's many Pulitzer Prize winners), Augusta Reed Thomas, Robert Morris, Allen Schindler, and David Liptak, strong voices quite different from one another who worked together splendidly, providing departmental majors with weekly private instruction set up in such a way that every student had, over the four years of undergraduate study, four different private composition teachers. I thought it important to move away from the Eastman orthodoxy of compositional style that had marked the school during Howard Hanson's long regime, and with the help of those listed above, I believe that goal was strongly accomplished. Each student, it has always seemed to me, represents a unique combination of skills and potentials that have been encouraged by musical mentors met along the way, each of whom has the possibility of opening up new ideas, new enthusiasms, new accomplishments, new contributions to music. A true school represents the potential for hundreds of human interactions among those possibilities — in which the faculty and students influence one another, just as faculty learn from one another, and encourage their students to do so as well.

Conducting

To the original group that included Donald Hunsberger, Gustav Meier, and Rayburn Wright, we added Sydney Hodkinson, David Effron (now head of orchestral activities at Indiana), Donald Neuen (now head of the choral program at UCLA), Philip West, Bill Dobbins, Fred Sturm, and Bill Weinert. The choral program was always a problem, involving a long series of very good choral conductors, most of whom did not make tenure. It is my own observation, having served as head of three quite different educational institutions, that the higher the quality of a voice faculty, the greater the problems for the choral conductor. After the departure from Eastman of yet another good choral conductor, I once proposed to Jan DeGaetani that we simply drop the choral program. Said she, "You can't possibly do that. The *St. Matthew Passion*, the *Mozart Requiem*, the *Missa Solemnis*, and the *Symphony of Psalms* are all such important masterpieces that all young musicians should know them well. You should understand, however, that my own students will be soloists, and thus should not sing in a chorus. No voice major should have to sing more than two hours a day." The idea of making a large chorus in 1973 out of Eastman and River Campus students was a complete failure, partly because of the distance between the campuses, partly because of the political problems that resulted from controversy about the school's possible relocation, and partly because while the Eastman students had better voices, the River Campus students had greater facility in reading music, resulting in continuing disagreements of the kind one meets in *Peter and the Wolf*, between a bird who cannot swim and a duck who cannot fly.

Humanities

To a group that included Alice Benston, Jessie Kneisel, Gilbert Kilpack, Mary Aversano, and Ruth Gross, all excellent people, we added some real stars, including David Roberts (who left to teach history at the University of Georgia), Douglas Dempster (eventually my successor as dean at the University of Texas at Austin), John McGowan (now director of the Institute for the Arts and Humanities at the University of North Carolina at Chapel Hill), Jonathan Baldo, Ann Sen, Ernestine McHugh, Jean Pedersen, and Timothy Scheie. The continuing national oversupply of very gifted PhDs in the humanities made it relatively easy to hire very good people in this area, one that I thought should be strong enough to persuade Eastman students that the abilities to read with nuance and to write and speak with power were important skills for a modern musician. I was eager for Eastman students, separated as they were from young people working in other intellectual domains, to experience daily the excitement that other human beings gain from the life of the mind. While Eastman taught French, Italian, and German, for example, those interested in Chinese, Japanese, or Russian pursued those studies at the River Campus. Eastman humanities faculty were sufficiently productive in their own disciplines that they were welcome guests to teach more specialized graduate courses on the River Campus, normally with the costs of such instruction covered by the Eastman School.

Music Education

To the original faculty of Everett Gates, Milford Fargo, and Donald Shetler, we added Roy Ernst (founder of the New Horizons Band movement, an inspired idea), Donna Brink Fox, Richard Grunow, and Louis Bergonzi. The original idea of Eastman's program was that the school's music education graduates would be good (if not virtuosic) musicians, intelligent people who were certified to teach music in the public schools of New York State. But, as elsewhere in America, the evolution after World War II of what had been teachers' colleges into research universities persuaded many of the nation's academic assessors that music educators should stress, not inspired music making, but statistically oriented treatises, often but marginally related to music. (The silliest music education dissertation I ever read was nearly five hundred pages long, filled with numbers, an investigation of whether the job description for a junior high school band director in Ohio should be the same as or different from that of the music director of the Boston Symphony. The conclusion—that differing job descriptions require different kinds of preparation—could, I thought, have been inferred at the outset, without a statistical apparatus designed to impress a true academic.) Thus, the words "OK for music ed" on an Eastman admissions file of my administration were a code for "nice person, plays decently, intelligent, can afford to pay," for the primary institutional goal was no more to train school teachers than would have been the case at the time at Harvard or Princeton, for example. Providing the nation's schools with teachers capable of leading inspired music making by young people remains, I think, a largely unfulfilled national goal. Persuading local school systems to hire inspired teachers, pay them enough that they will be persuaded to become teachers, and provide them with enough time in the curriculum to actually teach would be, I am persuaded, not only good for the future of music but also in the national interest.

When I moved to Texas in 1999, I dealt with a case in which the music faculty had failed a young music education violinist as the result of her freshman jury. In her visit of appeal with me, she said she knew she was neither Heifetz nor Perlman and that she wanted simply to be a public school music teacher in Texas. I told her what the faculty had urged—a philosophy with which I agree fully and which I hope permeates this book—that teaching music is a very special mission, one requiring excellent musicianship and a great deal of enthusiasm for music teaching and for children. I told her, "My colleagues and I think that you are an intelligent person but not a very promising musician. If you want to stay at the University of Texas, you can continue to study the violin, but you should major in philosophy, psychology, or physics, for example. If you insist on trying to be a public school music teacher, you will have to transfer to another university." She did so.

When I moved to Boston in 1996, I discovered that the New England Conservatory had a program with the Boston Symphony, WGBH, and the Boston public school system then known as the Boston Music Education Collaborative. Apparently a good idea, I neither invented it nor killed it. But I discovered, from annual springtime concerts in Jordan Hall that, while the participating students from Boston's inner-city neighborhoods were well behaved and well groomed, the general level of music making from three-quarters of the eighteen groups performing was so low in my judgment as not to merit the investment of student time. The question, I think, is not whether children should study music in elementary school, but whether the musicianship and pedagogic skills of the teachers guiding them are sufficiently high as to warrant the effort. I have come to believe that it is in our vital interest as a discipline that we make that effort, now and in the future. Part of the problem with the collaborative was that, of the 105 members of the Boston Symphony, only six were interested in presenting informances in the public schools, and of the six who were interested, only two were very good at doing so. When I offered free instruction at the conservatory on how to make attractive presentations in the public schools, no one in Symphony Hall was interested.

Musicology

Begun in the 1930s by Charles Warren Fox, this department in 1972 included Edward Evans, Hendrik van der Werf, and Jerald Graue, to whom we were able to add Jürgen Thym (long-term chair and builder of his department), Ralph Locke, Alfred Mann, Patrick Macey, Ellen Koskoff, Kim Kowalke, Gretchen Wheelock, Kerala Snyder, and Virginia Newes. This cohort of distinguished scholars offered not only broad historical coverage but also showed strong interests in performance practice problems and in ethnomusicology. When Abram Loft told me that he did not believe the Eastman undergraduate musicology curriculum served the interests of the school's string students, I sent him to Jürgen Thym, and reforms were quickly instituted that satisfied the members of both departments.

Music Theory

To a faculty that had been dominated for many years by Allen MacHose and a largely vertical approach to music theory, Robert Gauldin and I added David Beach, Robert Morris, Patrick McCreless (later chair of Yale's Department of Music), Dorothy Payne, Robert Wason, David Headlam, Matthew Brown, Steven Laitz, Elizabeth Marvin West, and Marie Rolf (current head of graduate studies at the school). The emphasis shifted from a philosophy dominated by Rameau (1683–1764) and by harmony to the more contrapuntal outlook of Heinrich Schenker (1868–1935) and to the impact of music theory on actual performance. Undergraduate emphasis remained strong in basic musicianship and ear training, while graduate studies turned to speculative and historical theory and to the relationship of theory to the performance of music. We knew we were making progress when graduate students not accepted in our doctoral studies program began to turn up among Yale's graduate students!

Organ

David Craighead and Russell Saunders, both gifted players, very successful teachers, and close personal friends, were the cream of American organ teaching in 1972. The only problem was that they were almost exactly the same age. And what I feared might happen eventually took place. David Craighead, whose wife became ill, decided to retire, and Russell Saunders, when only in his early seventies, suffered a fatal heart attack. The subsequent appointments of Gerre Hancock, David Higgs, Michael Ferris (who died suddenly while still very young), William Porter, and Hans Daviddson have allowed the school to continue one of its strongest and most respected programs, recently adding focus on historical organ construction. With the establishment of the Craighead-Saunders Organ (initiated by a very generous bequest in the will of Russell Saunders, furthered by Russell's nonagenarian mother, Hazel, who decided on the name of the instrument as a result of her son's close friendship with David Craighead) in Christ Church Episcopal, just south of the school on East Avenue, Eastman has completed an unusually strong ensemble of performance instruments. (In the mid-1970s, as part of the school's "short-term" renovation, we had turned what had been Howard Hanson's baronial office—which I used to call the Hall of the Mountain King—into a ninety-seat organ recital room with a two-manual tracker by Jan van Daalem, just what Professors Craighead and Saunders had wanted at the time, a move that helped impress the faculty that I was more interested in the future of the institution than in having an impressive office.)

Piano

The faculty of 1972 comprised Frank Glazer, Eugene List, Barry Snyder, and Brooks Smith; Cecile Genhart returned from Switzerland in 1974. Later additions included David Burge (giving the program, like much of the rest of the school, a much more contemporary tone), Robert Spillman and Jean Barr (successors in the art of collaborative piano playing to Brooks Smith), Anton Nel (now a highly valued colleague at the University of Texas at Austin), Natalia Antoniva, Tony Caramia, Rebecca Penneys, Alan Feinberg, Thomas Schumaker, and Nelita True, one of the century's great piano teachers.

Strings

To the original faculty of Millard Taylor, John Celentano, Carroll Glenn , Zvi Zeitlin, Francis Tursi, Ronald Leonard, Oscar Zimmermann, and Eileen Malone, we added the Cleveland Quartet (Donald Weilerstein, Peter Salaff, Martha Strongin Katz, and Paul Katz, eventually succeeded by Atar Arad, James Dunham, and William Preucil Jr.), Charles Castleman, Abram Loft, Sylvia Rosenberg, Catherine Tait, Lynn Blakeslee, Oleg Krysa, Heidi Castleman, George Taylor, John Graham, Robert Sylvester, Steven Doane, J. B. VanDemark, and Kathleen Bride. While the origins of the Eastman School facilitated close collaboration for many years with the Rochester Philharmonic, it was the sense in the mid-1960s that the nation's funding for the arts was on a dramatic upswing, produced by the nearly simultaneous development of the National Endowment for the Arts and eighty-five million dollars of support grants for American orchestras from the Ford Foundation, leading to what amounted to a divorce between the school and the orchestra. When David Zinman and I came to Rochester in 1972, myself as Eastman director and Zinman as the new music director of the RPO, I invited him for lunch, indicated that I wanted to develop a world-class music school, made plain that I had no interest in conducting, and showed that I was eager to work collaboratively with Zinman for the good of the community. I proposed that, in future searches involving orchestral instruments, Eastman search committees and I produce a list of five leading teachers of the instrument in question, while Zinman and his colleagues were to produce a list of five outstanding players, hoping to find the same name on both lists. When this suggestion toward rapprochement between the school and the orchestra fell on stony ground, with the orchestra going so far as to insist that any of its principal players had to be full-time RPO, I decided we would be best served by proceeding on our own, which as a well-endowed institution we could afford to do. (George Eastman's legal documents of the 1920s and 1930s specified that he wanted to endow a music school in his name as a division of the university, at the same time asking that the RPO, which he considered a community enterprise, not share in the income from the endowment he established.)

Especially in retrospect, a laissez-faire philosophy that permitted too many community not-for-profits went a long way toward undermining Rochester's potential, especially at a time when Rochester's principal industries were in decline. In addition to the University of Rochester and the Rochester Institute of Technology, a small city of declining population also supported Roberts-Wesleyan University, St. John Fisher College, Nazareth College, Monroe County Community College, and the Geneseo and Brockport campuses of SUNY. Besides the Rochester Philharmonic, there were Opera Theatre Rochester, the Rochester Chamber Music Society, the Rochester Chamber Orchestra, and a very good professional theater group known as GEVA, in addition to the Memorial Art Gallery, the Rochester Museum and Science Center, the International Museum of Photography, and the Margaret Woodbury Strong Museum. This many not-for-profits chasing a dwindling funding base was a recipe for continuing budget crises. (That such crises are not inevitable can be inferred from the spectacular success of Princeton, which strictly limits its size and has focused for many years on the liberal arts, taught and researched on an exceptionally high international level.)

Voice

The voice faculty I met in 1972, chaired by Leonard Treash, included Anna Kaskas, Helen Boatwright, Masako Toribara, and John Maloy. To these excellent people, we added Jan DeGaetani, Thomas Paul, Yi-Kwei Sze, Marcia Baldwin, Rita Shane, Dale Moore, Carol Webber, and Richard Pearlman, a faculty that helped produce some real operatic stars, including Rochester's Renée Fleming, for both sides of the Atlantic, as well as a large number of well-trained singers comfortable in the broadest range of musical repertory. The inclusion in the same department of Jan DeGaetani (a world-class artist with a necessarily small but very fine class) and John Maloy (a superb teacher who had not had a distinguished professional career but who did spectacular work as a teacher and as the chair of his department) emphasizes the advantage to a school of a dean (and provost) committed to institutional team building rather than on an insistence that one faculty profile fits all.

Winds, Brass, and Percussion

Because of the earlier collaboration with the Rochester Philharmonic, several world-class teachers had worked for both institutions, preferring a balanced life of playing and teaching in Rochester to all sorts of offered opportunities in larger cities. Flutist Joseph Mariano, oboist Robert Sprenkle, clarinetist Stanley Hasty, hornist-composer Verne Reynolds, bassoonist David Van Hoesen, trombonist Donald Knaub, tubist Cherry Beauregard, harpist Eileen Malone, and percussionist John Beck were the core of that group. Subsequent members of the department have included the flutists James Galway and Bonita Boyd; oboist Richard Killmer; clarinetists Charles Neidich, Peter Hadcock, and Kenneth Grant; saxophonist Ramon Ricker; hornist Peter Kurau; bassoonist John Hunt; trumpeters Barbara Butler, Charles Geyer, and James Thompson; and trombonist John Marcellus. They were all splendid players, but because most of them had but marginal relationships with the RPO, both institutions ended up paying higher salaries and necessarily requiring both higher teaching loads for full-time faculty members and greater stress on large-ensemble placement for Eastman students. (Frederick Fennell's inspired founding of the Eastman Wind Ensemble in the early 1950s was motivated by the fact that, even then, the school was unable to find enough large ensemble experience for wind and brass players, given the expense of string enrollment and the fact that Beethoven and Brahms symphonies require many more violins than oboes!)

FACULTY SALARIES

Recognizing that the faculty is the greatest capital you have as dean on which to build the reputation of a school, I always did my best to invest both thought and funds in the development of superior and loyal faculty. Partly, of course, this involves competitive compensation, which goes up as much as the school can afford. Because Eastman salaries had before my time been depressingly low, I made a point of determining the schools with whose salaries Eastman ought to compare itself. The Faculty Advisory Committee, the provost, the president, and I agreed that the comparison schools should be Indiana, Illinois, Oberlin, Michigan, Northwestern, USC, and Yale, adjusted in each case for the varying living costs of each locale. We agreed on an index for the salaries of assistant, associate, and full professors, averages that, during the course of my administration of the Eastman School, we matched or exceeded.

For the last dozen years or so of my Eastman administration, the best-compensated member of the faculty was oboist Richard Killmer. Though I never publicly identified him as such at the time, I have often described the characteristics that I thought made Dick Killmer so valuable a faculty member. To begin with, Killmer was a superb oboist, keenly interested in anything that had ever affected the oboe: the shawm, the English horn, the oboe d'amore, the oboe da caccia, or the heckelphone. He had cultivated, over time, an international network of friends who were also very good oboe teachers. All of these, including especially former students, were eager to see their own best students in Killmer's class, for which there were at most five annual openings, four for freshmen and one for a graduate student. As a result, the school normally received sixty annual applications from potential oboe students, of whom, from Killmer's point of view, any of what he called the top twenty were admissible. That made it possible for the admissions director to seek, among the five to be admitted, potential students with SAT scores of 1600 or with parents who earned one million dollars or more a year and thus did not need scholarship funds for their sons and daughters. Finally, the admissions director and I understood that, year after year, all of Killmer's students accepted our offers of admission, thus making it possible for the school to avoid admitting too many oboists simply as a way of balancing budgets. Killmer made it a practice to call the unsuccessful candidates and their teachers, to say how sorry he was that he had not been able to admit all of the top talents he had wanted, gently urging the teachers of unsuccessful candidates to try again in the following year. Once a student matriculated in his class, Killmer not only worked hard to help each of his students succeed as an oboist—through dedicated and personalized instruction—but also attended as many of the student's rehearsals and concerts as possible, conferring with ensemble directors on the perceived strengths and weaknesses of each young oboist and holding regular counseling

sessions on the students' evolving dreams and aspirations. From Killmer's perspective, winning a major oboe position, as a player or a teacher, was just fine. But, he believed, so was a career as a conductor or
composer, as a U.S. senator, or as the CEO of a major corporation. Because he felt it was productive of the greatest happiness to play the oboe,
he always urged those who did not go into music professionally to continue to play avocationally.

But salaries are not the only means of faculty development. Administratively supported projects toward professional development have a
major payoff in morale. At Eastman these included faculty appearances
on an annual series of four institutional concerts in Lincoln Center's Alice
Tully Hall, support for publications approved by distinguished university presses, support for recordings on a broad array of professional labels, and support for commissions of new work, both by faculty composers and for faculty performers. (An eventual bequest of two million dollars from the estate of Howard Hanson to found the school's Howard
Hanson Institute for American Music was very helpful in providing
funds for the latter.) Not to be forgotten is what I have always found the
most positive motivator of all: a few appreciative words from time to
time in recognition of faculty achievement and contribution. There is
nothing quite so powerful as an occasional pat on the back for expressing
thanks!

Very important for the functioning of the Eastman School was my
dependence on a strong group of faculty chairs, each of whom could be
counted on to build the strongest unit of which he or she was capable,
working constantly to find people who would help connect that unit to
the school's other departments. When a dean cannot find strong departmental leadership, it is your obligation, after consultation with the provost, to put that unit under receivership, running its faculty searches
yourself or through your associate director for academic affairs, until
strong departmental leadership can be recruited.

SHOULD A COLLEGIATE MUSIC SCHOOL INCLUDE A PREP DEPARTMENT?

A critical question for any music dean[4] is the role of a preparatory department or community education program. On the one hand, schools
that are parts of universities will deal with provosts who believe, quite
naturally, that such institutions represent the world of higher, postsecon-
dary education. On the other hand, the skills of execution and ear-training that a young musician should have developed by the time he matric-
ulates as a college freshman should best be started when a child is five or
six. At Eastman, this problem had been solved, during Howard Hanson's
administration, through a poorly paid faculty without academic rank that

taught children, adolescents, and adults—degree candidates and those who were not candidates for academic degrees. During Walter Hendl's time, when emphasis was put for the first time on the development of a ladder-ranked collegiate faculty capable of being tenured in a nationally competitive manner, the question of evaluating the teaching of children and adolescents became a thorny one. There developed, as a result, a special prep faculty, appointed yearly and paid less well than the collegiate faculty, without the application of annual subsidies from the school's endowment, a practice I also used in the summer session of the school's collegiate division. This sort of arrangement works well, so long as there is plenty of plant space to go around or if, as in the fashion used at New England Conservatory, the Prep Department functions mostly on weekends. At Eastman, Martin and Joan Messinger, a wonderfully generous trustee of the university and his wife, eager to build a closer link between the Eastman School and the Rochester community, bought the building immediately to the south of Eastman's main facility on Gibbs Street, renovated it, and then developed a much more ambitious community education program than had existed before, supported by the generous endowment of Jack L. Frank, an antiques dealer who oved studying voice with Nancie Kennedy. In its new facilities, this division of the school was renamed the Eastman Community Music School. A community education program of this kind will normally employ recent graduates, faculty spouses, and graduate students as its faculty, though the graduate students will normally represent a less skilled work force, lacking the experience of people who have dedicated themselves to this important work for many years; it should also operate so that expenses are covered by revenues. Inevitably, some of the leading collegiate faculty will recognize extraordinarily talented five- and ten-year-olds whom they are very eager to teach. My rule at Eastman for such matters was that such senior pedagogues could take on such pupils, but only if the collegiate enrollment of the studio was full and only for the hourly rate normally paid for teaching children and adolescents. Though faculty eager to teach a small number of prep students on that basis were joyfully encouraged to do so, the number of them was never very large. When a music school relies wholly on graduate students for instructional activities in a prep department, the graduate students learn a great deal, but at the expense of continuing musical instruction for the community's children and adolescents. Parents of exceptionally gifted children may wish to bear this in mind when choosing music teachers for their sons and daughters.

BRANDING: SHOULD ALL PROFESSIONAL MUSIC SCHOOLS PURSUE THE SAME GOALS?

In the early 1990s, Paul Boylan (then dean of the School of Music of the University of Michigan), Larry Livingston (then dean of what is now the Thornton School of Music of the University of Southern California), and I visited for thirty minutes with Samuel Hope, executive director for many years of the National Association of Schools of Music, at an annual NASM meeting in Chicago. We proposed that when NASM schools prepare their decennial reviews, each be required not only to respond to several dozen questions about what makes the school like all the other 637 NASM institutions but, in addition, to write a paragraph about what makes it *different* from all the others. Though no action within NASM that I know of has followed up on that initiative, the idea remains an important one in my view.

Relevant in each case are the history and geographic location of the school. The Berklee College of Music in Boston has long distinguished itself from other American music schools as a result of the repertories studied there. The Eastman School I helped build during the 1970s, '80s, and '90s comprised a very strong faculty in composition and performance, happily married to an equally strong group of scholars, all of whom supported the idea that musicians should learn how to think and to read as well as to play and to sing. The Butler School of Music of the University of Texas at Austin will inevitably have to deal with the fact that the very large university of which we are part fosters interdisciplinary activity, in a city that calls itself "the live music capital of the world." Texas's long border with Mexico is another central aspect of the Butler School's history and future, as is the importance of the urbanization problem in Texas, the tendency for our residents (and those of the Midwest in general) to leave the small cities and towns where they grew up and to move to the big cities.

A very important problem for our 638 NASM schools, as I see things, is that because New York City is the media capital of the nation, our faculties are more obsessed than they should be with the "Lincoln Center Syndrome." Too few faculty members tell their students that the world is full of competition winners, and that the number of management firms has withered in the past quarter century, as has the audience for classical music in America. While there are certainly firms that will take a young singer on commission, only a very small number of them work on a business model that requires large artists' fees from which a 20 percent commission earns enough to cover overhead and make a profit. Put another way, most of our young graduates who are self-employed will need to know how to develop and to manage their own careers.

But imagine how valuable a young musician would be who could conduct instrumental and vocal ensembles, play the piano well, and deal administratively with a mayor and a city council, the chair of the school board, the chamber of commerce, and the heads of the local churches, mosques, and synagogues. There is no reason why some of our 638 NASM schools should not focus on that sort of outcome, the development of young musicians capable of building a community's artistic life as a bulwark against urbanization, the continuing outflow of talent and imagination from our smaller cities and towns to our burgeoning cities.

Just as Texas focuses on Latin America, the University of California has an understandable interest in the Pacific Rim, and the University of Michigan, because of the large Arab population of Metropolitan Detroit, has a special interest in Africa and the Middle East. And there are other ways of thinking about new focuses. The Ewing Marion Kauffman Foundation of Kansas City has assets of two billion dollars, the income from which is to be divided equally between projects relevant to Kansas City, Mr. Kauffman's hometown, and the rest of the United States. Kauffman's goal was for entrepreneurial thinking to become part of the mainstream not only of business schools but also of all American higher education. I believe strongly that while young musicians can learn accounting and finance if they wish—and there are strong music business programs at Northeastern and at Miami, for example—undergraduate courses in entrepreneurial thinking should be a central aspect of many more American music schools than is presently the case. (Though many of the New England Conservatory faculty felt very negatively about my ideas along this line during my brief stay there as president, Tony Woodcock has in the meantime developed a strong entrepreneurial program at the conservatory.) This means not only the possibility of inventing new businesses but especially a musician's ability to recognize and thoughtfully explore and follow through on new opportunities as they emerge.

ADVERTISING: GETTING OUT THE MESSAGE

It is important to let the rest of the world know what is going on at your school. Schools in New York City, the media capital of the United States, get lots of publicity as a result of their location. But for schools in Rochester or Bloomington, for example, it will be important to find other means of communication. Howard Hanson understood this in the 1930s. He provided Eastman from those days forward with transcontinental radio broadcasts and an unending series of recordings by Eastman ensembles, including the Philharmonia and the Wind Ensemble, often featuring music by American composers. In the early 1950s, with support from the State Department, Hanson led a Philharmonia tour to the Soviet Union. I continued the tradition of recording, on a variety of professional labels of broad distribution, for faculty soloists and for the school's major ensembles, including CDs in which Eastman groups accompanied such major celebrities as James Galway, Benita Valente, and Wynton Marsalis. Our extensive recording program was ably led by John Santuccio, then assistant director for administration, later president of G. Schirmer and operations manager of the New York Philharmonic. Many of our recordings were produced by Grammy Award–winning alumnus Thomas Mowrey, who put together a very successful recruiting cassette entitled *Sounds of Eastman*. The Wind Ensemble, led by Donald Hunsberger and supported by Sony International, regularly toured Japan during June, with students paid a generous honorarium and their expenses. For many summers, members of the Philharmonia, under the direction of David Effron, made up (and were professionally compensated as) the resident orchestra of the Heidelberg Summer Festival for a score of opera performances, symphony concerts, and chamber music opportunities. We discontinued Eastman's Alice Tully series in the early 1990s when we discovered that the chances of a *New York Times* review, even for a program with a major premiere, were only about one in three. A broadly distributed series of recordings, Sounds from Eastman, publicized the school. Interactive samplers on the Internet, both in Rochester and at Texas, have likewise spread the message. Any serious decanal candidate should invest a good deal of time in comparing a variety of schools' Internet representations of their work. Appearances by distinguished visiting faculty not only bring excitement to the program but, if properly handled, also promote the work of the institution, nationally and internationally, through the positive reactions of the visitors.

CURRICULAR REFORM: REPERTORIES

Though the whole of my background is in classical music and the liberal arts, I have recognized since the late 1970s that the vast majority of current music school students in America have much broader musical interests than I do. (My marriage to Carol in 1976 helped begin to broaden at least some of the music I listen to.) Our students may study classical music at school by day, but I learned that when they return to their dormitories in the evening, they listen to the music that the rest of the nation enjoys. While we went through mayhem in Rochester during the early 1970s by imagining that putting music students in dormitories with liberal arts and engineering majors would change Eastman's culture in notable ways, at the University of Texas, while the fifty thousand non-arts students go to the east side of the campus for football games (in a stadium that seats one hundred thousand), almost none of them attends concerts of classical music. While Henry Lee Higginson and Serge Koussevitzky insisted that playing anything less highbrow than J. K. Paine's music for American elitists risked degrading the sensitivities of the players of the Boston Symphony, the most popular concerts of the Eastman School were of the Prism format, wherein we mixed a variety of repertories. Renée Fleming sings Schubert, Schumann, Wolf, and Brahms lieder for the body of a recital, but she often performs Broadway masterworks or pieces of contemporary rock for her encores, chatting amiably with the audience in a fashion that would have been altogether foreign for Elizabeth Schwarzkopf. Leonard Bernstein may have been denied the music directorship of the Boston Symphony partly because he had composed two Broadway shows, not a comfortable idea for tradition-minded Bostonians. But we now live in a millennium in which it is hard to imagine anyone trying to persuade our forty-fourth president that music with European roots is all qualitatively superior to music with American roots.

Although easy enough to think about, this truth has difficult implications for a modern music school dean, especially in a time of economic recession. Whom do you appoint when you have an open faculty position? A classically trained pianist in the mold of Lang Lang, the goal of any traditionally oriented piano search committee, or someone like Steven Mayer, who has recorded both the works of Charles Ives and the amazing difficult piano arrangements of Art Tatum? How will the dean assert needed leadership if the broad array of sociological and traditional concerns noted earlier in this chapter are allowed to dominate institutional thinking? Isn't there an opportunity here for some of the 638 NASM schools to distinguish themselves from one another by differentiating at least some of the repertories they study? There is, particularly if new deans are willing to reflect on the point that Boylan, Livingston, and I raised with NASM director Hope in the early 1990s, about working to make more American music schools distinct selling propositions instead of Juilliard wannabes.

The introduction to *Preparing Artists for the 21st Century*, the transcript of a three-day meeting held in 2002 by the Thomas S. Kenan Institute for the Arts and the North Carolina School of the Arts, contains information vital to the future of American music schools. It begins thus:

> The twenty-first century conservatory finds itself at a point of unprecedented questioning of purpose. Until now, the conservatory's role has been clear; to develop the essential skills for performing at the highest level in the professional arts arena, using predominantly the Western canon as a foundation of preparation. By the end of the last century, the technical aspect of this goal was being achieved by American conservatories at an exceptionally high level, possibly at the highest level in history. At the same time, a new set of essential skills was emerging that was not so easily defined. Conservatories have been struggling to identify this new set of skills; they have been experimenting with programs to address the ones that can be identified. There is little agreement about what these essential skills are or about the best ways to develop them. The twenty-first century demands more of the well

trained artist, and the conservatories that provide them training strug-
gle to sustain the high levels of technical accomplishment, even as they
expand the terrain of their responsibility.

There are major developments over the last century that impact the
arts and artist preparation. The population is changing, and audience
demographics, expectations, and interests are evolving and diversify-
ing. There are new literacies that change the way students and audiences perceive and deliver the arts. The global community is becoming
more available and influential on the arts as a result of the technology
revolution and specifically the Internet. Emerging audiences are less
connected to the Western classical tradition and more aware of other
cultures and traditions. Popular culture has been combining all types of
media, so students and audiences seek arts experiences that include
seeing, hearing, touching, and reading all at once. Audiences perceive
and learn in new ways.[5]

An especially inspiring book, Eric Booth's *The Music Teaching Artist's
Bible*, is enthusiastically recommended to music deans, faculty, and students. Booth maintains, and I certainly agree, that for all of us the most
vital act of our existence should be teaching music, not simply composing, performing, or, as scholars, discovering new information about the
canon of Western music, but drawing the many people who have not yet
felt the power of the music we care about into music's orbit. This idea, I
think, well deserves the reallocation of scarce resources to the budget of
any music school that is serious about the success of its graduates. According to Booth, an actor and an acting teacher at Juilliard,

> Conservatories tend to be conservative; there is a reason they aren't
> called progressatories or arts experimentariums. Yet these institutions,
> dedicated to retaining the best of the past as they move forward, are
> now recognizing what working musicians have long known—the skills
> to draw people into music and educate them effectively about music
> are not afterthoughts, are not luxuries for the few who get famous or
> the few who are naturally outgoing or garrulous or happen to like
> teaching. Advocacy is a responsibility for all. We all are educators all
> the time. And these abilities are not just natural gifts, personality tricks,
> or the refuge of the musically less gifted. Advocacy, entrepreneurial-
> ism, and education skills can be taught, can be learned and developed
> for a lifetime to enable even the shy or tongue-tied musician to become
> comfortable and effective in these roles.[6]

Referring to the conference hosted by the Kenan Institute for the Arts in
2002, cited above, Booth writes:

> The participants agreed that, overall, the technical preparation of artists
> is being accomplished at a higher level in America today than ever
> before in human history. There is increasing parity among musician
> training institutions but, they agreed, fine technical training isn't
> enough anymore. A new set of skills has become crucial to the success

of a twenty-first-century artist. What are these skills? The participants couldn't identify these additional skills with the same certainty and specificity as the technical skills, but they generally felt that education, entrepreneurship, advocacy, communication (verbal and written), and problem solving were the areas in which musicians and other artists have to develop proficiency to build fulfilling careers. The conference participants didn't agree on ways to incorporate these subjects into training programs—do you require new courses and take time away from studio practice, or do you make new classes voluntary for those who can squeeze them in? Participants argued about building a priority around these additional skills. The League of American Orchestras' representatives claimed that musicians with education skills were solid gold, essential to the future of orchestras—so why don't conservatories produce more of them? The conservatory honchos snapped back, "Then why are those skills completely ignored in all orchestral hiring? Consider these skills in hiring, and we will happily train them for that." Such testy episodes aside, the understanding I took away from the conference was that the music field as a whole now acknowledges that the "extra" skills are no longer extra. So here it is, musicians: your supplementary skills—as educator, entrepreneur, advocate, communicator—are as important as your musical skills to creating a full, rewarding, and sustainable career.[7]

He adds that artists attending the Kenan conference recognized the need for those additional skills in their own lives.

Although the artists attending the conference expressed appreciation for the arts education they received and complimented the caliber of their particular conservatory faculty (if they attended a conservatory), most admitted that they were not prepared for the professional world upon graduation. They did not feel they had the skills needed to create or sustain their own projects or to create in the realities they encountered. Service organization representatives underscored this lack by discussing how professional artists in the field need help with their writing skills and business plans, as well as how to create self-sustaining projects.[8]

Greg Sandow, a Juilliard faculty member who wrote about classical music for the *Wall Street Journal*, back in the days when the *WSJ* included such a column, has told me that, as a member of a Juilliard faculty committee concerned with curricular reform, he had been recently asked to research where all of this began. It was, he said, at Eastman in the early 1990s, a statement that reminded me of a walk of mine with two of our golden retrievers on the beach at Hilton Head in the spring of 1993. I had that morning begun to muse on the history of audience development in America, seeking to relate that in my own head to the incredible amount of performing talent my colleagues and I were developing. That musing led to the appointment of five Eastman faculty committees known as the Eastman Commission on Teaching Music, which led in turn to the Eastman Initiatives, then to the Shouse and Kauffman grants and to East-man's current program on arts leadership and to the Paul Judy Institute.

My own suggestions for future curricular reform include asking musicologists and theorists to change part of their focus from the evolution of compositional styles to the evolution of the institutions in which music has played a central role: the public schools, the professional music schools, the orchestras, the opera companies, the chamber music societies, the publishing and recording companies, and the firms that manage musical careers, for example. Relevant, too, is the history of audience development, together with the encouragement of practical experience on each campus about who the audience has been, who it might become, and on what we need to do as musicians to retain a better share of Americans' lessening leisure time, partly by refreshing the concert experience. In thinking about questions like these, surely we need to reflect while our students are still in school about how to interact with people and with institutions outside the realm of classical music. If music students fail to think about such matters while in school, it should not surprise us that they feel unprepared for the real world once they graduate.[9]

We should be thinking, too, about the balance between studio work and classroom studies, especially for students concentrating on performance for instruments of very narrow repertory. Perhaps it is advisable for a pianist to practice at least four hours a day, but it is hard to justify that sort of practice-room commitment for trombone and double bass players. Although such leading artists as Renée Fleming and Yo Yo Ma routinely include all sorts of repertories as part of their performances, the question of how to finance a faculty that can include performance instruction in many of those repertories is tricky, even in communities like Austin, Nashville, Seattle, New York City, and Los Angeles, where such instruction of high quality is readily available on an hourly basis, without the need of importing talent from out of town. This question implies a rethinking of how an ideal faculty is built, with a new focus in many institutions on a hunt for faculty talent that is versatile. The rapid recent evolution of distance learning certainly suggests that some of our fiscal problems in this area might well be addressed through new technologies. If, as Kevin McCarthy suggests, we will be left in a quarter century with but a dozen American orchestras that facilitate a decent living wage for their players, do we really need 638 music schools whose curricular backbones are built around the symphony orchestra? In university systems that maintain several state campuses, how many orchestral specialists can be justified in the evolving context? All of these questions could be profitably addressed, not only by music deans and directors but by music faculty, music students, and the provosts from whom fiscal support is most often forthcoming.

FUTURE STUDENTS

A matter of special importance for the future of America's collegiate music schools concerns international demographics. From the time of the Civil War to the onset of World War II, it was natural for the most advanced of our nation's young musicians to turn to London, Paris, Berlin, Leipzig, and Vienna for the completion of their musical educations, just as it has been understandable since 1945 that many young people from Europe and Asia have turned for the completion of their musical educations to the United States. But now that artists like Yo Yo Ma, Daxun Zhang, and Lang Lang have clearly demonstrated artistry at the highest level in Western art music, it is to be expected that young Asians will not forever wish to study in such large numbers as at present in American schools. Once Asia has learned what we have to teach, it is to be expected that the governments of China, Japan, South Korea, Taiwan, and Singapore, for example, will likely try to save money by keeping most of their students at home, something that I think we should also anticipate in the sciences and in engineering. I am told that, two years ago, there were three rapid transit subway lines in Beijing; now there are thirteen!

NEW WORK

Commissioning new music is not only an important means of helping stimulate community interest; it is also a vital stimulus to music and musicians.[10] Beginning with the Eastman School's commission in 1980 for Joseph Schwantner to compose *New Morning for the World*, I have had the idea that commissioned music should meet the needs of its potential audience, and I have never met resistance from any composer about proceeding in this fashion. If a particular composer doesn't want the commission, another one will.[11] Thus, when I first spoke with Schwantner, a faculty colleague at Eastman, about a work for a famous and highly intelligent African American baseball player named Willie Stargell[12] for a premiere in the Kennedy Center, I stressed the importance of thinking of music that would have immediate appeal for baseball fans and for African Americans. Though Joe hesitated for an evening, his ten-year-old son, Chris, assured him of what a fine and exciting human being Willie was, and Joe was instantly on board. *New Morning* was a huge success at the Kennedy Center, but equally successful at the Academy of Music in Philadelphia and in New York's Carnegie Hall, as the result of which the Eastman Philharmonia got the lead articles not only on the music page of the *New York Times* but on the sports page as well. We performed, too, in Pittsburgh's Heinz Hall, in Boston's Jordan Hall, and in Rochester's Eastman Theatre. The Kennedy Center premiere of *New Morning* was broadcast nationally by NPR as part of a program that included works by

George Walker, Walter Piston, Aaron Copland, and Samuel Barber. It was recorded for Mercury, and in the meantime, it has been performed more than two hundred times, all over America, by orchestras eager to create bridges to local African American communities. There are those who believe, for reasons I cannot understand, that composers who write for specific audiences are selling out, though Joe tells me that he has earned more from performances of *New Morning* than from the rest of all his wonderful music put together, a spectacular tribute to the importance of thinking about one's audience, at least some of the time! We had a similar success with a brass quintet for Christmas, commissioned from John Harbison and most ably performed on *CBS Sunday Morning* by Charles Kuralt and the Eastman Brass.

Any dean thinking of undertaking a project involving a speaker who is neither actor nor musician should know that Willie Stargell's huge success with *New Morning for the World* was partly the result of his own charisma and partly because he and I agreed from the outset about the importance of professional training for him in what was for him an entirely new field. This coaching was wonderfully delivered by Ben Shaktman, then director of the Pittsburgh Public Theater, who gave Willie regular instruction, not in an effort to emulate Dr. King, but to speak Dr. King's words in a fashion that was true to Willie's wonderful persona, while supporting the core of Dr. King's message.

Your Role in Accomplishing New Work Accomplishes All Sorts of Objectives

- It keeps composers and their relationship to performers vital and alive. Too many music schools concentrate on repertory composed between 1700 and 1950. At Eastman in the early 1990s, I persuaded the faculty to agree on policies requiring that all degree recitals include a substantial work written during the previous twenty years, a requirement changed in the meantime to the past forty years. When my friend Laurence Lesser wondered why we couldn't program Elliott Carter's Sonata for Cello and piano at Eastman, I responded that we could, of course, but that it had been composed in 1948, a long time ago. Performers who give compelling performances of living composers' work often find, as a result, that the composers become their active champions, eager to find performance dates for performers they believe in.
- It provides a path through which young music students can be introduced to exciting new repertories. Though Bach, Mozart, and Bartok all composed fine works for young people, much of the repertory performed in the K–12 sector leaves a lot to be desired. Ned Corman's brilliant work in bringing about more than four hundred classical and jazz new works for school ensembles (the commissioning project described in Corman's *Now's the Time: A*

Story of Music Education and Advocacy [Rhinebeck, NY: Epigraph, 2012]) accomplished a great deal for the musical perceptions of the young people who studied with Ned over thirty years in the public schools of Penfield, New York, a Rochester suburb. The costs of the new repertory, whose scores and recordings are safely stored in the Eastman School's Sibley Music Library, were modest, for Ned came up with the imaginative idea of commissioning many Eastman composition students, for whom a thousand dollars or two is a lot of money, not only to write the music but to prepare and lead initial performances, a thrill never to be forgotten, I'm sure, by any of the performers who participated over the years in Corman's project.

- It provides a way to honor the departed. Especially at a time when so few metropolitan papers employ music critics, presenting a local editor with a compelling story will often produce a major article, which can boost attendance and community enthusiasm. Allow me to cite a personal example. In memory of my dear father, the BSO double bass player, Carol and I asked Kevin Puts, an Eastman alumnus who taught at the time at the University of Texas, to write a companion piece for Schubert's "Trout Quintet," a wonderful piece for violin, viola, cello, double bass, and piano that doesn't get played often enough because concert sponsors are understandably reluctant to pay full fees for performers who play only half a concert. Turning to Karen Payne, then UT's very able assistant dean of fine arts, for fund-raising, I asked who operated the best seafood restaurant in Texas. Armed with the information that this was Paul Gaido, a UT alumnus whose family had founded Gaido's at the Seawall in Galveston, I had lunch with Mr. Gaido, inviting him and his family to contribute one quarter of the twenty-thousand-dollar commission. I said, "For 75 percent of the commission, I get to determine the composer, the instrumentation, and the shape of the piece. For 25 percent, you get to choose the fish." Paul consulted with his family over the weekend, calling the following Monday to let me know that the new work would be known as "The Red Snapper Quintet," a perfect twenty-three-minute companion piece to Schubert's "Trout." In addition, the new work provides a fine opportunity for chamber ensembles all over America to enlist the support of the finest seafood restaurant in town. I commissioned Jack Brannon, a UT colleague and a close friend, to write a poem entitled "The Red Snapper" (Texas's state fish), on which Kevin Puts, now a Pulitzer Prize winner, wrote a beautiful variation set.

> It hangs above the pier's rank bustle,
> Shimmering vermillion orb,
> Trophy stunning as a second sun,
> Gilt on the luster of day's last light.

A prize star fixed by unseen wire,
The fish outshines the sun-scorched anglers
Proudly caught in gleeful portraits
Lordly luminary: bright-prismed oval
Rivets our gaze on its heavenly form—
Sublime crown of crimson armor
Declined below fins to silver eclipse.
No prisoner of the sky's pale void,
This god springs like mighty Poseidon,
Violet sovereign over blue-deep realms
It rules iridescent, vanishing free.

With the permission of the UT provost, we changed the name of the University's Bates Recital Hall for the afternoon to the Baits Recital Hall and followed the event with a seafood reception, part of an effort to make concert music more playful, less formal, less anticipatable.

- My brother, Jim, the founder and music director of Philadelphia's Orchestra 2001 Plus, commissioned a twenty-minute work by Andrea Clarfield for violin and orchestra in memory of our mother. When Jim and I spoke about putting the two pieces by Puts and Clarfield in memory of our parents together on a compact disc, we decided to ask Gunther Schuller whether he would write a work for two pianos for the two of us to perform and to record. Gunther, an admirer of both our parents, immediately acceded to the idea. Once the CD is ready to be issued, I intend to work with the National Association of Retired People and *Readers' Digest* to publicize both our new recording and the idea that other American musicians commission new music in memory of *their* parents.
- It provides new work for repertory-poor instruments. Piano, voice, violin, cello, and flute are one thing. Viola, double bass, oboe, bassoon, trumpet, trombone, horn, and tuba are another. Shortly after coming to Austin, I asked Rebecca Henderson and Kristin Wolfe Jensen, UT's distinguished young professors of oboe and bassoon, respectively, to recommend a young female composer from UT whose music they especially liked. They suggested Jenni Brandon, who had just earned a master's degree in composition at UT. As dean, I commissioned Jenni to write a work for narrator, oboe, bassoon, and piano called "The Wildflower Suite." Dedicated to Lady Bird Johnson, on texts by Mrs. Johnson's closest friend, Betty Castro, "The Wildflower Suite" was premiered in Mrs. Johnson's presence in the spring of 2005 at the Lady Bird Johnson Wildflower Center in Austin, with Luci Baines Johnson as the work's very effective narrator. In the meantime, it has been recorded (by Luci Baines Johnson, Rebecca Henderson, Kristin Wolfe Jensen, and myself). Given the dearth of repertory for the instrumentation used in

the piece, I predict a continuing popularity for Jenni Brandon's suite, in Texas and beyond.

- It helps provide an aura of celebration for important events. The most important contribution of my six-year deanship at the College of Fine Arts of the University of Texas at Austin was to collaborate on the construction of the eighty-five-million-dollar Jack S. Blanton Museum of Art, the largest and among the very best American university art museums. For the dedication of the museum, I commissioned Donald Grantham, chair of composition at UT, to compose a new work for fifteen instruments called "Music for the Blanton," a kind of local "Pictures at an Exhibition" in which the museum's primary donors got to process, from one gallery to another, as a result of beckoning music performed by groups of three to five players in one gallery after another. The very effective piece showed off many members of the Butler School's faculty and student body. It will shortly be available on DVD to promote the work of the museum.

- It keeps the art of music alive, working against the idea, implied in the curricula of all major music schools, that the music anyone really wants to listen to ceased with the death of Debussy in 1918. If young pianists obsess about the Beethoven sonatas, the Chopin études, and the Brahms variation sets—all wonderful pieces of music—how can we help but give the impression that we are museum curators for an art whose best days are all in the past? What, after all, might the motivation be for attending live performances downtown when the wonders of the CD are available for listening while we are driving and the endless variety of performances on YouTube and Spotify are but three mouse clicks away when we sit down at our personal computers?

- It helps raise money. Long before I moved to Texas, I had been greatly impressed by the optimism, pride, and energy that informs the people of the Lone Star State. I had been particularly moved by David Higgs's premiere recital in 1994 on the new Lay Family Organ in the Meyerson Concert Hall in Dallas. For a packed audience of international organists and Texas dignitaries, Higgs played a wonderful first half, then gave a gracious speech at the close of intermission, thanking Ross Perot and Margaret McDermott for the money that had made the hall possible, thanking the Lay family for the money that had made the new organ possible, and thanking the Fisk Company of Boston for having built so fine a recital instrument. Seated again at the organ, Higgs was about to launch the second half of his program when, as the result of apparently sudden inspiration, he turned over his left shoulder and told the audience, sotto voce, "Dallas, I would be remiss not to acknowledge that this organ is, in my view, the very best recital instrument in the best concert hall in the United States." The audience leaped to its feet and applauded for ten minutes!

Back in Rochester I reflected on how I might harvest Texan enthusiasm in behalf of the Eastman School. Accordingly, I invited Todd Frazier, a fine young Eastman graduate from Texas who had in the meantime taken a master's degree in composition at Juilliard, to compose a new half-hour work for narrator and orchestra on what it means to be a Texan. With the help of Todd's mother, Rachel, I made contact with Don Carleton, director of the Dolph Briscoe Center for American History at UT Austin, who suggested Steven Harrigan (in the meantime a Texan celebrity as the result of his novel *The Gates of the Alamo* and professor of creative writing at the University's Michener Center) as a likely candidate to write the text. The work is now known as *Buffalo Altar*. Harrigan's text describes a Texan landsman, a man who for fifty years has been leasing land for oil companies to drill on. In *Buffalo Altar* the landsman finds an old farmer who owns several square miles of land in the northwestern part of the state but who refuses to lease his land for any amount of money. The landsman agrees to stay overnight, and in the morning walks with the rancher to the top of a hill, where they enter a cave. The text concludes:

> Pretty soon the sun started to slip up over the horizon. I could hear mourning doves calling, and there were swallows flying in and out of their mud nests at the top of the cave. Then this one ray of light started to travel across the plains, moving across the grass and then along the floor of the canyon like it was looking for something. Finally it came into the cave and settled on a pile of rocks a few feet behind where we was standing and lit it up like a Christmas tree.
>
> It was then I saw it wasn't rocks; it was bones. It seemed that somebody had taken a bunch of old jawbones and set them up on end, so that they made a kind of platform. And on the platform was a skull from some animal I'd never seen before. The skull was big and thick, and flat and prehistoric-looking, and it had two horns that swept out from either side like a longhorn steer's. The skull's eye sockets were as big as my fists, and they were staring out toward the plains. I had this strange feeling that those empty eye holes were watching the sunrise . . . just like I was. "What the hell is that?" I asked the old man. "By God, son," he said, "that's an altar."
>
> The man said the skull belonged to an old buffalo. Not the kind of buffalo we know about, but the kind that died out thousands and thousands of years ago. Way back in those times some fella had climbed up to this cave with this buffalo skull and very carefully set it up on those jawbones so that it was looking east across the plains.
>
> "Why do you suppose he did that?" I asked the old man. "Why do you think?" he said, looking out to where the sun was rising and the hawks were circling in the sky. "They didn't have no First Baptist Church back in those days. Where else were you going to go and do

your worshiping? Besides, a sunrise up here is a pretty sight, and I guess that old boy wanted the buffalo to see it. . . .

He never would let us drill on that bluff. We tried all around it, but all we ever got was dry holes; and that old man died without any royalty at all.

I come to this cafeteria for lunch pert'near every day, except for once or twice a year when one of the kids might fly in to visit. The girls behind the counter all know me and they treat me pretty well. They all pretend to flirt with me, but I tell em I ain't interested in any woman that wears a hairnet. And then I take my tray over to the same table by the window. I eat my lunch and then my jello and then usually I'll take out a geologist's report or a survey map and study it for a while. You don't want to get behind in this business. But my mind sometimes drifts, and these days it drifts mostly to that buffalo skull sitting there in that cave in Floyd County. I keep thinking about the old boy who built that altar. He was a Texan like me, I guess, though it was a hell of a different place back then.

Or maybe it wasn't. Maybe it's the same. Maybe all these cities and Taco Bells and Dairy Queens and outlet malls don't have a thing in the world to do with what Texas is. Texas is what connects me and that prehistoric fella and that old rancher and that dead buffalo. It's not just the place we live in; it's the place that lives in us—even after we're dead and looking toward the sun with empty eyes. [13]

- A piano vocal score for the piece has now been finished by one of my former graduate students, Hermes Comacho. Lucien Douglas, a wonderful professor of acting in our Theatre Department, a New Englander who speaks fluent Texan, will join me on a tour across the state performing *Buffalo Altar* as part of the university's current three-billion-dollar capital campaign.

THE JOYS OF FUND-RAISING

Besides a pride in your institution, you must be possessed by an insatiable enthusiasm for raising money. Russ Alan Prince's fine book *The Seven Faces of Philanthropy* and Francie Ostrower's excellent *Why the Affluent Give* should be required reading for a new dean. Both bring attention to what motivates Americans to give money away to causes they believe in. I have in my career as a fund-raiser dealt with all of these stereotypes:

- The self-absorbed donor. An Eastman alumna wanted to be known as the school's first graduate. Because she moved to Rochester from Syracuse for her senior year, she was in fact the only student to graduate in 1922! She expected me to call her every week or two for a two-hour conversation in which she did all of the talking (mostly reminiscing about bygone days). She caused no end of difficulty with each of the four presidents for whom I worked as Eastman director, for she loved to throw sand into the machinery. But she ended up by leaving her alma mater a bequest of ten million dollars, which she specified was to be used for a tower named in her honor.

- The bolt from the blue. A lady from the class of 1931 who made the school the only beneficiary of her will. An AIDS nurse in the South Bronx, she was a person whom I had never met nor corresponded with. My parents, who had graduated in the class of 1930, did not remember her at all. I can only guess that, never married, she read the alumni magazines and looked back with pride on the days when her life was filled with music, clearly the most inspirational part of a life of selfless service to others. She specified that her gift was to be used for undergraduate financial aid.

- The diplomat. A Rochester lady widowed while only in her early fifties. She filled her life with daily lunches with each of the many heads of Rochester's not-for-profit institutions: Mondays with the head of the RPO; Tuesdays with myself; Wednesdays with the head of radio and television station WXXI; Thursdays with the head of the Memorial Art Gallery; and Fridays with the head of the Rochester Museum and Science Center. She had a lifelong love of Rochester as a community and devoted herself to using her considerable influence toward getting us to collaborate on behalf of the community. She contributed a beautiful seminar room to the new Sibley Library that included a closet with a refrigerator and a locked cabinet with a good supply of the best gin, to which only she and I had keys! (She loved martinis.) She was also the sponsor of the Philharmonia's tour with Willie Stargell to the Kennedy Center.

- The Wallflower. An antiques collector who loved studying singing with a member of Eastman's Community Education Division. When I asked the faculty member whether she would arrange for me to have lunch with her affluent student, Jack L. Frank, she said he would prefer not to, for he was a shy person who did not like to make commitments. My taking her advice seriously resulted in a bequest of six million dollars.

- The community leader. In Austin a civic leader who, on our first meeting, decided he could trust me to the degree of offering to endow a million-dollar chair for a new violin professorship. I responded without delay, "But I already received one of those last week. How about an endowed string quartet?" He gulped, promised me he would think about it, and then, with his wife, two months later gave us half an endowed string quartet in exchange for my promise to raise the other half of what amounted eventually to a six-million-dollar endowment. This couple's interest in a string quartet came from my ability to convince them that such an ensemble would benefit our community. "If this works out as well as you say it will, UT will become the new Indiana, all the best young string players will come here, and we can continue to build the quality of the Austin Symphony without it costing the community funds that we could put into social services," he said.

- Important for the endowing of chamber groups is the "broken string quartet" syndrome, suffered in years past by the universities of Michigan, Illinois, and Indiana, for example. The provosts of the world get understandably anxious when they think of the consequences of a violist falling downstairs, subsequently able to teach but not to play, and thereby making nonfunctional the work of three colleagues appointed to make beautiful music together. In 1975 Paul Katz, cellist of the Cleveland Quartet, and I figured out how to accomplish such arrangements within the tenure framework of a modern American university.[14] Our legal arrangement provided first that the four members of the quartet were appointed to play and to teach; that if one of the members was either unable or unwilling to continue as a member of the quartet, his or her place in the ensemble would be taken by another person, suitable both to the quartet and to the university; and that the person leaving the quartet would be considered for a faculty position if one were available. The school would cover the costs of the search for a replacement, an expensive matter given the necessity of having each candidate stay in town a week, first to rehearse, then to perform with his or her potential new colleagues. Second, if two people decided, more or less simultaneously, to leave the quartet, the decision whether to try to rebuild from existing personnel would be up to the dean and to the university president. Over twenty years, this arrangement provided for three changes of membership in the Cleveland Quartet; then, with the simultaneous departure of both William Preucil Jr. and Paul Katz in 1995, for the ultimate dissolution of that great ensemble, a very sad experience for us all. An arrangement of the kind at issue here would have saved Virginia Tech and the Audubon Quartet all kinds of grief had they been sensible enough to come up with such a contract at the outset of their relationship. Because no one appears to have thought of such problems at the beginning of the quartet's relationship to the university, the lower three members of the ensemble eventually fired their first violinist, who then sued his colleagues for breach of contract. When he won in court, the other players were obliged to sell their instruments in order to settle their legal obligations.
- The Prankster. A lady in Beverly Hills who shared my last name told me the first time I spoke with her by phone that she never gave money except to benefit music in Southern California. When I responded that I would never dream of asking for money on the first date, she laughed and invited me to her home for lunch. "I like

your style," said she. Though the Eastman School never directly received any of her funds, she invited me often to stay at her place in Beverly Hills and to use one of her cars while in Los Angeles. A widow, she asked only that I accompany her from time to time to a Beverly Hills party (I was ever glad to meet new people in Beverly Hills!), for she loved the hostess's inevitably startled reaction at the front door when she announced, "Here come the Freemans!" While she was not interested in Eastman scholarships for students from Southern California, she did in fact contribute a generous commission for Christopher Rouse, then an Eastman faculty composer, to write a cello concerto, which Yo Yo Ma premiered with the Los Angeles Philharmonic.

- The red herring. *Fortune* magazine, listing the fifty wealthiest people in the world, included a well-known octogenerian music lover whom it posted as having a net worth of two billion dollars. Having checked with the American vice president of the international corporation the man headed, and being convinced that *Fortune* was right, I invited him to Eastman to give a speech, to conduct a concert of music he had commissioned by world-class composers, and to receive an honorary degree. He accepted and flew to Rochester on his private jet. The visit went beautifully, and he invited me to join him for a couple of days in Switzerland the following summer. He received me in July in the most gracious manner, and we had a wonderful lunch together, looking out at the Alps, and at the end of the lunch, I asked for a gift of ten million dollars to name the new building to which Eastman's Sibley Music Library had just relocated. My friend thanked me, said he would think about it, and invited me back for lunch the following day. I hardly slept that night! Before our lunch, he got right to the point. "I like you a lot, and I love your school. But what gave you the idea that I could give you ten million dollars?" I pulled out my *Fortune* listing. "Oh," said he, "I see. I should ask whether, on your way in today, you saw my adolescent son and daughter, the joys of my life. Didn't it occur to you that my late wife, who passed away in her early nineties, could not have possibly been the mother of those children?" I said that the thought had briefly crossed my mind but that I didn't think that that was any of my business. "Well," he said, "my late wife didn't much like that fact, and as a result I have enough to live on, and in good style, as you can see, but I was essentially disinherited, and thus am not in a position to give away ten million dollars, even for a cause I like." Our lunch proceeded in a friendly fashion, but in a quite different key. Once I returned to the United States, I visited my friend, the American vice president of the international conglomerate, who wrote, in my friend's honor, a check for one hundred thousand dollars for the general scholarship fund of the Eastman School. "I am really sorry about what happened," he said. "I thought *Fortune* was right and that you were really onto something important. Sorry it did not work out!"

- The personal friend. The widow of a distinguished Eastman alumnus in California gave the school funds, not only in memory of her husband but also in honor of Carol and myself. Because her gift in our honor came long after we had left Rochester, I had nothing whatever to do with the thoughtfulness behind the gift, though it was certainly deeply appreciated.

- The Western Maecenas. A wonderful man in California generously gives away nearly eight million dollars a year to several hundred music schools, orchestras, opera houses, and chamber music societies, in grants ranging from two thousand to one million dollars. He does this in public recognition of what he calls excellence and accomplishment, and it is perfectly true that the award of such a grant encourages others in an institution's community to be supportive—something along the lines of the National Endowment for the Arts grants and the awarding of *Good Housekeeping* seals of approval. I am ever trying to persuade him, as we both get older, that it lies within his power to leave a lasting legacy to music in America by thinking and working collaboratively with the heads of other American foundations that give money to music and the arts, about how to provide fiscal incentives that would help rebalance supply and demand in some of the ways recommended in this book. I was delighted a year ago to learn that he had made a grant of one and a half million dollars to the American League of Orchestras for the development of projects generated by what the officers of ALO recommend as best practices.

I was not personally involved with the biggest gifts ever made to the Eastman School and to what is now known as the Butler School of Music of the University of Texas at Austin, by George Eastman on the one hand and by Sarah and Ernest Butler on the other. George Eastman died three years before I was born, and the Butlers' gift, the second largest in the history of the University of Texas, came shortly after I retired as dean. The motivation of both of these gifts, however, seems to me essentially the same—a wish, through the inspiring power of music, to improve the quality of community life, attracting, to Rochester in the 1920s and to Austin in the new millennium, talent and ambition, among not only the fine young artists who will inevitably respond to such generosity but the additional imagination and entrepreneurial energy that such gifts bring to our community. At a time in American history when more people are moving to Texas than to any of the other forty-nine states (see the *Economist* of July 11–17, 2009), this is the kind of aspiration that makes Texas such an exciting place to be part of. The leadership of the university understands that, if we are to succeed as American leaders, we will need not only the liberal arts and natural sciences but engineering, the law, business, medicine, and the arts. We understand that the Elgin Marbles were not born at the British Library and that the treasures of the Metropolitan Museum of New York City were bought during the nineteenth century from Europe. Accordingly, if this is where the money and the energy are, this is where the arts will be as well, not in the fashion of mid-twentieth-century America, but with an eye to the future. When, a couple of years ago, the *London Times* called Texas one of the world's greatest fifteen universities, President Bill Powers, speaking for us all, responded, "While we're not quite sure how the *London Times* came to the conclusion they did, we take the compliment, and we are grateful. But I hope the *Times* understands that we mean in the long run to be the best university in the world. We just got a late start!"

Russ Alan Prince is right. American philanthropy, supported by our federal tax code, is a vital aspect of who we are as a nation. But it is important to remember that human beings respond to a variety of potential motivators in giving money away: in support of the development of a more vibrant community, to commemorate the contribution of parents and loved ones, to make a statement about one's own importance, to honor the work of a dedicated teacher, to remember joy from an earlier part of one's own life, to honor the contribution of a dean or president whom one especially admires. People give money to other people whom they like, people who are enthusiastic about the quality of the institution they serve. Those thoughts have inspired the fun of my work in fund-raising, which is a lot more like big game hunting than standing on the corner with a tin cup. I had the privilege in Rochester of a close friendship with Robert and Lois Orchard, a married couple from St. Louis, who gave tirelessly of their resources, energy, connections, and friendship, he as the chair of Eastman's Visiting Committee, she as a member of the University of Rochester's Board of Trustees. They engaged in philanthropy because they believed in music and in the potential of the young people we helped educate and train together, but they never asked to be publicly recognized. A similar pair of enthusiastic donors and personal friends were Eastman alumnus Fred Westphal and his wife, Hinda. I am ever moved by the fact that the most generous donors in the history of the University of Texas at Austin are another anonymous couple who never wish to see their names publicly recognized. They are simply proud of their great university, eager to see it help the Lone Star State achieve the dynamic leadership to which all Texans aspire.

VISITING COMMITTEES AND ADVISORY COUNCILS

Many music schools and departments are served by groups of distinguished outsiders, often appointed by the president of the university at the nomination of the dean, to ensure, from the perspective of governance, that the leadership of the school is honest and forward looking. These are called visiting committees, boards of visitors, or advisory councils. Whatever their label, they are as effective as the men and women who chair them: in my case Elliott Gumaer, Robert Orchard, and Edwin Colodny at Eastman; Lisa Boyd, Diane Schoch, William Nowlin, and Judy Tate at the University of Texas. At Eastman, Bob Sproull once insisted that I include the dean of another music school on our visiting committee, a proposition on which we compromised through the appointment of a *former* dean, someone who could be better trusted not to run off with our best faculty and fund-raising prospects. I have served myself on visiting committees for music and the arts at Harvard, MIT, Yale, Princeton, Howard, Middlebury, and Vanderbilt, interesting experiences in every case, from which I learned a lot. Most of these groups are established to assure the university board that its several schools are decently led. I was surprised, and delighted, at Texas to find that fund-raising was not an incidental byproduct of our advisory council but its primary raison d'être. At an early meeting of UT's Advisory Council for the College of Fine Arts, I was asked in public, "What is the principal mission of our council? When do we get to give you advice?" The chair of the council responded without the least prodding from the dean, "The principal mission of this group is to raise needed funds for the college. The more generous any of you is with funds, time, or both, the more access you will have for providing the dean with advice. Isn't that right, Bob?" That spirit, I must say, symbolizes why I have so much enjoyed my years in Texas.

PLANNING

It was Donald Engle, a distinguished Eastman graduate who later managed the Philadelphia and Minnesota Orchestras and directed the Martha Baird Rockefeller Fund for Music, who, shortly after I became Eastman director, introduced me to the value of long-range planning. Your taking responsibility for asking faculty, staff, students, and alumni to think about what the institution could become if we get our priorities right has an important payoff, both in the short and in the long terms. Larry Faulkner, the UT president who appointed me dean of fine arts in 2000, two or three years later put together what he called the Commission of 125, a group of 125 powerful and affluent Texans whom he asked, in celebration of the university's 125th anniversary, to think intensively for eighteen months about what our university should look like in 2028, then to write a report reflecting those ideas, and finally to help him and his successors as CEOs of the institution to raise the money to implement those ideas, a prelude to our three-billion-dollar campaign under President William Powers. At Eastman, I led three long-term plans, one for the 1970s, one for the 1980s, and one for the 1990s, each of which, involving extensive faculty and alumni participation, accomplished its goals: the recruitment of a world-class string quartet, the development of the "cultural district" that surrounds the school, new homes for the Sibley Music Library and the Student Living Center, and new ways of thinking about the supply of and demand for classically trained musicians in America. All involved the appointment of faculty committees and the development of a reiterative process that plots deliberative change in a positive way, with the support of most if not all concerned.

In the fall of 1996, there took place an event that filled me with pride, making it all seem worthwhile. I was welcomed to Vienna by the Rektor of Vienna's Hochschule für Musik und darstellende Kunst with the words, "It is a privilege to welcome to the classical music capital of the world the director of the world's greatest music school." And he went on to share with me how important he thought the idea that musicians' bear the responsibility of developing our own future audiences.

REVIEWS AND GOOD-BYES

While the faculty in a university music school will inevitably face promotion and tenure reviews, during the forty-year administration of Howard Hanson, the faculty of Eastman never reviewed the director. I was told at the outset of my Eastman appointment that, while I would have tenure as a professor of musicology, I would be reviewed by the faculty every five years. This perfectly normal practice for university deans and directors struck me at the time as entirely sensible, facilitating as it does an opportunity for the faculty to reassess its leadership, suggesting modifications of style or asking for the dean to be replaced if necessary. As with the reelection of a U.S. senator or president, a successful review provides the incumbent with renewed authority, with new political capital that can be expended in fashions that support the positive development of the institution. During the period 1973–1988, I underwent three successful faculty reviews of my stewardship as director, chaired successively by David Burge, Abram Loft, and Samuel Adler. When the provost of the university decided in the spring of 1996 that *he* wanted to chair the quinquennial review for what I had hoped would be my final five-year term as director, I anticipated no problems and moved my parents, then in their late 80s and in what turned out to be the last year of my father's life, to Rochester. But when the New England Conservatory tried for the third time to recruit me back to Boston as their president, it was immediately clear to me that President Thomas Jackson and Provost Charles Phelps, the fourth of the four UR teams I had served, would be just as pleased were I to move on, for they offered me a three-year term instead of the five-year term that would have taken me to sixty-eight, the age at which Hanson had retired. Within five days of my initial meeting with Jackson and Phelps on the subject, I decided to do so. Though my brief stewardship as NEC president turned out to be an unexpectedly wild ride, an experience I will get to a bit later, had I not left Rochester when I did, I would never have ended up at the University of Texas at Austin, a place where it almost never snows!

The issue at hand—length of time in office—is one of great importance for institutional development but one for which, now in my seventies, I don't see as clear a solution to as I wish I did. On the one hand, the current state of musical education in America is in desperate need of strong leadership, leadership that can only be sensibly developed through an effective deanship of at least ten years. But on the other hand, as Larry Faulkner once pointed out to me, it is probably a professional mistake to stay in a deanship or presidency for more than seven or eight years. While I worked well with Allen Wallis, Bob Sproull, and Dennis O'Brien as UR presidents, and while I thought I worked well with Thomas Jackson, I decided that I was not fulfilling whatever Jackson wanted of me and moved on, as did Jay Stein, the exceptionally effective director of the University of Rochester's Medical Center, a year or so later. Put another way, the dean (or director) serves in an academic enterprise as an interface between the CEO of the university and the faculty of the school, representing in good faith the interests of each to the other. Once the trust required in that relationship is in doubt, it is time to move.

Worth considering in this context is *how* to move to the next position when the time comes. It helps immeasurably, I believe, to develop a team of senior, respected men and women who know your work and think highly of it. At the time I moved from Boston to Texas, I was sixty-five years old, a time in life when a lot of people retire. It has always seemed to me, however, that life is a privilege, an opportunity to get something done that needs doing, and to enjoy the adventure of doing so. Important figures in my appointment at UT were Bob Sproull, to whom I reported for a decade and with whom I have stayed in touch as a close friend ever since; Bryce Jordan, whom I met after a meeting of the American Musicological Society in 1962 in the bar car of a Pennsylvania Railroad train on its way from Columbus to Philadelphia, a man who served as a member of the Eastman Visiting Committee and who transformed Penn State University as its president in the 1980s; Robert Kuhn, the polymath husband of a distinguished Eastman alumna pianist, a man who has had very successful careers in science, finance, communications, and writing (especially about modern China), who apparently called the UT provost for an extended conversation on my behalf from Beijing; and Daniel Neuman, dean of arts and architecture (later executive vice chancellor) at UCLA, who withdrew as a candidate from the UT search once he knew I was interested in the UT deanship. I am deeply indebted to all four, as I am to President Larry Faulkner and Provost Sheldon Ekland-Olson, the men who helped make my Texas deanship such a pleasure.

A VERY SPECIAL CASE

One of the problems I encountered in Rochester was the lack of any paper trail for the first half century of the school's existence. Howard Hanson, having been paid a generous salary without duties for nearly a decade after his retirement, had been allowed to take all the fiscal records with him, while Walter Hendl successfully resisted the urge to write anything down. I worked with Mary Wallace Davidson as Sibley librarian and with a professional archivist to develop protocols for what to keep and what to throw away, a trickier question then than now, for stored paper consumes real space and thus genuine resources. At a public university, this sort of thing is not a problem, because the overriding need for openness and transparency, especially in the capital of the state, has persuaded everyone at the University of Texas for many years that accurate record keeping must assume a high institutional priority.

My most serious Rochester problem concerned what I'll call intergenerational equity in real estate. Though the original campus of the University of Rochester, which called itself a university from the time it was established in 1851, was on Main Street, by the early part of the twentieth century it had moved to a campus on University Avenue, three-quarters of a mile northeast of downtown. When the Eastman School was opened in 1921, it was located on its own campus, two blocks to the east of the middle of downtown, a quarter of the way from downtown to the University Avenue campus. Then it was decided to build a medical center, three and a half miles south of downtown, and shortly afterward the River Campus, on a beautiful space that had heretofore been a golf course abutting the Genesee River, just to the north of the new medical center. It opened in the late 1920s, for male students only, and the University Avenue campus was renamed "the women's campus." In 1955, the university decided to move the women to the River Campus, thus restoring coeducation. But that left two blocks of semiurban real estate, including the Cutler Union, the original dormitories, and the university's Memorial Art Gallery, isolated from the rest of the institution. As a result, over protests from Howard Hanson, the part of the University Avenue campus that was not the Memorial Art Gallery was sold to the Eastman School for one million dollars, and along with it the continuing responsibility for operations and maintenance. Later, a chapel in Howard Hanson's honor was established in the Cutler Union.

Then my staff and I decided in the 1980s that the school needed a new home for the Sibley Library and a new student living center for undergraduates. Though I recommended a three-story, ten-million-dollar dormitory north of the Cutler Union, President O'Brien told me he wanted to build a sixteen-story dormitory much closer to the school, on the site of the old YMCA. I objected that building so high would be expensive and that I didn't believe the school should have to bear a twenty-million-dollar incremental cost for doing so. Naturally, I abandoned my objections when President O'Brien told me that the Eastman (now Miller) Place building (containing the Sibley Library) and the Student Living Center would end up costing forty-eight million, but that he would cover thirty million dollars of the total through university general funds. With professional legal help, we had a formal document drawn up, returning the Prince Street campus to the university in exchange for a thirty-million-dollar credit on the two new buildings, leaving me with but eighteen million dollars to raise.

All was well until President Thomas Jackson took office in 1994. After that, there was pressure to transfer much of the thirty million dollars back to the general fund, a procedure to which I objected on behalf of the Eastman School, but for which the school paid a price, I think, the next time I came up for a quinquennial review. Since then, much of the school's administration has moved into the new building, thus raising the school's operating costs in a fashion I had tried to avoid.

A related matter involved a large oil painting by Maxfield Parrish on one of the grand stairways of the Eastman Theatre. When a Japanese art firm decided in 1995 to stage an exhibit in Japan of the complete works of Parrish, Eastman was offered one hundred thousand dollars for a year's loan of the picture. With the permission of President Jackson, I arranged to have Eastman Kodak take so good a colored photograph that it was difficult to determine it was not the original painting, and working at night during the summer, I had the painting removed from inside an outside wall (where the painting had been subjected for seventy-five years to the annual expansion and contraction of the wall, the result of Rochester winters), with the original shipped to Japan. There it was shortly evaluated as being worth one million dollars, together with an offer to let the painting stay in Japan in exchange for the transfer to Eastman of that sum. I checked with President Jackson, who approved the sale of the painting. Then someone told the Memorial Art Gallery that the painting was about to leave Rochester for an increase of one million dollars to the Eastman School's endowment, and the gallery decided it wanted the painting for its collection. I suggested to the president that the Memorial Art Gallery could buy the painting for one million dollars, if it wished to. He countered that we should let the gallery have the painting, spacing out annual payments of one hundred thousand dollars over ten years. Though such an interest-free loan is not the sort of arrangement any of us could make for a mortgage on a home, I thought it a reasonable local compromise and signed off on the agreement as proposed by the president. Once I left Eastman, it was arranged that my successor *give* the painting to the Memorial Art Gallery "because it seemed like the right thing to do," he told me. Clearly, it is an important responsibility for the school's director—now called dean—to protect the school's assets, a more complicated matter at Eastman than at any other American academic institution I know of. It is striking in this context that in the ninety-year history of the Eastman School, there has never been an Eastman graduate on the board of the university. When President Joel Seligman, shortly after his inauguration several years ago, called me in Texas to ask what I thought about the idea of an Eastman graduate on the university board, I endorsed the idea wholeheartedly and suggested a couple of candidates. Such an appointment would go a long way, in my view, toward demonstrating to Eastman parents, faculty, students, and graduates that resources appropriate to the work of the school would not be inappropriately used in support of other units of the university.

A CAUTIONARY TALE: THE PROBLEM OF BOSTON,[15] THE "HUB OF THE UNIVERSE"

This chapter is replete with positive examples from my own experience of how music deans can improve their institutions. But leadership is not always sweetness and light, and I continue this chapter with a story about how things can go wrong.

At the New England Conservatory, my effort to develop a long-term plan (and the possibility of change) led quickly to chaos and the request for my resignation. Partly, this may have been the result of a lack of communication between myself and the board. I had been asked, at age sixty-two, to transform the conservatory and to lead a capital campaign. Because I planned to stay but six years on the job, I thought I had the board's support to move faster than, in retrospect, I think I should have. Part of the problem was that I was not well served by a provost eager to be president, a matter of overconfidence on my part, for I accepted the recommendation of the provost's appointment by the board chair without doing the necessary due diligence on trustworthiness of the proposed candidate. But part of the problem, I believe, was Boston itself, where but a small number in town accept the importance of well-considered change. Too few of Boston's institutions of culture and higher education work actively together in support of a positive future, and far too many Bostonians believe that the hinterlands beyond Route 128 are not worth paying much attention to. As a result, the physical plant of NEC, built during the final years of the nineteenth century and the early years of the twentieth, remains much as I left it in 1999, though a plan has now been established for badly needed renovation. The faculty has been strengthened and the financial aid resources improved, but the idea of musicians developing skills for spreading greater musical literacy among Americans was stopped for a decade at the pass. Russell Sherman, a fine pianist and wonderful piano teacher, writing in the summer of 1998 to the community as a whole, quoted the Harvard philosopher George Santayana in a fashion with which I disagreed, but out of respect for Sherman I failed to push back as strongly as I should have. Wrote Sherman, in a memo to the faculty:

> "Culture is on the horns of a dilemma; if profound and noble it must remain rare, if common it must become mean."
>
> The recently released results of the 1994 federal census indicate that five percent of the American public attends the opera while one percent plays classical music. The breach between the general culture and high culture is unfortunate, undemocratic, and largely intractable. NEC must have programs that reach out to the community. NEC should include in its curriculum courses that help certain students to develop careers in various para-musical areas corollary to the actual creation and performance of music. However, NEC should not adopt an accommodationist agenda—however generously intended—which dilutes our charter and tradition in order to facilitate jobs and to sweeten our image. That is a task for other schools. We are a conservatory.
>
> In pursuing and reinforcing this choice, our school should aim for the highest standards of artistic achievement. Ultimately, this will redound to NEC's benefit in the spheres of professional pride, reputation, and general support. In the end, our students will be both happier and more respected. And so will NEC.[16]

I have never believed that classical music is for a limited part of American society, for people who, like J. K. Paine, believe that if the music is of high quality, only people of high quality will be qualified to listen to it. I believe, rather, with the people of China, that it is a matter of the presentational and pedagogical skills that musicians can learn while young that will help them spread the message, in the fashion of what in Boston I called musical missionaries.

When accepting the NEC presidency, I was told I was being asked to make the conservatory into the kind of institution I had developed at Eastman, listed in the spring of 1997 by *U.S. News & World Report* as the music school with the best master's degrees in the nation, marginally ahead even of Juilliard and Indiana. (The magazine has not re-ranked music schools since then.) Accordingly, I began a planning process aimed to change and to energize long-term fund-raising for salaries, financial aid, and plant renovation. The process involved the faculty and staff, though I failed to realize how difficult such a process can be in a school where the large number of part-time people makes attendance at meetings difficult. Though this was badly needed in an institution with a $45 million endowment at a time when Eastman's endowment was $175 million, Juilliard's $275 million, and Curtis's $125 million, I did not properly understand the nature of rumormongering in an institution where many people were made nervous by the thought of change. After having turned down the George Eastman Professorship at Oxford in the summer of 1998, as urged by the NEC board chair, I was asked on March 15, 1999, to resign, for having, as a member of the executive committee of the board told me that day, "tried to turn NEC into a liberal arts college." Actually, I had made no new curricular requirements and had appointed no new humanities faculty. What I *had* tried to do was begin moving in a direction to require the students to think, at the end of their sophomore years, about whether they were really performers, and to question the problem raised by our issuance as a nation of more than 30,000 degrees a year in music without questioning where and how all these young musicians might find employment in the world of music.

Looking back on the period 1996–1999, I take joy in my contribution to the development in Boston of two forward-looking organizations: the Youth Orchestra of the Americas, a fifty-fifty mix of superb young musicians from north and south of the Rio Grande that tours every summer, and the remarkable radio program *From the Top*, which weekly presents some of the best of America's wonderful young performers, teenagers who not only play and sing with skill and artistry but also know how, as shown in Chris O'Reilly's able interviews, to use the English language in ways that promote interest in all kinds of music study. But my efforts to establish a series of weekly programs at WGBH-FM, in which the superb musical institutions of the Lowell Institute—the Boston Symphony, the Boston Philharmonic, the New England Conservatory, Harvard, MIT, Boston University, the Handel-Haydn Society, the Gardiner Museum, the Longy School, Wellesley, Brandeis, Tufts, and the Walnut Hill School—all competed with one another, not only for musical excellence but also for the skill with which members of those organizations brought new audiences to music through talks no longer than five minutes, came to naught. While that idea went nowhere in 1998, I hope that, under the new leadership at WGBH-FM of Benjamin Roe, something worthwhile along these lines can be accomplished in the new millennium.

At the time of my contretemps at NEC, I wish that I had had access to an article by Ronald A Heifetz and Marty Linsky, "Leadership on the Line: Staying Alive through the Dangers of Leading," published three years later by the Harvard Business School Press in 2002. The article begins:

> To lead is to live dangerously because, when you lead people through
> difficult change, you challenge what people hold dear—their daily hab-

its, tools, loyalties, and ways of thinking—with nothing more to offer than a possibility. . . . People push back when you disturb the personal and institutional equilibrium they know. People resist in all kinds of creative and unexpected ways that can get you taken out of the game, pushed aside, undermined, ostracized, or assassinated.

If you are willing to lead a music school into the next generation, please take note. You need at every moment the steadfast support of the person or people to whom you report if you are effectively to lead through what most American schools will need to survive in the years immediately ahead. The speed of change cannot be more rapid than the community to be led will tolerate, unless the leader has strong support from his or her superiors—in writing and frequently reiterated. Being ahead of the curve often exacts a price. In the fifteen years since I left NEC, much of what I had advocated in the late 1990s has begun, including curricular reform, longer-term contracts for the faculty, renovation of the facilities, and the development of a successful entrepreneurial program. What I worked on in Boston was not wrong. But I believe now that I probably tried to solve too many problems in too short a time span. As Bob Sproull used regularly to remind me, "Only one tiger at a time!"

INSTITUTIONAL PRIDE

This chapter concludes with what I have come to think of as a dean's most important task, the development of a sense of community cohesion and institutional pride. The University of Texas has developed this sense in the most noteworthy fashion for more than a century, through faculty, staff, and alumni loyalty, and a shared and powerful sense of institutional purpose. The "Hook 'em Horns" sign is one expression of this, as is the congregational singing, at the end of every formal ceremony, of what the university president will always call "our favorite song," a contrafact of "I've Been Working on the Railroad."

> The Eyes of Texas are upon you,
> All the livelong day.
> The Eyes of Texas are upon you,
> You cannot get away.
> Do not think you can escape them,
> At night or early in the morn.
> The Eyes of Texas are upon you,
> Till Gabriel blows his horn!

While it would be hard work institutionally to develop a song like "The Eyes of Texas" for a professional music school, the most moving memory I have of my years at Eastman came on the eve of commencement in 1983, when an original ballad by Neal Hampton, a member of the graduating class, was sung at the conclusion of a graduation concert in

Kilbourn Hall by a small chamber choir that included Renée Fleming, with composer Hampton at the piano. Without prompting from the director's office, Neal and his colleagues at that moment summarized exactly what I was trying to accomplish at Eastman. By the time the ballad was over, I was close to tears.

> We say "good-bye" for the very last time.
> I take your hand in mine and hold it tight.
> Don't close your eyes, just look back and smile;
> We've grown; we're different than we used to be.
> Where has it gone?
> The years have passed.
> And yet it seems like weeks since we first met.
> The time we've shared, the hope and pain is all behind us now.
> Time to begin again.
> Moving on,
> Take your dreams and leave this world behind.
> The path is long,
> Never knowing what you'll find around each corner,
> Or find within yourself.
> The time has come to say "good-bye."
> There's been some good, some bad; remember both.
> In these four years I've watched you grow into a person
> Better than you were when I first met you. Farewell.

NOTES

1. In my letter, I correctly anticipated Allen Wallis's reaction. When he introduced me to the Eastman faculty and students, in a packed Kilbourn Hall where I dedicated my administration of the school to music's future in America, he said, "While Robert Freeman never attended the Eastman School of Music, except as a Preparatory Department student when he was a boy, if it had not been for Eastman he would not exist at all, for his parents met here." The reader can imagine the pride of my mother and father, seated together on the stage.

2. Chancellor Wallis was ultimately correct. When Gilbert McCurdy, a UR trustee who was head of one of the community's leading department stores, decided to close the store's flagship branch in the downtown, two blocks from Eastman, there was no preliminary discussion, just an announcement in the papers.

3. Kristen Carmichael-Bowen, "The Legacy of Jan DeGaetani (1933–89)," PhD dissertation, Smith College, 2004. During the early 1970s, I wrote an article on repertory of the famous castrato Farinelli, published in a Festschrift honoring Arthur Mendel (*Studies in Renaissance and Baroque Music*, ed. Robert L. Marshall [Kassel: Bärenreiter, 1974], 301–30). In rehearsals for a recording with Jan DeGaetani, I mentioned the article, explaining that I had looked carefully through Farinelli's repertory for substitute arias and was disappointed that I had found almost none. Following the clues of parodists like Marcello and Martello, I had imagined that the motive for substitute arias came from eighteenth-century singers' pride and political power in an opera house. Said Jan, "The phenomenon you were investigating was real, but you picked the wrong singer. It isn't political power but musical illiteracy on the part of singers that brings about substitute arias. If you have trouble learning new music, you'll want to rely on repertory you already know. But Farinelli was a composer and a singer,

wasn't he? I can't imagine that he was the sort of artist who needed to use substitute arias." On the threshold of directing Eastman, I was instantly persuaded that scholars have as much to learn from performers as performers surely do from scholars.

4. I have no idea why University of Rochester president Rush Rhees and George Eastman chose "director" as the title for the Eastman School's first leader, Alf Klingenberg. In 1972 I accepted the fact of the title as a historical precedent that I saw no reason to try to change. At the faculty meeting in December 1996 when I announced my resignation, Provost Charles Phelps, sitting next to me, leaned over to tell me that he intended to change the title of Eastman's head to that of dean, to which I responded quietly that I did not see what purpose that change would serve. After James Undercoffler's appointment as my successor, it was announced that his new title would be that of dean, thus bringing Eastman in better alignment with the titles of the heads of the university's other six colleges, a period that began with Undercoffler serving as dean *and* director. At the time of my own appointment, many members of the Eastman faculty believed that Howard Hanson, as director of the Eastman School, ran a more independent ship than did the university's other deans. From my own perspective, it is the table of organization that counts, not the detail of the title. Clearly, one has to get along with one's boss. The times when this becomes critically important are in the approval of faculty appointments, promotions, and tenurings; the approval of annual budgets; and on the occasions of decanal (directorial) review for reappointment. I have never believed that the "independence" of Director Hanson's administration was especially strong. While the faculty was untenured, Eastman budgets from those days had unaccountably disappeared before the time of my directorship.

5. The Thomas S. Kenan Institute for the Arts and the North Carolina School of the Arts, *Preparing Performing Artists for the 21st Century*, June 6–9, 2002, B2.

6. Eric Booth, *The Music Teaching Artist's Bible: Becoming a Virtuoso Educator* (Oxford: Oxford University Press, 2009), 75. As the reader already knows, too many faculty at leading music schools misunderstand the etymology of the word *conservatory*, deriving as it does from the word's original use in this context to conserve female virtue in an otherwise dangerous environment. Modern music schools are called conservatory, school, institute, and college, without any apparent distinction of implication to go along with the noun in question. The degree of conservativeness in their curricula has nothing to do with the use of the term *conservatory*, as is illustrated by the differences among Oberlin, New England, and Curtis. The first two are called "conservatories," though NEC is a lot more conservative than Oberlin, not in the least a conservative conservatory. The most conservative of the triumvirate just listed is the Curtis Institute, where the repertory studied until very recently ended with the death of Debussy and where any study of the humanities was accomplished only as a way of achieving NASM accreditation, but where the performance standards are exceedingly high among all of the very limited number of students in the enrollment.

7. Booth, *Music Teaching Artist's Bible*, 74–78, 215–22.

8. Booth, *Music Teaching Artist's Bible*, 220.

9. Two anthropological studies of American music schools are highly recommended to those considering a career in their leadership. Bruno Nettl's *Heartland Excursions: Ethnological Reflections on Schools of Music* (Urbana: University of Illinois Press, 1999) reviews several of the nation's large Midwestern schools of music. Henry Kingsbury's *Music, Talent, and Performance: A Conservatory Cultural System* (Philadelphia: Temple University Press, 1988) presents a similar analysis of "The Eastern Metropolitan Conservatory," a thinly disguised version of the New England Conservatory. Among the questions raised by these two provocative books is whether every performance major needs to be put through the psychologically grueling torment of one or more solo recitals, performed from memory.

10. For a foundation whose focus lies with the commissioning of new work, see www.bethmorrisonprojects.org.

11. I once suggested to the president of the Heritage Foundation, a friend from days at the Bohemian Grove, that he commission a symphonic work dedicated to the mem-

ory of Ronald Reagan. He demurred. "Aren't most composers academics and aren't most academics liberals?" I responded that, while I thought he was right, I said it is also true that all composers have to pay their mortgages and plan for their eventual retirements, and that it would be perfectly possible for me to suggest to him and his friends composers whose recorded music he could audition in advance of a new commission. The project now belongs to a very able UT student of mine, Victoria Schwartz.

12. That I had made the right choice of narrator in Willie Stargell, not only a Hall of Famer but a truly great man, was clear on the night we played Philadelphia's Academy of Music and the critic of the *Philadelphia Inquirer* got past our security team to interview Willie ten minutes before he was to go onstage. Said the critic, "Mr. Stargell, this is a temple of high art. Serkin plays the piano here, Rostropovich the cello, and Isaac Stern the violin. Stokowski and Ormandy have conducted here. Doesn't it make you nervous, realizing how little you must know about high art, to go on stage here as a soloist?" Though my heart was in my mouth, Willie replied, "Is Steve Carlton here?" (Carlton was at the time the Philadelphia Phillies' most successful pitcher, himself a Hall of Famer.) "If Carlton were here, there would be something to be nervous about. He's struck me out more often than I can remember. Which reminds me, though the clothes I am wearing tonight (white tie and tails) look pretty silly, I don't suppose they are sillier than the costume I used to wear playing baseball. The real difference is that baseball fans knew when I screwed up; and because they knew I was getting well paid for doing so, they'd begin booing, then they'd throw things at you, especially in the outfield. But when I was about to go onstage last night at the Kennedy Center, David Effron told me, 'Whatever happens, it's vital that you look as though you know what you are doing. I think you will do splendidly. But should anything happen, please remember that I will know as conductor, and Joe Schwantner as composer will know. Bob Freeman may know. But the audience has never heard the piece before, and they will not know. So when you get to the end of the piece, shake hands with me warmly, then go around the front desks of the string section, and embrace all of the young women who have just performed with you. When we go offstage, don't wait to be recalled, simply do an about-face and get back onstage.' Actually, nothing unplanned happened, and we had a wonderful response from the audience. The whole experience taught me that the biggest difference between baseball and classical music is that baseball fans know what's happening while classical music fans appear not to."

In David Halberstam's book *The Teammates*, the author describes a trip made by Johnny Pesky, Dominic DiMaggio, and Bobby Doerr, all members of the pennant-winning Boston Red Sox team of 1946, who drove together from Boston to Florida to visit with Ted Williams, the great star of that team, during the final months of Williams's life. There Pesky speaks of Willie Stargell, a young member of the Pittsburgh Pirates during the early 1960s, when Pesky was a coach for that team. Says Halberstam, "To this day, when Pesky spots a ballplayer he likes not just as a ballplayer but as a man, he uses Stargell as his measuring rod, the requisite qualities being uncommon inner strength and human richness." Stargell once told me, after our tour with him, that the opportunity to perform Joe Schwantner's *New Morning for the World* with the Eastman Philharmonia under David Effron was the most wonderful thing that ever happened to him, "for it gave me the opportunity to help forward the important message that Dr. King had given his life for."

At a private dinner with my son John, then a hard-hitting, strong-armed eighteen-year-old catcher who was considering try-outs for the Pirates and the Reds, John told Willie that he thought himself too slow a runner to aspire to a career as a professional baseball player. Willie responded that he was proudest of the only National League record he still held: striking out more often than anyone else in the history of the league. "You see, John," he said, "striking out is an art that one has to learn in order to succeed—in the arts, in politics, in sports, and in business. None of us hits a home run each time at bat. Most people lose courage when they strike out. What each of us has to learn is how to fail, then to stand up from the dust to try again." Though John did not become a professional player, he is in fact a man of inner strength and courage of whom I am very proud.

13. *Buffalo Altar, a Texas Symphony* has been recorded by J. F. Brazos Enterprises with Barry Corbin as narrator and Todd Frazier conducting the Houston Ballet Orchestra.

14. Katherine Millet, "Bargaining Power: Artists in Academe," *Chamber Music* 24, no. 6 (December 2007): 38–46, 79.

15. See Martin Green, *The Problem of Boston* (New York: W. W. Norton, 1966). Shortly after news of my NEC resignation was announced, I had a call from my old friend Thomas W. Morris, at that time executive director of the Cleveland Orchestra. After Morris asked me what had happened, he said that he had heard the story from other sources: "In Boston, you are not supposed to change anything, for too many of the people there have trouble looking beyond Interstate 495."

16. Letter from Russell Sherman to the NEC community, summer 1998. Once in Texas, I invited Russell to perform an evening of Beethoven piano sonatas as part of a conference that the College of Fine Arts staged with the university's Law School, using the concept of artistic authenticity as a lens through which to consider the Constitution of the United States, described at the time as "a wonderful artistic work by James Madison, performed in the meantime by several generations of artists called attorneys for an audience called the courts—and American public opinion." Russell, a wonderful pianist and teacher, left me with his fabulous complete recording of the Beethoven piano sonatas, which he dedicated to me as "a man for all seasons." I was deeply flattered.

EIGHT

Advice for Provosts and Presidents

Leadership for the Music School of the Future

Your music dean or chair has just resigned, died, or retired, and it is your responsibility to find a new one. Before you do anything else, read Kevin McCarthy's *The Performing Arts in a New Era* (2001), the Thomas S. Kenan Institute's *Preparing Performing Artists for the 21st Century* (2002), *The Creative Campus* (a report of Columbia University's 104th American Assembly, 2004), Eric Booth's *The Music Teaching Artist's Bible* (2009), and Joseph Horowitz's *Classical Music in America: A History of Its Rise and Fall* (2005)—all previously discussed in this book—and reflect on the educational outcomes that would take place on your campus were you able to find visionary leadership for your music school.

If there is a message for you in this book, it is that because musicians are normally trained to specialize in composition, performance, or scholarship, they almost always earn doctoral degrees whose subject matter has relatively little to do with reaching the other students on your campus, your musicians' potential future audience. Since American universities have long been in the business of selling doctoral degrees, it is to be anticipated that many of your candidates for the deanship will have PhDs or DMAs in music and that your faculty search committee will, as a matter of course, tend to reject candidates whose life histories depart from an imagined norm that includes a doctoral degree. It will be important to choose the chair of your search committee with unusual care and to speak with him or her about the importance of looking for candidates who have a vision for the future of music in America and of the particular role that your institution can play in musical education. Of course, you will ask that you be included in the review of all résumés from minority group members and from women. I believe you should also ask to see professionally prepared materials that depart in one way or another from what many a committee will consider the safe, current subdisciplines of music. It is important that you remind your committee that Howard Hanson had no doctoral degree when he was selected at age twenty-eight to be Eastman director for a deanship that lasted forty years, that I had no previous administrative experience when selected at age thirty-seven to be one of Howard's successors, that Joseph Polisi had no doctoral degree and very little experience when selected in his midthirties as president of Juilliard, and that Gunther Schuller had neither a doctoral degree nor administrative experience when selected at age forty for a ten-year term as president of the New England Conservatory. You are looking for someone, perhaps rather young, who has a dream about new ways musicians need to be trained and educated, a person relatively well connected in the larger world of music, someone who understands how the history of your institution relates to those of other leading music schools, someone who has a dream for how your school might separate itself from your competition, someone who cares not only about the music majors but also about the musical education of those who will be the music majors' audience, and someone who at least at the outset has the strong support of the faculty.

As you know, it is very important for you to understand who your real competition is, for faculty members and for students. When the University of Rochester used to speak of "the universities with which we like to compare ourselves," I tried to remind the speaker that the challenge is really to identity the institutions with whom others compare us. While I like to compare my piano playing with that of Murray Perahia and Maurizio Pollini, it is a problem if no one else wants to. In my view, you are competing favorably with your competition whenever more than 50 percent of the students admitted to your school and to those of your competition matriculate in the fall on your campus, owing the same net tuition to either school.

For more than twenty-five years, books like those cited at the beginning of this chapter—along with the present volume—have been advising you that the narrow training of innocent young musicians who lack skills in thinking, reading, writing, and speaking condemns them to repeat a past that has not worked for some time and that gets more problematic for most of your music graduates every day. You should remember, too, that the potential audience for your young musicians comprises the other students on your campus and that an important aspect of your music unit should be the development of that audience.

I believe that you should strongly consider appointing the successful dean of one of your university's other schools to read the books mentioned above and to become a member of your search committee. The interviewing process can still run normally, so long as you can assure yourself that you are getting to see the candidates whose backgrounds especially interest you. Among the questions I think you should try to get the finalist candidates to answer for you are the following:

- In view of the serious imbalance between supply and demand for professional musicians, what do you believe an optimal balance between undergraduate and graduate enrollment ought to be in our school? (Note to the provost: The faculty will press for a 50–50 split because well-prepared older people play and sing better than younger ones, though it is much easier on financial aid budgets for you to press your dean toward a 75–25 division of enrollment. Keep in mind that successful undergraduate musicians are attractive candidates for medical, business, and law schools. They can become a vital part of an avocational musical community that supports the work of the professionals, and the music faculty does not have to find jobs for them.)
- What kinds of musical repertories will your students work on? Nothing but classical music, in the fashion of the Curtis Institute of 2000, say, or the kind of musical balance seen in front of the Lincoln Memorial on January 19, 2009? While in the short term you may not be able to represent American music very aggressively on campus, I'd like to hear your thoughts on intermediate-term planning toward a larger repertory for your students. If necessary, I can imagine using funds from the provost's office to help you accomplish this.
- Please share with me your thoughts on the potential support of your school and faculty for the non-music-concentrators on this campus. Will you appoint senior faculty to think about the best ways to engage your potential audience among our students in musical activities? How will you allocate studio, practice room, and ensemble placement opportunities with respect to concentrators and nonconcentrators? Because I want to be certain that fiscal pressures related to enrollment income don't influence you too heavily in this area, I am prepared to help you accomplish jointly agreed-upon goals in this area.
- Leon Botstein, the remarkable president of Bard College, editor of the *Musical Quarterly*, and music director of the American and Jerusalem symphony orchestras, has developed what seems to me a very interesting program, as a result of which an undergraduate in a five-year residence at Bard can end up, while studying with first-class music teachers, with a bachelor of music degree *and* a bachelor of arts degree.[1] (Bard has recently announced its acquisition of the Longy School of Music in Cambridge, thus providing the entrepreneurial Dr. Botstein and Bard with a new window on a major city, and all sorts of new curricular possibilities.) Please share with me

your views on the possibility of implementing such a program on this campus.

- I would be grateful if you would share your thoughts on intellectual collaboration between the music school and other colleges of our university. (Note to the provost: The University of Texas at Austin strongly encourages a collegial relationship among its prospective deans, arranging for a luncheon for each decanal candidate with the current deans. This is a strong assist to effective institutional fund-raising, under the leadership of an effective vice president for development. At Texas, great care is taken to provide deans with "hunting licenses" on major donors, licenses that expire with the passage of several months unless renewed by the vice president for development. It is also part of normal procedure in Austin that every meeting with a potential donor be summarized online, immediately after the meeting, in a message available for inspection by the other deans, the president, the provost, and vice presidents. As a result, fund-raising in Texas is a team sport, not the result of chance interaction among Somali pirates, as happens in some American universities.)
- What would you think about seeing to it that the music undergraduates were housed with majors from other colleges of the university, thus ensuring that your students have plenty of opportunity, while still students, to proselytize other disciplinary majors for the music they care about. In their essay "Music, Mavens, and Technology," Steven Tepper, Eszter Hargittai, and David Touve argue that articulate music majors can, as undergraduates, have a powerful impact on their non-music peers by acting as articulate advocates for music in your dormitories and social centers.[2]
- For provosts of universities, like the University of Texas at Austin, that include a performing arts center that brings in music, theater, and dance from the outside, for the benefit of your campus and the community of which you are part: What do you think is a rationale for the repertorial differences between what our arts students are learning and what our community seems to be willing to pay for? (Note to the provost: If there is a huge difference between the two, I think you should consider adding to your subvention of the performing arts center while asking yourself why your students are working on repertory that your community seems not much interested in. It is clear in any case that there ought to be a single dean in charge of both your music school and your performing arts center, with a view toward keeping you abreast of what is going on in the world of the performing arts. Kathy Panoff, the excellent new director of Texas Performing Arts at UT Austin, has recently brought in a $475,000 grant from the Andrew W. Mellon Foundation to help

underwrite the difference in Austin between the otherwise diver-
gent artistic and fiscal pressures just cited.)
- Do you regularly follow Greg Sandow's excellent blog on classical
  music? Will you comment on the curricular revolution now ongoing in the School of Music at DePauw University in Greencastle,
  Indiana, as described in a Sandow blog post on October 2013? The
  director of the School of Music, with the support of the president of
  the university, has charged each of the faculty chairs with recommending entrepreneurial changes in each of the institution's several music curricula.
- I would be grateful, finally, to have your views on how music and
  the other arts should be financed in America's future.

THE ARTS NEED NOT BE SO MARGINAL AS THEY ARE IN THE UNITED STATES

I believe it should be part of your goal, in the appointment of a new dean,
to think about the long-term role your university might play in developing for our country the kind of societal role that music plays in Scandinavia, for example. In 1994 I was invited to chair an international commission comprising the head of the Paris Conservatory, the head of Vienna's
Hochschule für Musik und darstellende Kunst, the president of the University of Göteborg, and a professor of musicology of the University of
Helsinki. We reported to Finland's minister of education on the future of
Finland's Sibelius Academy, one of the world's great music schools. After
a week of listening and interviewing, our group drafted a report in which
we told the minister that while the faculty and students were splendid,
working at a very high artistic level, the fact that the several departments
of the institution were located all over Greater Helsinki meant that, in
effect, there was no school. At the end of the week, I met with the minister to deliver our recommendations. I told him that we thought it important for Finland to build a new facility for the whole school, in downtown
Helsinki. "What do you suppose such a facility would cost?" he asked.
When I estimated one billion dollars, he leaped to his feet and embraced
me warmly. "You recommend it and we will do it!" "But," said I, "you
are in the midst of a serious recession, in a country of only five million
people, with 15 percent of your population unemployed." "That means
that this is a great time for building, the result of lower construction
costs," he said. He told me that in the view of the government, there were
three forces that had a strong impact on the Finnish people: alcohol, sex,
and music. (He went on to specify that by music, he meant classical
music, folk music, early music, new music, jazz, Broadway, church mu-
sic, rock, choral music, and wind music, among others. All kinds of mu-

sic!) "The government has believed for many years that music is the only positive force among these three!" said he.

When he asked where our commission thought the new facility ought to be located, I suggested "between the Finlandia Hall and the State Radio and Television, but that is where you have the marshaling yards for the state railways." He promised to move the marshaling yards. And since then Finland has accomplished exactly what we recommended, investing nearly one billion dollars in a brand-new facility for the Sibelius Academy that opened in 2011.[3]

While the United States is a much bigger and more complicated country than Finland, it has also given birth to a lot more music than has Finland, music that could represent the United States in the most positive ways as a social force, to ourselves and to the rest of the world, if only we would begin to reflect on the values that our country stands for. The music program of your university could make a major contribution to the realization of that dream. Its accomplishment depends upon a strong faculty, to be sure, but the energy that will move your program from a mindless repetition of existing goals to something much more ambitious belongs to the new dean you will choose, a man or woman who will not be able to succeed without your strong support.

THE RULES OF ENGAGEMENT

Once your new dean is appointed, especially if he or she is administratively inexperienced, do not confront him with an immediate crisis. Allen Wallis knew what a bombshell he was presenting to an inexperienced dean when he insisted on his own way in the Eastman relocation question of 1973, a political situation that he made much worse by forcing the issue. Self-doubt overwhelmed me before I had gained my sea legs, and it came very close to persuading me that I was in the wrong profession. Bob Sproull was a mentor who saved my administrative life. He could be demanding, but he was direct in letting me know, once he was CEO, what he thought I needed to do. He provided me with both guidance and latitude for action, persuading me that deaning could be fun. Having gone through a divorce and remarriage, I decided in the late 1970s that it was time for me to look for another job, and as a result was offered the deanship of the very distinguished music school at the University of Michigan. When Sproull asked me whether I wanted more money, I said I did not, adding that what I really wanted was to get along better with him. I may have said something like, "You're the boss and you get to decide, but I'd be grateful if you would begin by letting me make my case first." We agreed on that modus operandi and became good friends. From Sproull's point of view, my responsibility as dean was to frame a potential problem, to present him with at least three different ways of dealing with the problem, and to propose one of the three as my favorite course of action. As my supervisor, he then got to agree or to disagree. If he disagreed, I had as many minutes as I needed to present why I disagreed with him, after which I was expected to proceed as he directed, within a week, unless I uncovered new evidence that suggested a viable alternative.

Equally important is the willingness of the provost and president to block end runs. Early in the administration of Sproull's successor, the president made the mistake of taking a meeting with a professor of musicology who believed that Sproull and I had been seriously underpaying him. After the meeting, the president called me with the message, "I have decided that _____ is seriously underpaid, and I call as president to direct you to raise his annual salary by ten thousand dollars." I responded that I work for a living and that, of course, I would thus proceed, whether I agreed with the idea or not. Within a month, the same professor came to my office with further nonnegotiable demands for office space, clerical assistance, and financial aid support for his graduate students. I told him that it was silly to waste his time and mine. "The president is your friend. You should go to see him." Within a day, the president called with his white flag raised! Said he, more sensibly, "You're the dean. I'm the president. From now on, I promise not to interfere with your decanal function." And we became friends, then and ever since.

Problematic at the University of Texas has been the fact that the dean of the College of Fine Arts, an institution that goes back seventy-five years, is continually subjected to end runs by leaders of some of the college's units, more than one of whom has argued over time that he or she ought to report directly to the provost. In an institution with fifty-three thousand students, seventeen deans, and three thousand faculty members, a level of middle management is critical. Without it, the provost would never get to go home, subject, as he would be, to forty or fifty direct reports instead of twenty-five, itself a much larger number than desirable. Not to recognize the existing table of organization subjects the whole institution to entirely unnecessary strain while wasting time and energy better reserved for other matters. The goal is to persuade one's boss to advocate enthusiastically for the resources one needs.

There exist a variety of plans for deciding who gets to make the final decision on faculty tenure. Certainly, all faculty members need to understand out front and in writing the terms of appointment and what they have to do to be promoted and to attain tenure, if that is an available institutional option. And the untenured faculty deserve an annual private conference with the dean for a report on their progress as individuals toward that goal. At Rochester, Bob Sproull's system involved a recommendation by the dean, supported by the tenured faculty of the department; the tenure case involved all sorts of internal and external documentation on teaching, professional work, and service. That package had to be presented to an anonymous ad hoc committee of tenured faculty, advisory to the provost and appointed with the consent of the dean. Only once in twenty-four years did the ad hoc committee present a recommendation different from my own, on the tenuring of a very good violin professor who was not, in my view, however, the best violin teacher at the time in the school. When the president asked me, in a final conference, whether he ought to follow the recommendation of the ad hoc committee or of the dean, I handed him my letter of resignation, indicating that it was impossible for all of the violin faculty to be equally attractive, for some of them had to teach violin students not acceptable in the studios of some of the others but whom we needed in the school. As I expected would happen, the president did not want to accept my letter, and an important point had been established: whereas I was happy to follow protocol, I could direct the work of the school only were I in charge, at least in this vital area.

FUTURE STANDARDS FOR MUSIC EDUCATION

Of special importance, I think, is a provost's consideration of the standards according to which music education faculty are evaluated. Certainly, there is room in the world for statistics-oriented studies on public-policy development in school teaching. These, however, ought not to be substituted for a person's enthusiastic accomplishment in bringing children and adolescents to music, with excitement and artistry. If a K–12 music teacher is a good musician who generates enthusiasm for music making and listening in young people, he or she is generating an interest in the beautiful that can become a lifelong passion for the students. If a music teacher is not a good musician, in the judgment of the music faculty, I would greatly prefer that he not be let loose to direct the musical activities of the young and innocent. Musically uninspired teaching may be a way of making a living, but it does great damage to the fabric of music all over the nation.

DIFFERING STANDARDS FOR APPOINTMENT, PROMOTION, AND TENURE?

While the doctoral training of scholars goes back to mid-nineteenth-century Germany, the idea of doctor of musical arts degrees for performers goes back to the collaboration of Howard Hanson and Earl Moore in the middle 1950s. This was a mission undertaken at a time when the number of music positions in a growing number of American colleges and universities was increasing rapidly, and it was the aim of the farsighted director of Eastman and dean of Michigan to see to it that all the new positions were not taken by scholars. At the best of the nation's comprehensive music schools, our DMA programs have produced performers of international distinction, men and women who can hold their own on any stage in the world while supported by communications skills and habits of mind that would make them ideal faculty members anywhere. The late David Burge, who took his DMA at Eastman, was not only a superb pianist, especially for new music, but a prize-winning writer of many books and articles on music, a composer, a conductor, a novelist, and a poet. UCLA's Robert Winter, who took a PhD in musicology at the University of Chicago, is not only one of the world's leading Beethoven scholars but a splendid pianist, an engaging developer of future audiences, and a technological entrepreneur of the highest accomplishment and potential. Charles Rosen, a concert pianist and recording artist of the first rank and the author of a dozen brilliant books on music of the eighteenth, nineteenth, and twentieth centuries, took his PhD at Princeton in French literature. The provost's insistence that music appointments go only to the specialist holders of doctoral degrees would, of course, preclude contemporary appointments for people like Shakespeare, Beethoven, Da Vinci, or Diaghilev. And many faculty would be intimidated by the multiple talents of Burge, Winter, and Rosen.

A related problem involves institutional self-definition, a proper solution of the congruence of faculty talents and development to an institution's real goals. If everyone tries to be Harvard, where disciplinary specialization is the normal order of the day, no one but Harvard will succeed. An institutional insistence on emulating Juilliard, if undertaken elsewhere, is bound to fail for the same reasons. The Butler School of Music at the University of Texas is a first-rate, well-endowed institution, but I believe its future lies not in ideals generated at Lincoln Center but in the exploitation of two strengths closer to home: the University of Texas at Austin and the city of Austin itself. Put another way, distinguished liberal arts colleges will have music faculties of between six and twelve, many of whom should be generalists who strive for artistic goals different from those of Harvard and Juilliard. Since it will be difficult to recruit world-class specialists to such remote locations as Tuscaloosa, Alabama, Grand Forks, North Dakota, or Fairbanks, Alaska, provosts at those and similar universities would do well in my view not to fall prey to the inevitability that some faculty will be eager to emulate Harvard or Juilliard. The importance of defining your own institutional mission, realistically and with integrity, should manifest itself in the development of goals for faculty career building and tenuring that have, in turn, a positive impact on the future design of the university and of the students it teaches. As a wary provost, you will, of course, wish to be sensitive to the extremely conservative nature of accreditation by NASM, the great majority of whose members regard change with trepidation. While the professional loyalty of doctoral degree holders will normally be to the musical subdiscipline of their doctoral degree—musicology, music theory, piano, music education—the kinds of faculty who teach at institutions of the kinds just alluded to should be especially concerned with the future of music itself. Certainly, the goal of every dean and provost should be to see to it that the right people are appointed and promoted, providing for the faculty realistic goals that support the musical development of statewide and local communities, especially among the young musicians who study there. As a sensitive provost, you should bear in mind, too, that faculty need not all be cut from the same cloth, that one size does not fit all—that there should be room both for international artists who while young teach relatively light loads, and for fine teachers and able department chairs who teach heavier loads that involve much less travel.

NEW FACILITIES FOR MUSIC SCHOOLS AND DEPARTMENTS

While it is to be expected that presidents and provosts will continue to receive requests from their music units for more space for concert halls, classrooms, faculty studios, and practice rooms, it is hard to think of a single American college or university that includes the kind of inexpensive facility herewith recommended for any campus that enjoys an abundance of good weather: an outdoor concert shell in the middle of the campus. As indicated earlier, the fifty thousand UT students who regularly visit the east side of campus for football games very rarely attend musical events at the Butler School of Music, a mere two hundred yards north of the stadium. Because so many of the Butler School students play and sing on so high a level, it has for some time seemed to me that we ought to invest in a music performance shell in the midst of our very beautiful campus. There, two or three times a week during the academic year's fine weather (September to mid-November, late February to mid-May), one might put on forty-five-minute student musical, theater, and dance presentations in the middle of the day. Some of our students perform so spectacularly that it is hard for me to imagine their informal performances in the open air not stopping large crowds of their fellow students from other parts of the university. One would need, of course, carefully designed sound-projection equipment and special arrangements for the protection and security of keyboard instruments. But the investment of funds needed for such a purpose would be rewarded, I am sure, not only by improved attendance at music school events but also by a much greater willingness, a generation or two ahead, for enthusiastic and generous participation on the boards of the region's professional not-for-profit performance groups. Such institutions as Miami, Florida, Florida State, Louisiana State, Rice, Texas, SMU, Arizona, Arizona State, and UC San Diego, Irvine, Los Angeles, Riverside, and Santa Barbara might thus, in the midst of their campuses, create incipient, local, low-cost, student-centered Tanglewoods!

ISSUES OF THE DAY

In my continuing quest to make the arts a more integral part of the life of the modern American university, I helped set up a project at Texas in 2006 that almost became a reality. That it did not was the result of my stepping down as dean at the same time that my boss left his position as provost. The program that we worked on with great enthusiasm together was called "Issues of the Day," and it involved at the time the provosts of the University of California, Berkeley, UCLA, the University of Michigan, the University of Illinois, and the University of North Carolina at Chapel Hill. I was delighted to be informed in February 2013 that all five of the other universities had followed through on "Issues of the Day," a project whose results I will follow eagerly.

The original idea was to use a combination of provostial and decanal funds amounting to two hundred thousand dollars for each of three years, for a campus total of six hundred thousand dollars, to commission a major new work of art—an opera, a play, a piece of choreography, or a visual work—though I think we both liked the idea of beginning with a new opera. An opera, for example, might have been commissioned from a major American composer on an issue of the day, to be picked by the provost, working with his seventeen deans. (Informally and preliminarily, the provost and I had decided on immigration as a fine potential topic for Texas.) With the kind of money we were talking about, we could have commissioned a truly major composer, who would have been asked to choose his or her own librettist. The university was then to invite the librettist to be in residence for a spring semester, working on a text for the opera. But during the semester immediately beforehand, the provost was to commission immigration courses to be taught all over the university—in literature and history, in law and government, in nursing and social work, in business and communications, in visual art and theater. Then, during the spring semester, the faculty and students working on immigration were to confer with the librettist, who, at his or her own discretion, would work at weaving into the new work aspects of the topic that the librettist had heard about from those involved in the immigration courses. Produced as a major event on campus, the work would then tour to other collaborating campuses all over America, advertised as a piece reflecting the contributions of many fields. The University of Michigan, for which the Islamic population of Metropolitan Detroit is a major constituency, was thinking about the role of women in the West and in the Middle East as its issue of the day. The Eastman School might commission an opera on the very dramatic life of George Eastman, an American

Horatio Alger who cared about capitalism, employee relations, the impact of industry on community, education, technology, health, music, and the world's view of the United States. I am grateful to acknowledge a recent heads-up from Matias Tarnopolsky, the able executive and artistic director of Cal Performances at UC Berkeley, that that great university has followed through with a series of academic courses, linked to the work of Cal Performances, as follows:

- "Music and Literary Modernism," taught through the Department of English by Serena Le, under the supervision of Professor Eric Falci. This course focused on the connection between major modernist writers of the early twentieth century as they grappled with the political, social, and technological backgrounds of the early twentieth century. Performances connected with the course took place by Anne-Sofie von Otter, mezzo soprano, and Emanuel Ax, piano; by the Martha Graham Dance Company; by Gerald Finley, baritone, and Julius Drake, piano; by Venice Baroque with Philippe Jaroussky, countertenor; by Jonathan Biss, piano; by the Calder Quartet; by the Vienna Philharmonic Orchestra; by the Jerusalem Quartet; by Jestyn Davies, countertenor, and Thomas Dunford, lute; by the Kronos Quartet—"A Meditation on War"; and by Marcus Shelby Jazz Orchestra in "The Legacy of Duke Ellington: Fifty Years of Swing." This course culminated with the creation of a synthetic project—integrating both a written and aural element—by members of the course, as well as an associated colloquium during which each student had the opportunity to present his or her work.
- "Vienna 1800—Vienna 1900: Art and Modernity of the Turn of Two Centuries," through the Department of Music, taught by Professor Nicholas Mathew. Structured around two pivotal historical moments in one cultural center, this course posed questions about the construction and reconstruction of musical modernism at the end of two centuries. The urban space of Vienna itself circumscribed the repertory under consideration: concerts, including music by Schubert, Brahms, and Schoenberg, as well as a series of performances by the city's own Philharmonic Orchestra. Students were exposed not only to written texts but also to examples from contemporary visual culture. In that way, the course aimed to immerse the music of these two periods in a rich and complex intellectual context, all in order to tease out connections between this pair of storied fin de siècle moments in Vienna's history. Students attended concerts by Richard Goode, piano; by Anne-Sophie Mutter, mezzo soprano, and Emanuel Ax, piano; by Gerald Finley, baritone, and Julius Drake, piano; by Jonathan Biss, piano; by the Calder Quartet; by the Vienna Philharmonic; by Yo-Yo Ma, cello, and Emanuel Ax, piano;

by Pinchas Zuckerman, violin, and Yefrim Bronfman, piano; and by the Mark Morris Dance Company.

- "Thinking Critically about Dance," through the Department of Theater, Dance, and Performance Studies, taught by lecturer Jenefer Johnson. A survey that spanned a broad range of dance styles while cultivating a variety of analytical skills, this course offered students a framework for thinking about gesture. Over the duration of the semester, students attended seven dance performances on the Cal Performance season, providing written responses to those events. To promote the development of vivid gestural awareness, students were required to present their somatic reactions to readings and performances in the form of "movement phrases" and other such assignments. A crucial component of seminar meetings involved interactions with visiting artists, such as Marni Wood of the Martha Graham Company and Mark Morris during his company's production of *Acis and Galatea*. These exchanges provided students with invaluable artistic insight while presenting new scholarly lenses through which to consider dancing and the moving body. The students attended performances by the Martha Graham Dance Company, Cedar Lake Contemporary Dance, Ballet Flamenco with Eva Yerbabuena, the Trey McIntyre Project, Les Ballets Trockadero de Monte Carlo, the Alvin Alley American Dance Theater, and the Mark Morris Dance Group in *Acis and Galatea*.

James Leija, associate dean of the College of Literature, Science, and the Arts at the University of Michigan, also contributed a much appreciated summary of Ann Arbor's plans for their use of a similar grant from the Andrew W. Mellon Foundation. The plan that follows is based, Leija writes, on a preexisting infrastructure of close academic relationships already developed at the university, encouraging intercollegiate collaboration. In May 2014, the University Musical Society will host its first Faculty Institute on the Arts and Academic Integration. They will be working with a cohort of twelve faculty fellows, across rank and from a broad range of academic disciplines to share best practices on incorporating performance and arts-based learning strategies into their teaching. Each participant will either create a new course or substantially revise an existing one to integrate the arts into their teaching plan. The initial intensive two days will feature workshops with staff from the Center for Research on Learning and Teaching, U of M faculty, and visiting scholars and artists. Over the course of the 2014–2015 academic year, the cohort will meet with UMS staff several times to gain insight into the season-planning process and learn about upcoming performances, as well as continue to refine their arts-integrative syllabi. The cohort will then implement their syllabi in the 2015–2016 academic year. Participants will receive two thousand dollars in course development funds to support their work. The grant provides funds for three iterations of the Faculty Institute. As partners, UMS; the School of Music, Theatre, and Dance (SMTD); and LSA are launching an ongoing, dedicated, UMS-related course to be offered each year, beginning in winter 2014. The topics for these dedicated courses will be developed in close consultation with participating faculty, integrating academic themes in LSA with related threads in UMS programs, and drawing from the academic experience of SMTD. Some of the faculty partners have already suggested possible topics for a UMS/SMTD/LSA courses, including a focus on creativity and innovation, or theories of spectatorship (with emphasis on lenses such as globalism, race, gender, cultural criticism, and international cultural forms), or the creative arts for community organizing and cultural change. They anticipate that students who already have an interest in the arts will naturally seek out the dedicated courses; however, the primary target population is students who may not have a prior inclination toward the arts, particularly students who are not otherwise likely to encounter the arts during their undergraduate years. The Winter 2014 iteration, "Engaging Performance," will be taught by Yopie Prins (English) and Matt Thompson (SMTD) and will meet the LSA requirement for Humanities. The course will focus on seven UMS performances and offer a range of opportunities for pre- and postperformance reflection and processing. The UMS Faculty Insight Group will engage with UMS's programming and education staff to explore curricular connections with prospective offerings for future seasons, to help raise awareness about the academic role that UMS plays within U of M, to advise staff on best practices for arts integrative learning, and to help plan and recruit faculty for the Arts/Academic Integration Faculty Institute. Faculty Insight Group members, representing a broad range of schools and academic disciplines, will meet regularly throughout the year to view UMS performances, discuss season planning, and explore opportunities to more deeply and systematically integrate programming into the academic life of the university.

If the process of making art seems remote to most Americans, it seems to me that we ought to expand the number of our citizens who have had, at least as students, the opportunity to work with the materials of art (words, notes, clay, oil, the human body) to make them moving, expressive, and beautiful. Gaining such experience—a much easier matter than it used to be as a result of rapidly developing technologies—should lead in only a small number of cases to the idea that the nascent artist should try to make a living through the world of art. We understand as a society that while athletic activity is good for children, adolescents, and adults, there is no point in encouraging us all that such activity is beside the point unless we become professional athletes.[4] Especially relevant to this point is Joanne Lipman's article, "Is Music the Key to Success?" published in the *New York Times* of October 12, 2013. There the author reports on her interviews with a number of celebrities in fields other than music who attribute to their musical studies all sorts of credit for their eventual success in other domains: Condoleezza Rice, Alan Greenspan, Paul Allen, Paula Zahn, Chuck Todd, Steve Hayden, Woody Allen, Andrea Mitchell, Roger McNamee, Larry Page, Steven Spielberg, and James D. Wolfensohn. And she summarizes what the people just listed attribute to their music studies: opening pathways to creative thinking, the abilities to listen and to collaborate, a continuing drive for perfection, the ability to connect disparate or even contradictory ideas, and the power to focus simultaneously on the present and the future.

NOTES

1. *Chamber Music* 22, no. 4 (August 2005): 18–25, 89–90.
2. Steven Tepper, Eszter Hargittai, and David Touve, "Music, Mavens, and Technology," in *Engaging Art: The Next Great Transformation of America's Cultural Life*, ed. Steven J. Tepper and Bill Ivey, 199–220 (New York: Routledge, 2008).
3. See Leona Hyvärinen, ed., *Institutional Evaluation of the Sibelius Academy* (Helsinki: The Academy, 1995).
4. For an inspiring message on involving the whole of a modern industrial society in the making of art, see Seymour B. Sarason, *The Challenge of Art to Psychology* (New Haven, CT: Yale University Press, 1988).

NINE

Some Suggestions for Foundation Directors and for the National Endowments for the Arts and Humanities

How to Work at Increasing Demand

Precisely because the world's fiscal resources are finite while its needs appear infinite, it troubles me to see so much fiscal effort wasted or misdirected, creating a yet greater supply of musicians without giving much thought to the development of demand for music. This book is an effort to describe an imaginary musical ecosystem for the future of the United States that would deploy limited resources more strategically. It is not my aim in what follows to criticize past decisions, which were often made as a result of donor intent. I have tried not to suggest how to redirect who gets to eat bread but, if possible, to bake more loaves that could better feed more people, with more positive results.

Certainly, the nation's creative artists need support for their work, but the federal government is not an effective means for accomplishing that. Because artistic freedom is a vital matter, it makes no sense either to ban the creation of works by men like Mapplethorpe and Serrano, or to encourage the government to commission new work that, by its very nature, will cause counterproductive controversy. If part of the function of art is to create social criticism, to do so through the federal government only inflames the politicians, without accomplishing much that is positive. More sensible would be for the National Endowment for the Arts, perhaps through a White House conference on the arts convened by the president, to urge interested foundations and the nation's 4,200 colleges and universities to work together at commissioning new work, particularly if such funds could be used to persuade the faculty and students of an entire institution to embrace the excitement that a new artistic masterwork can help engender, in the fashion that Sheldon Ekland-Olson and I had in mind with our "Issues of the Day" project at UT Austin.

GRANTS THAT INDUCE INTER-ISLAND COLLABORATION

At Eastman, I was able to bring about a sense of institutional purpose by creating a one-hundred-thousand-dollar annual fund available to small groups of the twelve departmental chairs, as long as they were willing to work together instead of each concentrating on his individual island. I would strongly recommend to private foundations and the NEA that you do the same, seeking ways of bridging music's islands in order to accomplish larger societal goals, especially the creation of an avocational musical society more enthusiastic about music and much more eager to support the work of a smaller number of professionals. The recently announced "Academy" formed by Carnegie Hall and the Juilliard School is an exciting example of the sort of thing I have long had in mind and could easily serve as a model for outstanding music students in other cities.

My goal of reducing the number of professional musicians is part of a larger objective: to create more professionals in areas where we need them (schoolteachers, especially of science and math, general practitioners in medicine, speakers of such crucial languages as Chinese and Arabic, scientists and engineers of an entrepreneurial bent), while reducing numbers in areas where we are producing too many people (PhDs in the humanities and social sciences, attorneys, medical specialists, and bankers, for example). In an era dominated by modern technology and the Internet, when the number of Americans who purchase musical instruments without knowing what to do with them is rising rapidly, we should be providing net-based instruction on musical coherence, available without cost. As Clay Shirky says in *Here Comes Everybody*:

> Though some of the early utopianism around new communications tools suggested that we were heading into some sort of post-hierarchical paradise, that's not what's happening now, and it's not going to happen. None of the absolute advantages of institutions like businesses or schools or governments have disappeared. Instead, what has happened is that most of the relative advantages of those institutions have disappeared—relative, that is, to the direct effort of the people they represent. We can see signs of this in many places: the music industry, for one, is still reeling from the discovery that the reproduction and distribution of music, previously a valuable service, is now something their customers can do for themselves. The Belarusian government is trying to figure out how to keep its young people from generating

spontaneous political protests. The Catholic Church is facing its first prolonged challenge from self-organized lay groups in its history. But these stories and countless others aren't just about something happening to particular businesses or governments or religions. They are also about something happening to the world.[1]

And in the meantime we have been experiencing the so-called Arab Spring.

EL SISTEMA

For the past quarter century, I have followed with growing interest the development in Venezuela of El Sistema, a web of more than two hundred youth orchestras of which a marvelous ensemble called the Simón Bolívar Youth Orchestra of Caracas is, as the result of competitive auditions, the very best. The inspiration of José Antonio Abreu (b. 1939), a Venezuelan pianist, economist, educator, activist, and political leader, El Sistema has been generously supported by seven consecutive Venezuelan regimes of both the Right and the Left. It provides youngsters from the Venezuelan barrios with excellent instruments and fine age-appropriate musical instruction, developing in them not only a very high level of musical accomplishment but also, with the collaboration of teachers and parents, admirable skills in working with others, the desire to work hard, the esteem of their peers, rising levels of self-confidence, community-building skills, and joy in making and listening to all kinds of exciting music, from both sides of the Atlantic. Gustavo Dudamel, the brilliant young music director of the Los Angeles Philharmonic and an alumnus of El Sistema, has made a notable and very positive impact on the musical life of Southern California. As a result, Abreu's truly remarkable accomplishment in Venezuela is increasingly recognized in the United States. Mark Churchill, for many years the highly esteemed dean of primary and continuing education at the New England Conservatory, was put in charge of the development of classes of Abreu Fellows at NEC, opening the possibility of establishing a dozen or so El Sistema centers in other important American communities. Because no one has seriously studied the extent to which El Sistema also develops skills in reading, writing, and speaking, it is not known how many El Sistema graduates go into business, medicine, or the law, rather than simply adding to the supply of unemployable viola players. From the anecdotal account of Lisa Wong in *Scales and Scalpels*, however, it appears that El Sistema develops an unusually large number of physicians.[2] Thus, while it is premature to suggest that a strengthened American network of youth orchestras will improve the balance between supply and demand in America advocated by this book, the phenomenon is well worth continuing study by leading foundations for serious fiscal support in the years ahead.[3]

The long-term goal, in every case, should be to make music study a more central aspect of the general education of as many Americans as possible, emulating the ways professional sports—especially baseball, basketball, and football—have developed not only lots of young people eager to be professionals but also a vast audience eager to watch their heroes (and heroines) perform. And, as this book goes to press, I have just learned of something similar to El Sistema now taking place in Colombia. It is called Il Batuta, recently a feature of Christopher O'Reilly's wonderful weekly radio program *From the Top.*

SUPPORT FOR PUBLIC POLICY RESEARCH IN THE ARTS

Foundations ought to do more in support of public policy research in the arts. No doubt because France centralized early as a nation while Germany was relatively late in doing so, the French fund culture centrally while the Germans insist on doing it locally. This might give rise to studies on how the arts are funded in the world's other nations. If our tax laws promote private philanthropy within our own borders, might it not make more sense for us to persuade students from abroad to help revise their own tax codes in a fashion more like our own? At a time of national recession, what sense does it make for our tax code to permit fiscal breaks for affluent Americans who contribute funds for the arts and education in other countries? Wouldn't it be more prudent at a period of large national deficits to encourage such activity only when a partner nation encourages *its* citizens to make fiscal contributions to not-for-profit organizations in the United States?

POSSIBLE COLLABORATION WITH EDUCATIONAL TESTING SERVICE

During the 1980s, when I served as a member of the music test development committee for advanced placement by Educational Testing Service (ETS), I was impressed both by the excellence of their test in music theory and ear training (which is even better these days) and by the relatively small number of young Americans who took the test each year, so low a number that it was not really in the interest of ETS to continue administering the test. In the interest of national musical literacy, it would be a major step forward were some foundation to dedicate an endowment of fifty million dollars, say, to four-year college scholarships for high school seniors who get top marks on the ETS music theory and ear training test. At 5 percent, such an endowment would yield two and a half million dollars a year, providing full-tuition scholarships and more for as many as fifteen annual four-year scholarships of as much as $160,000 each. Were these fifteen very generous scholarships properly publicized *and made available to students who matriculated at any accredited American college or university and for whatever field of concentration the student chose,* I have no doubt that many American parents would press their school boards to offer AP instruction in music theory and ear training, thus helping develop what would be a sizable annual cadre of young Americans who knew and loved music, irrespective of their profession, with aural skills developed at a more appropriate time in their lives than is normally the case now. It goes without saying that an interested donor could try out such a program for five years, say, before endowing it; could put his or her own funds together with those of other donors; and could raise or lower the number of scholarships, depending on their dollar value, whether or not they covered all four years of undergraduate study. The numbers just cited are for purposes of illustration only. In any case, the amount of money allocated would represent but a drop in the bucket of the financial aid already allocated each year to the students of the 638 NASM schools.

I am especially enthusiastic about financial aid for collegiate music students that requires a focus on programs connected to the local community, especially those wherein the students play and sing for audiences in schools, prisons, retirement communities, and hospitals, for example, not simply performing the music but, in the fashion recommended by Eric Booth's *The Music Teaching Artist's Bible,* also finding ways of connecting the music performed with the interests and perceptive powers of their audiences. Such informances ought also to provide students with experience in booking such engagements, thereby gaining skills relevant to the management of their own careers. Greg Sandow told me recently of a very successful experiment he tried last fall at Juilliard, at 9 a.m. of the first class of a semester, telling two dozen Juilliard students that they would fail the course if they were unable to return to class by noon having booked a recital for him or herself. "While there was much weeping and gnashing of teeth at 9:15, every one of the students returned by noon with a recital successfully booked," Sandow said.

Further inspiration on potential leads in this area will come from the published results of the Strategic National Arts Alumni Project, the Surdna Foundation's studies on career outcomes from artistic education. Support for the "Issues of the Day" project, as described in the previous chapter to provosts and presidents, would also be helpful. Howard Fineman's *Thirteen American Arguments* is a pregnant source of ideas in this area. I hope that my own brief review of American values that follows may be of influence as well.

MUSIC AND AMERICAN VALUES

On September 16, 2007, I listened to a televised discussion of signal steal-
ing by Bill Belichek, coach of the New England Patriots, along with a
discussion of penalties later imposed by NFL commissioner Roger Goo-
dell. It occurred to me that the incident was not only a continuing problem in American sports but also in American life generally. I fear that too
many Americans have come to accept the idea that the end justifies the
means and that the only justifiable end is to win at any price, whether in
sports, politics, business, or world affairs. Some even equate the wish to
win at any price with American exceptionalism. In what follows, I try to
imagine the kind of America I would like to see us strive for, a nation in
which there is broader recognition of the rightness of the propositions
listed and of the possibility of achieving such a discussion, in important
measure, through new works of art commissioned for our college campuses. Such practices would help us consider what it means to be an
American. Far too many prominent voices in our political discourse insist
that what is exceptional about America is that one can make unlimited
amounts of money here—I am not sure to what end. I believe we should
aim instead toward a national discussion of American values beyond
winning and making enormous amounts of money. I would rejoice if
such a discussion could involve the following:

- We are governed by the Constitution, under the rule of law. While
  there is a lot of jabbering these days about the Constitution, it
  would be of great value for more Americans actually to read the
  Constitution and its amendments, and to think about it, perhaps as
  the result of American works of art.
- The checks and balances among the three governmental sectors—
  executive, legislative, and judicial—are a central matter, especially
  when we are under attack.
- The freedoms of speech and religion, along with the separation of
  church and state, as provided for by the Founders through the First
  Amendment of the Constitution, and the tolerance of nonviolent
  opinion, are central to what we are about.
- Freedom of opportunity—the possibility that anyone, given a willingness to work hard, can succeed—has helped make us who we
  are. This should not mean, of course, an absence of regulation, recognizing as we do that most human beings are a long way from
  perfection and that greed remains an important human motivation.
- Despite our history, the civil rights of all men and women are vital
  to our future.
- We spend more on defense than all of the rest of the world put
  together, and, for reasons that seemed justified at the time, we are

still the only nation in the world to have used atomic weapons in warfare.

- We have not yet provided equality of opportunity for everyone, and it is a serious economic drain on national productivity to have to incarcerate more than two million Americans annually, another activity in which we lead the world.
- We would be vastly better off, in an increasingly small world, by gaining the trust and admiration of others, through the United Nations or alternative means.
- It is a vital national interest that we educate our young people as well as we possibly can, for a world that will get a lot more competitive with the rapid industrialization of China and India.
- Arts education, delivered by dedicated and expert teachers, provides the population as a whole with a central set of experiences. (Rahm Emanuel's experience as a dancer during his high school and college years not only kept him lithe but probably contributed to his relentless pursuit of political achievement.)
- It is very important that our population be kept healthy, in part by minimizing infant and maternal mortality, improving our longevity rates, and by educating all Americans about the importance of exercise, diet, and avoiding smoking, recreational drugs, the excessive use of alcohol, and promiscuous sex.
- The problems imperiling the global environment, partly as a result of the impending industrialization of much of the rest of the world, are threatening to all of humanity, of which we are part.
- We are a nation of immigrants. Thus we should understand and appreciate the increasing strength immigrants of the past and future provide to the nation as a whole.
- It is important for children to be born into families that will welcome and encourage them while providing supportive nurturing and education—a true pro-life policy that also acknowledges women as the people best able to make decisions about their own bodies.
- Higher education is not only a private good but a public benefit as well.
- Selling goods and services through constant allusions to sex and violence undermines our own sense of national decency while providing extremists who do not like us with a rationale for focusing on our least positive characteristics.
- The values fostered by the arts—in the skills of listening, collaborating, understanding with nuance, seeing, experiencing empathy, and working hard toward the perfection of the product at hand—are critical to understanding who we are, and why.

- Though we speak endlessly about American exceptionalism, very little attention is given to understanding our history and to what makes us exceptional.

While it would be preposterous for anyone to think of defining American values for the nation as a whole, the idea here advanced is to use foundation funding for the arts to encourage a national *discussion* of American values, especially through the commissioning of new American work that opens broader consideration of who we are as a nation, thereby following through on the question Jeanette Thurber asked Dvorak in the early 1890s about how to define a truly American music. A word of caution: While there will always be those who promote art for art's sake, the opportunity to teach courses on the history of German opera and of the German lied has shown me—and some of my students, I think—how easy it was in the twentieth century for Germans to use the philosophy, literature, poetry, drama, and music of their immediate past as support for a political agenda that twice brought calamity in the twentieth century to a highly sensitive and artistic people.[4]

ENCOURAGEMENT FOR AVOCATIONAL INVOLVEMENT

If music study is, among other things, a way of helping young Americans learn to work harder while watching television less, why shouldn't American universities help undergraduate music majors learn to work harder, encouraging double degrees at the undergraduate level? It would be one thing if learning to play the clarinet really well for every undergraduate clarinet major were in the national interest. That we continue to develop such intense focus on really superior undergraduate musical performance when most such graduates are unemployed in the professional world of music seems to me a misplaced emphasis, as it does to Blair Tindall, Kevin McCarthy, the Kenan Institute, the participants in the Creative Campus conference, and Eric Booth. In this context, shouldn't someone be encouraging more avocational competitions like the Cliburn Avocational, but for organists, violinists, oboists, trombonists, and string quartets? The goal ought to be to make music a continuing and vital part of the lives of many people. Clearly, growing numbers of human beings are interested in music. The U.S. census figures of 1990 show one person in four as owning a musical instrument. That the figure changed in 2000 to one person in three demonstrates something of music's potential!

FUTURE INTERDISCIPLINARY FOCI

While the establishment of a strong disciplinary focus lies at the root of human intellectual and artistic achievement, I have become during the past quarter century more and more interested in interdisciplinary activity. Six areas of potential research will be of special interest for future work and its support:

1. **Scientific research on music and the brain**, especially with respect to brain plasticity in children and adolescents. Because technological advances in recent decades have made it much easier to study the living, working brain, it is now possible to better understand the impact of music on the human brain, especially in connection with the development of nonmusical cognitive skills. Researchers like Mark Tramo and Gottfried Schlaug have begun important work in this area, as have Isabel Peretz, Robert Zatorre, and Todd Frazier. If Howard Gardner is right that musical intelligence is one of humanity's basic forms of intelligence, and that music needs to be understood better from a scientific as well as artistic perspective, it is vital that the research of the pioneers just cited and of those who follow them be well supported in the new century. It is now possible to follow up scientifically on what have long been the serious interests of music therapy, that is, exploring music's positive impact on stroke victims and on those who suffer from Alzheimer's disease as well as on prematurely born infants. Yet more interesting from my perspective are the questions of how the brain processes music and on how, as the human being develops from infancy to maturity, it is possible to accomplish such goals as a performance from memory of the Rachmaninoff Third Piano Concerto. Clearly, a great deal of very high-level digital dexterity is required, necessitating a great deal of thoughtful piano practice. But in the interests of not overpracticing, it should ultimately be possible to understand better what instrumental practice optimally consists of and how to make it most effective, using the least amount of time. That so many musicians subject themselves to the unprescribed, unsupervised use of beta-blockers as a way of diminishing stage fright should also be a subject of ongoing research.[5]

Three years ago, I attended a meeting of the board of the National Center for Human Performance at the Texas Medical Center in Houston, where Colonel Lex Brown, an officer of the U.S. Air Force stationed in San Antonio, spoke about a problem encountered by the Air Force as a result of the predator drone planes that our country has been using in Iraq, Afghanistan, and Yemen.

Colonel Brown told us that it is a great step forward for the United States to be using predator drones, for when one of them crashes, our people are not injured. The problem is that the predator drones crash much more often than do manned planes, and that each drone costs the taxpayer several million dollars. Once the Air Force investigated why the drones were crashing so often, it discovered that there were two major problems, the first of which was easily solved. Though electronic signals travel very rapidly, their transmission is not instantaneous, a phenomenon known as latency. To reduce latency, the people who were operating the planes by remote control were moved from Nevada to the Persian Gulf.

The second problem, however, proved much more difficult. While the Air Force normally uses two drone operators to monitor such matters as altitude, speed, distance from target, incoming missiles, and remaining fuel, there are in fact about forty such variables, some of them reported visually, some of them aurally. But the two monitors have terrible trouble, under time pressures, synthesizing what the several variables are reporting. In training these personnel, the Air Force began to look for the kinds of human beings who can synthesize multiple variables under the pressure of time. And after a lot of research, they came to an interesting conclusion. The answer is concert pianists.[6]

These are the people in American society who, in performing on stage, not only have to hit all the notes, in the right order and in a big hurry, but to do so while taking into consideration the fact that the conductor may beat a measure of two when he is supposed to beat three, that the second bassoon may come in a measure early or the dampers of the piano malfunction. While a batter has to guess whether the pitcher is going to throw him a ninety-five-mile-an-hour fastball, an eighty-nine-mile-an-hour curve, or a seventy-five-mile-an-hour change up, once the pitch has been hit or missed, the batter gets a chance to gather his thoughts for ninety seconds before the next pitch is on its way. A concert pianist has no such option, for the piece he is playing goes on inexorably, for twenty minutes at a time, without pause, in a situation where what was ten seconds ahead fifteen seconds ago is now five seconds in the past.

Clearly, there is no time for reflection on wrong notes already played. Not only is there nothing to be done about wrong notes, in retrospect, but thinking about them undermines what is to be done immediately ahead. Frankly, the Air Force doesn't begin to understand how this works, but since so much depends on our finding out, they are working hard on the problem. They wonder how it might be possible to teach human performance, under pressure, to schoolchildren. Ought we not make all our soldiers experts in human performance? What ought the contribution of our public schools and universities be to learning more about this phenomenon?

2. **Music and cognitive development.** Because of the very strong work of UCLA's James Catterall, there exists a good deal of recent

information about the contribution of the arts to keeping at-risk students in school, improving their self-esteem, improving cognitive function, and improving their abilities to collaborate with others. While I believe from personal experience that this is all true, we all know that while some music teachers are inspiring, knowledgeable, and enthusiastic, that is not true of all of them. It would be very helpful were we to able to control Catterall's excellent work through better knowledge of the role that really excellent music teaching makes in such circumstances. It is, I believe, the quality and enthusiasm of the instruction, not simply its existence, that makes the difference.

3. **Music and children.** Because Jeanne Bamberger's research on how small children learn music, conducted during her days as a member of the MIT faculties for music and artificial intelligence, has been published in journals unknown to most musicians, too few in music education have read and thought about what she has learned. Now living in Berkeley, California, strongly influenced by early work of hers with Arnold Schoenberg and Roger Sessions while thinking about the work of Jean Piaget, Bamberger remains a fertile source of imaginative ideas that should have a more mainstream influence than they do. This lack of influence is due in my view to her teaching career at the University of Chicago and at MIT, neither of which is much involved in hands-on musical work with children in the nation's public schools.[7]

Because so many American K–12 schools now offer a curriculum that concludes at 3 p.m. while working parents are only able to pick up their children at 5 or afterward, there exists a hole in the schedules of many American children that might sensibly be filled by elementary instruction in musical literacy. This is, I believe, an excellent opportunity for one or more foundations to collaborate with community music schools and the nation's K–12 sector.

4. **Music and cultural diplomacy.** The work on cultural diplomacy initiated in Iraq by John Ferguson and Mark Thayer deserves much more enthusiastic support than it is getting. There appears to be a hunger in the world for all kinds of American music, especially in parts of the world that were closed to American cultural influence during the Cold War. Teaching Arab teenagers in Lebanon, Kurdistan, Iraq, and Afghanistan, Ferguson, Thayer, and their colleagues also perform with local musical artists all over the Mideast, in repertories that synthesize American music of all kinds with more local musical repertories. Those interested in what can be accomplished, with the expenditure of very modest sums of money, are referred to Ferguson's impressive DVD *Jazz Bridges, Afghanistan*, available through DVD Video and Pal NTSC, or through Ferguson's website, www.americanvoices.org. To follow through on Fer-

guson's imaginative initiative, however, we will need a generation of excellent American musicians who play all sorts of American repertories, unafraid of collaborating with local musicians in other countries.

5. **Music and Psychology.** To perform on the stage without getting paralyzed by stage fright, young musicians are urged to practice much more than I think they need to, going too mechanically through unending hours in the practice room to be able to perform with but half of the capacity they would exhibit while playing privately. I hope that work begun at the University of Texas at Austin in the School of Music, the School of Pharmacy, and the Phobia Avoidance Clinic of the Department of Psychology will be followed up on, there and elsewhere, in such a fashion not only to inform future musicians but also to influence outcomes for the Pentagon, for example. Put another way, stage fright is a phenomenon that undermines the lives of all sorts of people, in all sorts of vocations, though perhaps most obviously in the work of musicians where the tolerances are so much narrower.

6. **The Future of American Orchestras.** As the son of a Boston Symphony member and as the head of three schools that have produced many fine orchestral players, I view with special concern the deteriorating situation of American orchestras, a primary icon of what classical music in America has stood for.[8] The serious budget problems announced recently for the Cleveland, New York, Philadelphia, Atlanta, Detroit, Indianapolis, Louisville, Denver, and Honolulu orchestras, and the recent collapses of the New York City Center Opera and the Minnesota Orchestra, underline the findings of the Mellon Foundation's Orchestral Forum and of Robert J. Flanagan's new book, *The Perilous Life of Symphony Orchestras.*

While the hundred or so players of an orchestra understand incredibly well how to play together to achieve artistic excellence, the seven constituent parts of an orchestra (music director, executive director, players, board, press, audience, and community) appear to have no sustainable modus operandi for keeping most such organizations afloat during the quarter century ahead.[9] Herewith is a brief list of what I think of as some of the most pressing problems to be solved:

- A shortage of fine conductors, especially of conductors born in the Western Hemisphere. It makes no more sense for a really fine conductor to preside regularly over more than one orchestra than it would for Joe Girardi to manage both the Yankees and the Red Sox or for Carly Fiorina to have presided simultaneously over both Hewlett-Packard and Apple. The music director is responsible not only for the quality and ensemble of the players but for planning the programs in a way that makes artistic and educational sense to the audience and for representing the organization to the community of which the orchestra is a part. This entails musical, administrative, fund-raising, and public-relations skills.

- A general lack of understanding of the institution's table of organization. Does the music director report to the executive director or vice versa? How is the orchestra represented to the board, or at least to its executive committee?
- The possibility of involving the players in activities other than orchestral playing. How much should the institution try to accommodate the interests of some of its members in solo or chamber music performance? How far should the orchestra go in assessing the administrative and public speaking abilities of members who play instruments that are often not on the stage—piccolo, English horn, bass clarinet, trombone, tuba, harp, some of the percussion players, for example? What would happen were several orchestras not only to audition potential new members but to interview them as well? Might not some of those players also undertake administrative responsibilities if they were trained to do so? Relevant in this connection is the fact that, while American orchestra members are paid at about the same salary levels as American university professors, the job satisfaction of the former is much, much lower than that of the latter?[10] What would happen if prospective orchestra members were required to read John Spitzer's *American Orchestras of the Nineteenth Century* and Robert J. Flanagan's *The Perilous Life of Symphony Orchestras* before participating in their first audition-interviews? What would happen were growing numbers of American orchestras to rid themselves of the very conservative perspective of the American Federation of Musicians and the International Consortium of Symphony and Opera Musicians, as recently took place in Charleston, South Carolina? What sense does it make for a union to exercise control over an industry where prices are escalating while demand is sinking?
- The size of the board. While the members of the board should certainly be affluent and influential members of a community in which they take pride, should they not have a strong interest in music, thus obviating the problem of board membership as a means to sell vacuum cleaners or real estate?
- A better understanding of audience members and the multiple motivations for their presence. How does the audience relate to the whole of the community that the orchestra serves? What sorts of experiences are *they* looking for? Given that the community of which the orchestra is a part has multiple uses in the new millennium for its finite philanthropic dollars, the members of the orchestra should join the board and management in reflecting on and

discussing what will generate demand for the orchestra in the years ahead. At a time in American history when labor unions have been in decline for more than a quarter century, what sense does it make for the players to depend on the International Conference of Symphony and Opera Musicians and the American Federation of Musicians for the success of a product that is, at least for the moment, in apparently declining demand?

The fact that there are no agreed-upon solutions to these questions suggests the following foundation-supported solutions. Suppose a foundation, perhaps in collaboration with the NEA, were to employ for six weeks in the summertime an orchestra otherwise without summertime employment for the training of a new generation of American conductors. Those in charge of the instructional program might include such people as Leonard Slatkin, Daniel Lewis (formerly head of orchestral conducting at the University of Southern California), David Effron (now head of orchestral conducting at Indiana University), Larry Rachleff (former music director of the San Antonio Symphony, head of orchestral conducting at the Shepherd School of Rice University), Marin Alsop (music director of the Baltimore Symphony), and Gerhart Zimmerman (music director for many years of the Canton Symphony, current head of the orchestral program at the University of Texas at Austin). These able people are offered as examples of the kind of talent I have in mind. For five three-hour morning sessions a week, talented young conductors in their twenties would lead rehearsals of a professional orchestra, supervised by one or more of the senior conductors just listed. Then, in the afternoon, all members of the orchestra might participate in mandatory classes of fifteen or twenty, in which a curriculum would be addressed, devised by senior officers of the League of American Orchestras, to make the players the owners of their orchestras' problems—in the fashion already undertaken by the Berlin Philharmonic. Instructional materials would include, though by no means be limited to, Eric Booth's *The Music Teaching Artist's Bible* and David Wallace's *Reaching Out*, focusing on fund-raising, press relations, audience development, the commissioning of new work, and the development of a closer and more symbiotic relationship among the music director, the executive director, the players, the board, and the audience. The classes themselves would be videotaped, and results edited and distributed as DVDs both to American university libraries and to the boards, staffs, conductors, and playing personnel of American orchestras, with a view toward making each American orchestra a more effectively operating organization. While I am sure that the readers of this book could easily come up with a broad array of other ideas for making this notion more viable, the basic idea is that without thinking about how to make our orchestras more effective organizations, the mindless repetition of the status quo is bound to lead toward further frustration for all hands.

Because the integrity of our national not-for-profit sector depends entirely on the energy, enthusiasm, generosity, and far-sightedness of affluent Americans, I think it would be a good idea, too, for half a dozen leading American universities, partnering with two or three leading American foundations, to offer regular three-day symposia on the qualities and habits of mind needed for members of *any* not-for-profit board of directors.

NOTES

1. Clay Shirky, *Here Comes Everybody: The Power of Organizing without Organizations* (New York: Penguin, 2008), 223. The Belarus phenomenon mentioned by Shirky three years ago has in the meantime exploded into the so-called Arab Spring of 2011.

2. Lisa Wong, *Scales to Scalpels: Doctors Who Practice the Healing Arts of Music and Medicine* (New York: Pegasus Books), 198.

3. For more on El Sistema, see the following links: http://www.ted.com/talks/jose_abreu_on_kids_transformed_by_music.html; http://www.ted.com/talks/astonishing_performance_by_a_venezuelan_youth_orchestra_1.html; http://www.boston.com/news/local/massachusetts/articles/2009/10/23/famed_venezuelan_music_education_program_adopted/; http://www.boston.com/ae/music/articles/2010/04/16/conducting_a_movement/?page=full; http://www.boston.com/ae/music/articles/2010/07/18/inspired_by_a_venezuelan_music_program_two_prepare_to_bring_its_benefits_to_boston_kids/; http://www.boston.com/ae/music/articles/2010/07/25/reflections_on_the_upbeat_to_a_new_movement; https://www.youtube.com/watch?v=eEYSfn2-P9k. See also Eric Booth, "Thoughts on Seeing El Sistema," unpublished paper, May 26, 2008; Eric Booth, "El Sistema's Open Secrets," unpublished paper, April 2010; NEC President Tony Woodcock's talk at a Salzburg Seminar last spring: http://fora.tv/2010/02/24/Music_with_a_Mission_El_Sistema_Comes_to_the_US. For a hundred-minute DVD on El Sistema, see *El Sistema*, directed by Paul Smaczny and Maria Stodtmeier (EuroArts 2056958). Daniel J. Wakin ("Conservatory Is to Cut Ties to Children's Music Project," *New York Times*, January 22, 2011) reports on the New England Conservatory's cancellation of its further involvement with El Sistema.

4. For a very good example of how differing national ideologies affect the most disparate worlds, see John Dizikes's *Sportsmen and Gamesmen* (Columbia: University of Missouri Press, 2002), a comparative history of British and American sports. Dizikes argues that the British have, until recently, engaged in sports as a way of developing young bodies while inculcating sportsmanship in the population, while in the United States we engage in sports, as in everything else, to win. (As a Rochester Little League coach in the mid-1970s, I engaged in such practices myself. The Cobbs Hill Little League Angels were the terror of our division, racking up successive undefeated seasons of which I was very proud at the time. In the meantime, I have come to question the values I was implicitly teaching to a group of talented eleven-year-olds, including my son John [our all-star catcher], before they were old enough to think about such matters, and at the educational expense of the six members of our team who were not starters, kids whose time on the field I tried to minimize in the interests of winning.) Wasn't that the sort of problem we had in getting out of Vietnam without winning? Isn't that part of the problem that now confronts us in our relationship to the Middle East? What might be the role of the arts, including music, in getting young Americans to discuss such matters and to make thinking about them part of our evolving national life?

5. See Wong, *Scales to Scalpels*, 208.

6. Unpublished talk for the Advisory Board of the National Center for Human Performance at the Texas Medical Center in Houston, according to the reminiscence and notes of the author.

7. What I think are the most important works of Professors Catterall and Bamberger are mentioned in notes 5 and 6 in chapter 4.

8. Philip Hart's excellent *Orpheus in the New World: The Symphony Orchestra as an American Cultural Institution — Its Past, Present, and Future* (New York: W. W. Norton, 1973) concludes, "Theodore Thomas's eagerness to 'go to hell' for a permanent orchestra must strike a responsive chord among many — orchestra musicians as well as trustees, conductors, and managers — who have survived the symphonic turmoil of recent years. They must, on many occasions, have asked themselves whether their time, effort, and money were worth the cause. If the moral uplift of Thomas and Higginson strike us these days as faintly Victorian, the same sentiment has been cast in more modern terms by Sir Hubert Read, when he said, 'Genius is a genetic chance and history a confused clamor, but life persists. It is a flame that rises and sinks, now flickers and now burns steadily, and the source of the oil that feeds it is invisible. But that source is always associated with the imagination, and a civilization that consistently denies or destroys the life of the imagination must inevitably sink into deeper and deeper barbarism.' In this life of the imagination, so indispensable to our civilization, the symphony orchestra must play an essential role and the efforts of all its dedicated workers find their ultimate justification."

9. For a marked exception to the passive role taken by too many music directors in the solution of their orchestras' problems, Leonard Slatkin deserves special kudos for his *Huffpost Arts and Culture* posting of November 26, 2013, here quoted in full.

The most important question American orchestras face is: How do we reach new audiences? You all know the complaints:

The average age is increasing.

Classical music has little relevance today.

The economic market cannot sustain an orchestra.

The list goes on. But in my hometown, we have found a way to buck the trend. After a six-month strike, during which many in the industry wrote off the Detroit Symphony Orchestra as yet another casualty in the Motor City, we have bounced back with new initiatives that have helped to address these concerns.

One method in particular has been a boon for us: Internet broadcasting of virtually all our subscription concerts. As a result of cooperation among the musicians, the board, union, and management, a deal was reached that allows this to occur with very little outlay of cash resources. Through the generous support of the Ford Motor Company Fund and the John S. and James L. Knight Foundation, and in collaboration with Detroit Public Television, we have been able to reach thousands of viewers around the world, most of whom previously did not know of the DSO.

In my mind, much of the thinking has to do with the realization that the definition of the word "audience" has changed, at least for this orchestra. No longer does it consist of just those people who come to Orchestra Hall, but it now includes music lovers in homes, hospitals, and even automobiles. Clearly, this is a throwback to the days when people would tune in, for example, to broadcasts by the New York Philharmonic. As a youngster growing up in Los Angeles, this was my audio window to a special musical world. Being able to listen with my family was very special indeed.

How does this new technology solve the so-called "crisis"? Clearly, the age of this audience is mostly younger. We know this through the comments we receive each week. They love not only the programs but also the additional content. Sometimes we feature voiceovers about the music to be heard, other times we feature interviews with the artists or composers. We also give them a few glimpses into the arts scene of the diverse Detroit metro area. Last year, I was able to have a friendly web competition with Michael Tilson Thomas, as to whose baseball team would win the World Series.

A few weeks ago we presented the American premiere of *Cyborg* by the Barcelona-based composer Ferran Cruxient. He was not able to make it out to Detroit for the performance, but he watched it with his father, to whom the work was dedicated, from his home. I gave him a cyberspace show.

For Thanksgiving week, we will present the American premiere of David Del Tredici's only opera, *Dum Dee Tweedle*. Although we expect good attendance at home, most others, including journalists, cannot attend. But many will be watching from their own base of operations, and a few will actually review the concert, covering not only the musical content but the televised quality as well.

Because the idea seemed so unique and relevant, we have been able to secure the needed funds that allow us to do these broadcasts. It does not put very much money into one's pockets, as the proceeds mostly go to the production costs. Starting in January, we will have robotic cameras which will provide us with more flexibility in the way viewers will see the orchestra.

After two years of these webcasts, we are still learning what works and what does not. Most of the time we get it right. As with any live television event, there are moments of fragility, but these are offset by the sheer joy of each concert. We are building our audience on a worldwide scale yet continue to reach those who come—week in, week out—to experience the marvelous acoustics of Orchestra Hall. Who knows what the next development with the global audience will be?

Stay tuned!

One can only imagine the positive impact that such worldwide telecasts have on the international reputation of Detroit, a community that these days needs as much economic and political support as the arts can provide.

10. See J. Allmendinger, J. R. Hackman, and E. V. Lehman, "Life and Work in Symphony Orchestras," *Musical Quarterly* 80 (1996): 194–219.

TEN

Epilogue

Orpheus, the legendary musician of Greek mythology, was said through his music to be able to charm birds, fish, and wild beasts, to make trees and rocks dance, and to divert the course of rivers. When his bride, Euridice, was bitten at her wedding reception by a venomous snake, she died, quickly and sadly, and as we know from the treatment of this subject by several composers over the course of operatic history, the wedding party grieved. But Orpheus, blessed with a special talent for music, traveled to the underground River Styx, which separated the world of the living from the world of the dead, yearning to meet again with his bride and to bring her back to the land of the living. Though Charon, guard of the underworld, was not supposed to allow living humans to cross from one bank of the river to the other, Orpheus so overwhelmed Charon with his singing that he was allowed to cross.

When I heard that story as a boy, my reaction was something along the lines, "Wow! Music must be a pretty powerful medicine to accomplish that. People who have died are supposed to stay that way. I wonder how Orpheus was able to do that. He must have been a great artist!"

Shortly afterward, I was sitting in the backseat of my dad's car, listening to him chat in front with a colleague who lived nearby, an amiable man in his fifties who had just, under Koussevitzky's direction, performed as principal bassoon with the BSO in what had seemed to me a shattering performance of Tchaikovsky's Sixth Symphony. Said the bassoonist to my father, "What are you doing tomorrow? It's Sunday." My father, then in his late thirties, replied, "We're having some friends over and will be playing chamber music." "Oh," said the bassoonist, a wonderful artist, "have you plans for a concert?" When Dad said there were no such plans, the bassoonist asked, "Well then, are you forming a group so that you can set up some concerts?" When told that there were no such

plans, the bassoonist asked why anyone would want to spend an afternoon playing chamber music. My dad answered, "Because it's fun. We
like it!" The bassoonist concluded the conversation with the question,
"Are you crazy?" He retired from the Boston Symphony when he was
only sixty, in the midst of what seemed to his colleagues a highly successful career, moved to Cape Cod, never again listened to music, and was
rumored to have driven a spike through the heart of his valuable Heckel
bassoon, nailing it to the space over his fireplace.

   Though the attitude of the bassoonist was perhaps extreme, it struck
me at the time that something terrible must have happened in the bassoonist's life that had turned such a decent human being and fine player
so sour about his work. Why, I wondered, are so many orchestral musicians in their fifties such a generally unhappy lot, tired of the music that
meant so much to them when they were young? Part of that malaise, I
think, comes from playing the same works over and over again, sometimes under less-than-gifted conductors. Part of it, too, I think, has to do
with most orchestral musicians having a job description that allows them
but minimal contribution to the whole. In making chamber music, each
player's individual views really count, while in an orchestral situation
there is simply no time for individuals to take the orchestra's time asking
questions. And part of it has to do with the way too many musicians are
trained and educated, for having succeeded in getting one of the very few
decently paying orchestral positions in the United States, such fortunate
musicians are scarcely in a position at age fifty to begin again in a new
discipline. Thus, those who are bored stay bored, and become cynical and
jaded as well.

   Something more reminiscent of the way Orpheus must have felt about
music is apparent in a brief address given by Bishop Matthew Clark at
the dedication of a new pipe organ in St. Anne's Roman Catholic Church
of Rochester in the early 1990s, an occasion on which my own speech just
beforehand had stressed the church's leadership in Western music during the millennium that followed AD 500. Bishop Clark concluded his
remarks as follows:

> As you know, I believe deeply in the power of music in the worship
> experience, because I believe deeply in the power of music. A decade
> ago, my brothers, sisters, and I were called to the bedside of our dear
> mother, suffering from a very painful kind of cancer and close to the
> end of her life. We gathered around her, held hands, and prayed for
> her release. But though we all prayed hard, her painful breathing con-
> tinued unabated. At length, my older sister suggested that we sing to
> her, together, some of the songs she had taught us as children. Before
> long we came to "You Are My Sunshine." As soon as we began that
> song, her breathing became more peaceful. And by the time we had
> reached the end of a second verse, she had died, peacefully. It did not
> take us long to realize what had happened. We all bowed our heads

and prayed silently, in gratitude, for her life and for the power of music. We all understood that music is one of God's greatest gifts to humanity, that making music together had somehow suggested to our mother the peace and love of family that had been her aim for all of her children.

Reminiscent, too, of the impact I think Orpheus must have had is an essay by Lewis Thomas from his *Late Night Thoughts on Listening to Mahler's Ninth Symphony*. Dr. Thomas, an MD from Harvard, served as dean of the Yale Medical School and as president of the Memorial Sloan-Kettering Cancer Center in New York City.

> I cannot listen to Mahler's Ninth Symphony with anything like the old melancholy mixed with the high pleasure I used to take from this music. There was a time, not long ago, when what I heard, especially in the final movement, was an acknowledgment of death and at the same time a quiet celebration of the tranquility connected to the process. I took this music as a metaphor for reassurance, confirming my own strong hunch that the dying of every living creature, the most natural of all experiences, has to be a peaceful experience. I rely on nature. The long passages in all the strings at the end, as close as music can come to expressing silence itself, I used to hear as Mahler's idea of leave-taking at its best. But always, I have heard this music as a solitary, private listener, thinking about death.
>
> Now I hear it differently. I cannot listen to the last movement of the Mahler Ninth without the door-smashing intrusion of a huge new thought: death everywhere, the dying of everything, the end of humanity. The easy sadness expressed with such gentleness and delicacy by that repeated phrase on faded strings, over and over again, no longer comes to me as old familiar news of the cycle of living and dying. All through the last notes my mind swarms with images of a world in which the thermonuclear bombs have begun to explode, in New York and San Francisco, in Moscow and Leningrad, in Paris, in Paris, in Paris. In Oxford and Cambridge. In Edinburgh. I cannot push away the thought of a cloud of radioactivity drifting along the Engadin, from the Moloja Pass to Ftan, killing off the part of the earth I love more than any other part.
>
> There is a short passage near the very end of the Mahler in which the almost vanishing violins, all entangled in a sustained backward glance, are edged aside for a few bars by the cellos. Those lower notes pick up fragments from the first movement, as though prepared to begin everything all over again, and then the cellos subside and disappear, like an exhalation. I used to hear this as a wonderful few seconds of encouragement: we'll be back, we'll be back; keep going, keep going.[1]

As the authors of *The Performing Arts in a New Era* made clear in 2001, the central problem for concert music in America is that we are continuing to develop a large oversupply of too narrowly trained young musicians who will have minimal opportunities for professional employment in organizations of the kind we have thus far developed. Because I believe so deeply in music's powerful message, I have spent the whole of my professional life working at limiting supply while stimulating demand, helping each young musician to think of himself as an individual entrepreneur, a person with professional skills and interests that are both more flexible than and different from those of his contemporaries. I believe that this goal is attainable by changing some of the ways in which young musicians are trained and educated, an especially important matter at this moment in American history when laws like No Child Left Behind focus our young people on tests that take time and resources away from social studies, physical education, music, and art—the third, fifth, sixth, and seventh of Howard Gardner's multiple intelligences.

While there are many positive goals that can be achieved through music study, beginning when one is a child and continuing throughout life, I believe it a mistake to send young people to music schools without making them aware at the outset of the problems outlined in this book, and without providing as many of them as possible with a sufficiently broad undergraduate education so that they gain the skills that will be necessary for them to succeed, in the very likely event that they are not the concert stars of the future. Otherwise, the promise of Orpheus loses its force with them as they grow older. Because a great many musicians will become teachers, especially of music, young musicians should be thinking much more than they currently do about what constitutes good teaching, about the glories of being a dedicated teacher, and about what the individual needs of their students and of music itself will be a generation or two ahead. But if a musician has a good high school education and the benefit of a strong liberal arts education in college, there is no reason why such a person ought not to attend graduate school in some other discipline—medicine, law, politics, or business, for example, while continuing to enjoy musical performance, sometimes at a very high level, as an avocational musician or as a very active listener. The notion that one should give up music making simply because one doesn't make a living at it is a terrible idea in my view, like giving up golf because one doesn't play on the PGA tour.

Because so many young Americans are now college educated and the beneficiaries of a great deal more leisure time than was available a century ago, there is every reason for musicians and for those who care about music to think harder about how to teach music to those who are already adults. Because we have focused so much on performance rather than on music itself, there has been too little thought till now on how to use emerging technologies as a means to develop better habits of listening to music. A major roadblock impeding the development of new audiences has been the prejudice that because one didn't study music as a child, one simply doesn't have what it takes to become an attentive listener as an adult.

Just as this book was about to go to press, I had the privilege of meeting Claire Chase, a recent Oberlin alumna, a superb young flutist, and the founder of the International Contemporary Ensemble (ICE). The recent winner of a MacArthur genius award, Claire's compelling musicianship, her incandescent passion in making music, and her entrepreneurial imagination and accomplishment make a compelling package. ICE's current million-dollar budget enables Chase and her colleagues to commission new work, to pay the participating musicians decently, and to perform in all sorts of venues (from the Lincoln Center to warehouses and retirement homes), without charge to their inevitably enthusiastic audiences, on all seven continents of the world.[2] Claire Chase and young musicians like her are breaking the mold for what is needed in the new millennium, suggesting how badly musical education of the kind advocated in the book you have just read is needed if American music schools and the young musicians they try to serve are to survive in the years ahead.

I close with a very personal account that I hope will continue to inspire those who carry forward the work I have been engaged in since my appointment as Eastman director in 1972. As a Milton Academy student in the early 1950s, it was my privilege to be friends with the late George Oldberg, a horn player a year younger than I whose father, Dr. Eric Oldberg, a distinguished Chicago brain surgeon, was the son of Arne Oldberg (1876–1951), an American composer and pianist, a professor of composition for many years at Northwestern, and a teacher there of Howard Hanson. Arne Oldberg was a man whose romantic and very tonal orchestral works were regularly performed in the 1920s, '30s, and '40s by the Chicago Symphony Orchestra under Frederick Stock. At the time George Oldberg and I were Milton students, my father played in the Boston Symphony, and George's father was board chair of the Chicago Symphony Orchestra, the man primarily responsible for having brought Fritz Reiner to the music directorship of that great orchestra. As adolescents, George and I performed often together, arguing proudly of the relative merits of our fathers' orchestras.

George and his mother were, alas, involved in a serious automobile accident on Storrow Drive in Boston, shortly after we graduated from college, and both George, an only child, and his mother died not long afterward as a result of the accident. Once I became Eastman director, I got to be friends with George's father, who was moved by the serendipity, he told me, of my relationship to his family through George and through Howard Hanson. As a result, several Eastman colleagues and I were invited to perform Arne Oldberg's beautiful Sextet for Piano and Winds at Chicago's Goodman Theater. Then, a week before Dr. Oldberg's death in his late eighties, I was called to his bedside in Lake Forest, where we spent an afternoon reminiscing and listening together, as Dr. Oldberg had planned, to CSO recordings of the four Brahms symphonies. Afterward, with tears in his eyes, he told me that his father, knowing how difficult it is to make a decent living in music, had steered him into medicine, and ultimately into brain surgery, where he had had a very successful career. Said he at the end of our time together, "I don't know whether any of us ever gets to come back for a second try. I just want you to know that I believe there is nothing in the world like music—and that, if I get a second chance, I plan to return as a composer, conductor, and pianist."

NOTE

1. Lewis Thomas, *Late Night Thoughts on Listening to Mahler's Ninth Symphony* (New York: Penguin, 1980), 164–66. For more on the finale of the Mahler Ninth, see Leonard Bernstein's yet more expressive Harvard lecture, posted on YouTube. And for a similarly sublime presentation on music's potential contribution to humanity, see Yo Yo Ma's Nancy Hanks illustrated lecture athttps://www.youtube.com/watch/?v=TWsdrjUhol4.

2. ICE's web address is www.iceorg.org.

Appendix A

Appendix A: How to Evaluate Music Faculty

What follows is a memorandum from an excellent committee of the faculty of the Eastman School of Music on the evaluation of teaching, a central matter for any good music school. This memorandum appeared in the mid-1980s.

To: Robert S. Freeman, Director
 From: ESM Committee on the Evaluations of Teaching (Professors Averill, Effron, Graue, Lister-Sink, Maloy, Morris, VanDemark)

I. PREAMBLE

Roughly a year ago, this committee accepted your charge to examine and evaluate technique used in the evaluation of teaching at Eastman, and to recommend changes if they seemed appropriate. The willingness of the committee members to apply themselves to this task stems from the importance that all of us attach to teaching, from your assurance that teaching should be considered the *most* important activity of the faculty, and from our dissatisfaction with past and present methods used for evaluation. It has become clear that the act of teaching is regarded by many members of our faculty as an extraordinarily sensitive and personal phenomenon, and any recommendations that we might make seem certain to be controversial or to meet with some resistance. We request, therefore, that our recommendations be disseminated widely, so that the whole faculty has an opportunity to refine, revise, or reject any of our suggestions.

It has not been our intention to homogenize or standardize criteria for fine teaching. Our recommendations are based on a number of basic assumptions within which the style and personality of the individual teacher may still operate freely. Our basic assumptions have been:

1. Fine teaching should be rewarded by the university as much as are research and publication, public performances, or other service to the university.
2. Teaching excellence often does not figure as prominently in decisions on retention, promotion, or tenure as it ought to, perhaps because evidence of superior teaching may appear to be unscientific or flawed in some other way.
3. It is impossible to devise a single tool for the evaluation of teaching that will be fair, constructive, and true for every case.
4. As delicate as the issue may be, university professors should be held accountable in some way for their performance as teachers. Academic freedom should not be construed as carte blanche for weak teaching.
5. There are no universally canonized criteria for the definition of excellence in teaching, but university teachers may be the group most qualified to recognize it when it exists.
6. If any formal devices are employed for teaching evaluation at Eastman, they should address all types of teaching that occur in the school, so that no type of teaching activity is scrutinized less rigorously than another.
7. The compilation of evidence of teaching effectiveness is *most* necessary for faculty members being considered for unlimited tenure and for promotion to associate professor, since these decisions determine to a large extent the makeup of the permanent faculty. If, therefore, techniques are adopted that require so much time and energy that they cannot apply to the entire faculty, the groups that face watershed decisions should be given attention first.

The committee has interviewed a large number of our faculty colleagues, perused the literature on teaching evaluation, and reviewed procedures at other institutions. All of these resources have dramatized the complexity of the issues and the elusiveness of solutions. Our recommendations are made with a keen appreciation of the need to nurture and reward a widely varying array of teaching styles and circumstances. A number of tools or techniques are suggested, and each may gain in value through corroboration by other techniques. The tools themselves will need to be adapted to the many different settings within which teaching takes place at a school like ours.

Our goals, in the end, have been to assist the university in rewarding the many fine teachers in our midst and to stimulate within the faculty a continuing discussion of issues associated with our teaching responsibilities. If the framework we recommend is not the best that could be conceived, perhaps it may lead toward even better policies in the future.

II. TECHNIQUES

The information that could bear on an Eastman teacher's promotion, tenure, or salary in the past could contain several types of evidence on teaching effectiveness: (1) student opinionnaires, (2) jury performance by students, (3) concerts by the school's ensembles, (4) successes of students in competitions or in other professional settings, (5) the teacher's "popularity" as measured by enrollments or requests for study, and (6) hearsay. Each of these categories of evidence offers something of value, but each also raises the possibility of misinterpretation or manipulation. Should a classroom teacher strive to be "popular" by giving high grades and light assignments, in order to elicit favorable responses on student questionnaires? Should a new assistant professor in a performance department be judged by his or her student's showing on jury examinations, even if weaker students had been assigned to the studio? Should a few loud complaints by disgruntled students have a sharp effect on a faculty member's salary or longevity? All of these are serious objections to the traditional sources of information. Each source can be tainted by suspicions of political or noneducational manipulation. A new policy toward teacher evaluation should not only discourage the possibility of politically colored judgments, it should also avoid the *appearance* of vulnerability to political motives.

We recommend that a full and fair evaluation of a faculty member's teaching should include information gathered in several different ways—from the teacher himself, from colleagues, and from students. Chief among these procedures are a system of observation by senior colleagues and the use of student course questionnaires. Some additional methods of assessment can be used as well, at the discretion of the department chairman, the associate director, or the person being reviewed.

A. Student Opinion

Student questionnaires are among the most widely used tools in judging teaching effectiveness. Nevertheless, at Eastman and elsewhere, many faculty members express strong reservations concerning their usefulness. The particular forms used at Eastman in the recent past receive low marks from many of our colleagues. They are often viewed as simplistic, mechanical, and inflexible. They list categories such as "punctuality" and "knowledge of subject matter" with equal prominence, for example, and they are arranged so that negative and positive responses are all lined up on the left and right extremes of the columns, respectively. It can be argued that the format of the exercise discourages careful, thoughtful response by the student. The forms allow little space for prose statements by the student, so that responses are often difficult to interpret, because frequently the student's intelligence and literacy are not revealed.

Questionnaires have often been distributed near the end of a semester, before students have received their grades. To elicit more mature and objective responses from students, forms should be distributed at the beginning of each fall term, asking for students' comments on their teachers during the preceding academic year. The temporal distance between the student's experience with a teacher and his evaluation of it may lead to more carefully thought-out responses than have been given in the past.

Evaluation forms used in the past have been problematic, but we believe that no single form could address the different types of learning situations that exist at Eastman in a uniformly effective way. Each department should be allowed to develop forms suitable to the teaching activities within that department. We have no designed forms to be used as models (though they do exist). If some departments prefer not to devise forms, they should be asked to express their preference among a number of prototypes that can be offered.

B. Faculty Observation

Both the faculty in general and the committee feel that the most desirable means of achieving fair and constructive evaluation of teaching is through direct observation of a teacher's work by faculty colleagues. The settings in which teaching takes place at Eastman are so diverse, however, that the means by which teachers are observed cannot be made uniform. We suggest, therefore, the following steps to ensure that observation may take place with the positive effects:

1. Teachers will be observed by a committee of three senior colleagues. Two of these will come from the teacher's own department (unless that is impossible), and one will be from a different department.

2. At the beginning of the year in which a teacher is to be observed, the chairman of that department will meet with the associate director for academic affairs to construct a committee of three persons. These three names shall then be shown to the person being reviewed, and that person will eliminate one name from the list and replace it with a senior colleague of his or her choice. This step is important as a guarantee of fairness in the construction of the committees.

3. The committee members will visit the classes (or lessons, rehearsals, etc.) of the person being reviewed upon at least five occasions. If these visits occur in rapid succession, an appreciation of the continuity and cumulative effect of that person's teaching may be gained.

4. Visits by the committee will be announced in advance to the person being observed.

5. The observers will submit a confidential report to the associate director for academic affairs, who will share it with the director and the chairman of the department concerned. As is policy for ad hoc committees on tenure, any member of a committee may submit a separate report if his perceptions vary significantly from those of other observers.

6. If the logical outcome of a series of lessons or rehearsals is to be a public performance, the observers should also attend the performance.

7. Teachers who object strenuously to the potentially disruptive presence of faculty observers may be invited to provide the committee with videotapes as a substitute.

8. A teacher being observed has the right to submit to the committee, either just before or just after a visit, a brief written explanation of his pedagogical aims for the class, lesson, or rehearsal in question, along with copies of the course syllabus, handouts, exams, and so on.

In order to ensure candor and confidentiality, and to promote faculty harmony generally, it is felt that the committee reports should *not* be shared with the person under review. All the same, it is highly desirable for department chairmen to communicate constructive advice to each member of the faculty whenever possible. It is equally desirable to develop an atmosphere in which teaching techniques and strategies can be discussed freely and frequently among colleagues at all levels.

C. Other Techniques

While the solicitation of faculty and student evaluation may form the principal bases for judgment, other techniques may also be employed, if they are requested by the faculty member, the department chairman, or the associate director. Some of these techniques are listed here, though this is by no means a comprehensive summary of the possibilities.

1. A faculty member may prepare a written self-evaluation of his or her teaching for the use of the department chairman and the associate director.

2. A faculty member may submit a summary of his or her teaching activities that might otherwise go unnoticed and unrecorded. Such activities as informal coaching, private counseling with students, and guest lecturing might be included here.

3. Any faculty member may request that written evaluations of his or her teaching be solicited from alumni of the school. In this event, a

representative sampling of alumni could be assembled by the department chairman.

4. Evidence of teaching effectiveness that is gained through student enrollment patterns, requests for individual teachers, or jury performances by students should be treated with great caution. While large or small class enrollments, requests to secure or to avoid the services of a particular teacher, and high or low showings on jury exams may be significant in some cases, such data is so difficult to interpret and so much subject to external considerations that it should not be viewed as definitive evidence in any case. If such issues are treated at all in someone's review, they would require extensive interpretive comment by the department chairman and the associate director.

III. IMPLEMENTATION

The conscientious application of the techniques outlined here may well require handsome expenditures of time and energy by Eastman's faculty and administration. The committee does not desire to create a system so cumbersome and complex that it will sap the strength of the faculty or die quietly because of its very weight. All the same, the seriousness of the task demands that it be performed as well as possible.

Appendix B

Appendix B: Convocation Address by Robert Freeman

I gave the talk that follows in November of 1972. It introduced me as the new director of the Eastman School of Music and was delivered to a student- and faculty-packed Kilbourn Hall. This talk takes clear pride in Eastman's notable history while it discusses achievable goals for the future. I was personally thrilled at its conclusion to join the distinguished Chinese basso Yi-Kwei Sze in a performance of Schubert's wonderful song "An die Musik."

To stand here in Kilbourn Hall, looking out upon so many fellow musicians, is a very moving experience. This fine school, having recently celebrated its fiftieth anniversary, is justly famous for its distinguished contributions in a great many areas to the musical life of the United States. Blessed with George Eastman's generous endowment and with such excellent facilities, its alumni command respect throughout the country as performing musicians, as teachers and administrators, as scholars and theorists. Two generations of American composers have been educated here; a large number of very fine recordings have been made; the development here of so fine a symphonic wind ensemble has given rise to a whole new repertory and to a host of imitations; the finest university music library in the country continues to improve. The Eastman School has accomplished much in which one has a right to take great pride.

Some of you may have read recently that, as a person with relatively broad background in music, I take great challenge from my belief that here at Eastman we together have a possibility of retaining high professional standards while giving rise to a new and broadened education for musicians. Many of us are familiar with musical scholars who mistrust performing musicians, often imagined to be mindless practitioners of an art they do not understand. And there exist, as you know, large numbers of performers who mistrust academicians for judgments about music that sometimes seem based on faulty musical perception. I shall not maintain that there is often not good reason for mistrust on both sides. But at

225

Eastman, with distinguished faculty and students in so many areas, it is my dream that specialists may learn to work together, and that in doing so, we will all become better musicians for it. It happens in many a conservatory that a student of a particular instrument, working with a single professor very skilled on that instrument, misses the opportunity to gain from the experience of others who are teaching and studying the same instrument in an adjoining studio. It happens in many a university that young composers, however good their guidance and instruction from mature composers, miss the opportunity to hear regular performances of their new works and to gain from the hearing as well as from the potential comments and advice of their performing colleagues. It often happens that a music historian, working by necessity in a dusty archive, misses the chance to hear and to evaluate in the context of a live performance the work which he has discovered. These and many similar missed opportunities cannot be helped in many an institution; but the Eastman School provides us with an environment where the opportunities need not be missed.

It is among the tasks of the music historian to clarify the composer's intention. But we historians have done our task so well that a great many performing musicians now believe we know more than we really do. Conscientiously made editions are important, and performers are fortunate to have growing numbers of them available. But the scholar's search for historical authenticity must not blind us to the fact that, in any style, there is broader latitude of dynamic, articulative, and agogic possibilities, for example, than earlier musical notations can possibly indicate. The historian can, in a given situation, exclude a range of performance possibilities which would be clearly inappropriate. But, for any given work, there exists a much broader spectrum of stirring (and no less historically authentic) performances than many a performer presently conceives of. It is the work of the speculative theorists to chart those largely unexplored region for us. The analysis of a musical work often seems of questionable relevance to performers. It need not. Questions of orchestral balance, of variability of tempo, and of hierarchies of climax, for example, are vital to the best performances. There are some fine musicians who intuit well about such matters; but there are other colleagues whose music making, I think, could be liberated through such considerations as these.

There is much for us to learn from one another: students, certainly, from faculty, and faculty and students from their colleagues. I know, too, that many of the Eastman faculty will share my experience as a teacher when I say that issues which I had never even conceived of have often been clarified by the open questions of some of my students. There is a remarkable community here of practicing artists; some are designated faculty and others students, but in a broader sense we are all students of music, an art which as musicians we will all go on *studying* for the rest of our lives.

In a human sense it will be impossible that my door always be open, but I shall do my best to provide you with an administration that takes the counsel of faculty and students. I do have a vision of what the Eastman School could become, but that vision includes a great many different kinds of roles for faculty of varying combinations of talents and outlooks, of students pursuing a variety of curricula better tailored to the needs of the students as individuals. Above all, it includes a faculty of distinction requiring and attracting students who are themselves first-rate.

The school has various constituencies; the City of Rochester and the University of which we are part, the alumni, and the world of music generally are all important. But nothing is more important than the sense of students and faculty that we are all participants in an adventure whose future belongs to us all.

One final word about our opportunities and our responsibilities. Many of Eastman's students have come here with the dream of becoming concert artists. But because of the economic realities of today's musical world, the limited opportunities of yesterday for such careers are becoming more and more limited. Eastman musicians of the future will have the opportunity, I know, to develop their capacities as performers to the fullest possible extent. But bearing in mind that a great many of you will become performers and teachers—privately or as faculty members of colleges and universities, conservatories, secondary and primary schools all across the United States, it is important, I think, that you be educated partly toward the fulfillment of what may be your ultimate responsibilities as musicians. Those of you who may one day become teachers of small children, for example, have a much graver musical responsibility than you may realize. If new music continues to be the special province of a small group, it is clear that the gulf which exists between many of the composers and most of the audience will continue to widen, that the concert hall will continue evolving toward what the opera house has in large measure already become—a museum. The so-called classics are admirable works, but while one's perception is improved through repeated performances, it is not true that one can go on performing the same work indefinitely without, as veteran orchestral musicians will often tell you, in some measure dulling one's enthusiasm for the work. If the future of new music, the lifeblood of music, depends to an important degree upon the inclinations of future audiences, it is the responsibility of those of us who teach music, especially of those who teach the young, to provide the very best instruction we can possibly devise. Music education is, thus, a field of immeasurable importance; and it lies within the Eastman School's potential to vitalize that field for the benefit of all music.

From an economic point of view, music has never been an easy field, for the supply of musicians has always been well in excess of the demand. Writing more than two hundred years ago, the German flutist, composer, and theorist Johann Joachim Quantz, in a chapter entitled "Of the Qualities Required of Those Who Would Dedicate Themselves to Music," admonished his readers as follows:

> He who wishes to excel in music must feel in himself a perpetual and untiring love for it, a willingness and eagerness to spare neither industry nor pains, and to bear steadfastly all the difficulties that present themselves in this mode of life. Music seldom procures the same advantages as the other arts, and even if some prosper in it, this prosperity is most often subject to inconstancy. Changes of taste, the weakening of bodily powers, vanishing youth, the loss of a patron—upon whom the entire fortune of many a musician depends—are all capable of hindering the progress of music. Experience sufficiently confirms this, even if we think back only about half a century. . . . At many courts, and in many towns where music previously flourished, so that a good number of able people were trained in it, now nothing but ignorance prevails.

But whatever the economic situation—and there is much we can try to do to modify even that—we are musicians, drawn together by those wonderful combinations of tones which move men as do few if any other human experiences. Schubert's friend, the poet Franz von Schober, in eight lines of verse summed up something of the way we all feel about music in a poem entitled "An die Musk"—"To Music."

> O blessed art, how often have you,
> in hours of darkness when life oppressed me,
> kindled new love in my heart
> and taken me to better spheres.
> A sigh from your harp,
> a sweet, sacred chord has often
> opened to me the haven of better days;
> O blessed art, O music, I thank thee!

However moving the words of the poem, to a musician they are pale when compared with Schubert's musical setting of that poem. It seemed fitting to me that we conclude this afternoon with a performance of that brief Schubert song, an affirmation of the ideals that have made the Eastman School what it is, and in the dedication to whose mystery lies our common future. I am grateful to Yi-Kwei Sze for joining me this afternoon.

Index

Abravanel, Maurice, 7
Abreu, José Antonio, 197
Adler, Guido, 18
Adler, Samuel, 10, 43, 123, 124, 136, 166
Afghanistan, 203, 205
Africa, 46, 66, 147
Alarm Will Sound, 25, 84
Allen, Paul, 110, 192
Allen, Woody, 110, 192
Alsop, Marin, 208
Ambros, August Wilhelm, 18
American colleges and universities, 91–92, 92, 96; junior faculty, 104; music faculty, evaluating of, 94–95; music faculty, balance, importance of in, 104; public universities, departments of music, 16; tenure, 94, 95. See also higher education
American exceptionalism 9.17 9.35
American Federation of Musicians, xxi, 207
American League of Orchestras (ALO), 163
American Musicological Society, 41
American orchestras, 7–8; collapse of, 206; future of, 206–207
American Orchestras of the Nineteenth Century (Spitzer), 207
American values, 200–202
Anderson, Chris, 107
Andrew W. Mellon Foundation, 92, 182, 191; Orchestral Forum, 206
Antoniva, Natalia, 140
Antwerp (Belgium), 14–15
Arad, Atar, 140
Aristotle, 13–14, 19
Armstrong, Louis, 66
The Artist as Citizen (Polisi), xxivn5
Arts and Culture in the Metropolis: Strategies for Sustainability, 78

Arts, Inc.: How Greed and Neglect Have Destroyed Our Cultural Rights (Ivey), 66, 78
Asia, 1, 2, 66, 153
Atlanta Symphony, xix
Aubry, Pierre, 102
Audubon Quartet, 161
Austin (Texas), 107–109
Austria, 14, 40
Aversano, Mary, 137

Babbitt, Milton, 10, 12n7, 88n4, 123
Bach, J. S., 48, 65, 73, 102, 154
Bailey, Robert, 100, 103
Bain, Wilfred, 66
Baker, David, 66
Baldauf-Berdes, Jane, 14
Baldo, Jonathan, 137
Baldwin, Marcia, 142
Balsam, Artur, 37, 74
Bamberger, Jeanne, 41, 49, 205
Bang on a Can, 25
Barber, Samuel, 153
Barcelona (Spain), 14–15
Bard College: Longy School of Music, 181
Barlow, Wayne, 136
Barr, Jean, 140
Bartok, Bela,, 48, 65, 132, 154
Bay, Peter, 81
Beach, David, 139
Beauregard, Cherry, 142
Beck, Jean, 102
Beck, John, 142
Beckerman, Michael, 10
Beethoven, Ludwig van, 18, 65, 102
Beglarian, Grant, 124
Belichek, Bill, 200
Beloved Tyranna (Rezits), 118n3
Benedictines, 14

242

Index

"Who Cares If You Listen?" (Babbitt), 10
Why the Affluent Give (Ostrower), 159
Wiesner, Jerome, 43
"The Wildflower Suite" (Brandon), 156
Williams, Ted, 176n12
Wilson, Woodrow, 92
The Winner Takes All Society (Frank and Cook), 52–53
Winn, James A., 26n2, 114
Winter, Robert, 10, 186
Wolfen, James D., 192
Wolfensohn, James D., 110
Wolff, Konrad, 69
Wolf, Hugo, 73, 110
Wong, Lisa, 197
Woodcock, Tony, 147
Wright, Rayburn, 66, 67, 136
Wuorinen, Charles, 25

Yale University, 16, 143; Yale School of Music, 16–17
Yates, Sydney, 25
Yemen, 203
Ying, David, 81
Ying Quartet, 25, 81
Youth Orchestra of the Americas, 172
Yo Yo Ma, 152, 153, 161

Zahn, Paula, 110, 192
Zatorre, Robert, 203
Zeitlin, Zvi, 140
Zhang, Daxun, 153
Zimbalist, Efrem, 129
Zimbalist, Mary Louis Curtis Bok, 16
Zimmerman, Gerhart, 208
Zimmerman, Oscar, 140
Zinman, David, 140
Ziter, Richard, 109

About the Author

Robert Freeman, who graduated from Harvard with a summa in music, did his graduate work at Princeton, where he earned MFA and PhD degrees in music history. He taught at Princeton and at MIT before his appointment in November 1972 as director of the Eastman School of Music, which he led until 1996. (Eastman was listed by *U.S. News & World Report* in 1997 as the best music school in the nation and by *Newsweek* in 2013 as America's "hottest music school.") During the period 1996–1999, he served as president of the New England Conservatory in Boston, "Hub of the Universe," and from 1999 to 2006 as dean of the College of Fine Arts at the University of Texas at Austin, "the live music capital of the world." Administrator, educator, music historian, and Steinway artist, he studied piano with Gregory Tucker, Artur Balsam, and Rudolf Serkin.

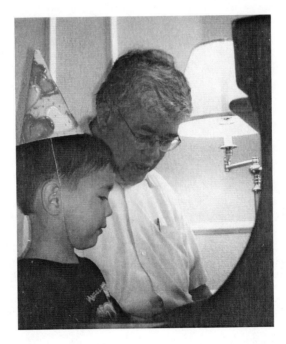